26-69

26-69

ROCK

From the Beginning

ROCK
From the Beginning

NIK COHN

STEIN AND DAY/Publishers/**New York**

Printed in the United States of America
Designed by Bernard Schleifer
Stein and Day/*Publishers*/7 East 48 Street, New York, N.Y. 10017

SBN 8128-1919-0

ACKNOWLEDGMENTS: Photographs on pages 67–82 used with permission as
follows: The Beatles: Donald McCullen; Tina Turner, Little Richard,
Pete Townshend, Phil Spector and Frank Zappa: Baron Wolman/Rolling
Stone; Jerry Lee Lewis, Elvis Presley (smiling), P. J. Proby, Cliff Richard,
Bill Haley, Ray Charles and Otis Redding: Topix; Johnnie Ray: H.
Leonard/Camera Press; The Everly Brothers: M. Sharrat/Camera Press;
Bob Dylan: Jerrold Schatzberg; The Supremes: David Montgomery,
courtesy of the *Sunday Times;* James Brown: Arnold Schwartzman/Redif-
fusion Television Ltd.

1495358

To Jet Powers,
Dean Angel,
and Johnny Ace

NB: The words "type" and "hustle," as used in this book, carry no pejorative implications. In most cases, they only mean that the person involved works hard.

Contents

1.

The Beginning

MODERN POP began with rock 'n' roll in the middle fifties, and basically, it was a mixture of two traditions—Negro rhythm 'n' blues and white romantic crooning, colored beat and white sentiment.

What was new about it was its aggression, its sexuality, its sheer noise; and most of this came from its beat. This was beat, bigger and louder than any beat before it, simply because it was amplified. Mostly, pop boiled down to electric guitars.

Of course, electric guitars were nothing new in themselves; they had been around for years in jazz and R & B (rhythm and blues) and had even been featured on some white hits, notably those by Les Paul, but they had never before been used as bedrock, as the basis of a whole music. Crude, powerful, infinitely loud, they came on like space-age musical monsters and, immediately, wiped out all of the politeness that had gone before.

Pre-pop (from the thirties on) dance music had gotten bogged down in the ballroom age—the golden era of the big bands, when everything was soft, warm, sentimental. When everything was make-believe.

It's one of the clichéd laws of showbiz that entertainment gets sloppy when times get tough, and what with the depression, the war, and its aftermath, times had gotten very tough indeed. Hemmed in by their lives, people needed to cling tight in the dark of dance halls, to be reassured, to feel safe again. Reality they could very well do without.

Always, that's the kind of situation that Tin Pan Alley thrives on; songs about moonlight, stardust, roses, and bleeding

9

hearts were duly churned out by the truckload. The big bands lined up strict and formal in penguin suits, the crooners slicked their hair back heavy with grease, the close harmony groups went oo-wah oo-wah in the background, and everybody danced. It was warm and snug like a blanket.

Sometimes, the big band era caught an odd freshness, an innocence, an atmosphere a bit like a Fred Astaire film. But when it was bad, which was almost always, it was only dire.

The worst thing was that it all dragged on so long without changing. Most dance eras last a few years, a decade at most, but the war froze everything as it was, gave the big bands a second life; by the early fifties, the scene had come to a standstill.

All this time, the music industry was controlled by middle-aged businessmen, uninterested in change of any kind. They were making money as things were, so they made no effort to find anything very new. They'd switch a few details, dream up some small novelty gimmick, and leave it at that. And the only reason they got away with it was that nobody offered any alternatives. Mostly, showbiz survived on habit.

There was no such thing as teenage music then, nothing that kids could possibly identify with. The business was structured in such a way that singers were generally well into their thirties by the time they made it. There'd be occasional novelties, cute comedies, but basically teenagers had to put up with the same songs their parents liked.

The nearest thing to an exception was Frank Sinatra.

In the early forties, when he first happened, Sinatra was still in his middle twenties, a novice by the standards of that time, and he was the first heart-throb.

He was hardly a teen idol—he was a conventional balladeer, he was backed by an ordinary big band, he sang the same songs as everyone else. But he was also good looking, he had soulful eyes, and almost all of his fans were women. They screamed for him, rioted for him, even swooned for him, and this was something new. Of course, film stars had always been treated like that. Sinatra was the first singer to join them, that's all.

As a prototype for pop, though, Johnnie Ray was much closer, the Nabob of Sob, the Million Dollar Teardrop himself. If Elvis Presley was the great pop messiah, Ray played John the Baptist.

Born in Oregon, 1927, he was tossed high in a blanket at the age of ten, landed on his head, and became about fifty per cent deaf. According to his press releases, he also changed from a happy, well-adjusted child into a full-time introvert, solitary and sad. At any rate, by the time he became a singer, he was wearing his neurosis like a badge. The gimmick was that when he got toward the climax of his stage act, he would collapse into helpless sobs. Not just once or twice but every time he performed. It was a ritual.

His big breakthrough year was 1952, and the record that did the trick was a double-sider: *The Little White Cloud That Cried* on one side and just plain *Cry* on the other, titles that more or less summed him up.

Anyhow, he caused riots, real live ones—he had his clothes ripped off, his flesh torn, his hair rumpled—and the police kept having to rescue him. He sang the same trash as everyone else, even a bit worse, but he contorted himself, he buckled and gulped, and that released an intensity of aggression that nobody else had stirred.

Johnnie Ray upped his earnings to four thousand dollars a week and sold records by the million—and all this time, he did nothing but cry. "I've no talent, still sing as flat as a table," he said. "I'm a sort of human spaniel: people come to see what I'm like. I make them feel, I exhaust them, I destroy them."

He was underrating himself. He couldn't sing, true enough, but he generated more intensity than any performer I ever saw in my life, and it was impossible not to feel involved with him.

He was a very skinny man, and when he moved, his limbs jerked out sideways as clumsily as puppet strings. He'd start his act slowly, out of tune, and he'd be almost laughable, whining and amateurish, gangling around the stage like some fevered crab. But then, just when you'd dismissed him, he'd launch himself into one of his major agonized ballads, and suddenly everything would come alive.

He'd hunch up tight into himself, choke on his words, gasp, stagger, beat his fist against his breast, squirm, fall forward on his knees and, finally, burst into tears. He'd gag, tremble, half strangle himself. He'd pull every last outrageous ham trick in the book, and he would be comic, embarrassing, painful, but still he worked, because under the crap, he was in real agony, he was burning, and it was traumatic to watch him. He'd spew himself up in front of you, and you'd freeze, you'd sweat, you'd be hurt yourself. You'd want to look away and you couldn't.

Frail as he was, thin and deaf and sickly, his fans would be twisted into paroxysms of maternal hysteria by him, and they'd half kill him. All around, it was the kind of orgiastic exhibition that simply hadn't happened before, and it was entirely pop. The music wasn't; the atmosphere was.

Ironically, considering that he'd helped pave the way for pop, he was destroyed by it. As soon as rock came in, he sounded hopelessly dated and melodramatic, and he stopped having hits. He kept on touring, but he sagged.

He had bad publicity, too: in Detroit, 1959, he was charged with soliciting a man in a bar. Amid frantic ballyhoo, he was acquitted, and having heard the verdict, he fainted dramatically on the courtroom floor. When he came around, he cried, "My prayers have been answered." "Oh, that poor boy," said the jury forewoman. And Ray fainted again.

In theory, he'd triumphed—but then it turned out he'd been found guilty on a similar charge in 1951, and that did him no good whatever. Altogether, he had it rough.

Still, he keeps going in cabaret, and when he turns it on, he's as fierce and agonized as he ever was.

All the time that moonglow ballads were dominating the white market, black music, as always, was bossed by the blues. The old country blues, raw and ragged and often wildly emotional, had been increasingly replaced by rowdy big city blues, by electric guitars and saxes, and right through the forties and early fifties, the movement had been toward more noise, more excitement. Beat came in, passion went out, and somewhere along the line, the new style became known as rhythm 'n' blues, R & B.

What this usually involved was a small band—five or six pieces, maybe more—belting out a succession of fast twelve-bars. Styles varied, of course, but generally the trend was toward the jump blues, loose-limbed stuff played by people like Louis Jordan, Lloyd Price, Wynonie "Mr. Blues" Harris, and Fats Domino.

It was good-time music, danceable and unpretentious, and by comparison with the mushiness of white music in the same period, it was like a window opened to let out some bad air.

It was straight about sex; it used no euphemisms about hearts and roses. A lot of the time, in fact, it was downright filthy: Hank Ballard's *Work With Me Annie,* Billy Ward's *Sixty Minute Man,* and the Penguins' *Baby Let Me Bang Your Box* were typical. All of them were big hits in the R & B charts, and predictably, all of them got banned by the white radio stations.

Just the same, R & B somehow began to filter through to white kids, and they liked it. In 1951, a DJ called Alan Freed launched a series of rhythm reviews at the Cleveland Arena and immediately drew crowds three times the capacity.

These shows featured colored acts but were aimed at predominantly white audiences, and to avoid what he called "the racial stigma of the old classification," Freed dropped the term R & B and invented the phrase rock 'n' roll instead.

Right through the early fifties, white stations persisted in blocking R & B off their airwaves, and the biggest names were still people like Doris Day, Perry Como, and Frankie Laine.

Black hit songs were usually covered and castrated for the white market—Pat Boone did Fats Domino's *Ain't That A Shame,* for instance, and Dorothy Collins assassinated Clyde McPhatter's *Seven Days*—and even multimillion R & B sellers like Joe Turner, Ruth Brown, and Bo Diddley never made the pop charts.

Pop and R & B apart, there was also, throughout the South, a massive market in country 'n' western, jogalong stuff to be sung through the nose. In England, this was thought of as cow-boy music and didn't sell much. But in the States, people like Hank Williams, Slim Whitman, Eddy Arnold, and Tennes-see Ernie Ford rated as big as anyone and often appeared in the top ten.

Each of these musics—country and R & B and Tin Pan Alley—had its own hit parade. Sometimes, of course, these would intertwine—LaVern Baker's *Tweedly Dee* was a hit in both pop and R & B markets—but mostly they ran independ-ently, and it was quite possible for someone like Eddy Arnold, say, to sell fifty million records and still mean hardly anything on the national charts.

So these were the musical ingredients that made pop hap-pen—the white ballad tradition, the exhibitionism introduced by Johnnie Ray, the elaborate sentimentality of C & W, the amplified gut-beat of R & B. Among them, they would have been enough to produce a major craze.

What made rock 'n' roll more than a craze, what turned it into a small social revolution, was nothing to do with music.

Basically, it all came down to the fact that in the affluent society teenagers now had money. If they were white, if they came out of anything but the worst slums, they weren't going to go hungry. More likely, they were going to get solid jobs and make money. They were even going to get time to spend it.

Even more important than any factual economic changes was the shift in atmosphere. For thirty years back, both in America and Britain, most working-class kids had come out of schools with a built-in sense of defeat. They might be headed for some dead-end job, they might be sent off to win wars, they might wind up in bread lines. Whatever happened, they weren't going to have much fun.

By comparison, the fifties were lush. Of course there was always the chance that everyone would get blown sky-high by an H-bomb, but that was too huge a concept to be really frightening, and at least, there was no depression now, no blitz, no rationing. It wasn't just a matter of keeping afloat any more —teenagers could begin to call cards.

The only snag was that, when they went looking for things

to spend their bread on, they found absolutely nothing. They had no music of their own, no clothes or clubs, no tribal iden-tity. Everything had to be shared with adults.

It was tough. After all this time, teenagers had finally made it through to the promised land, and they'd found it barren. Definitely, it was frustrating. They had all this money, nothing to do with it, and they went spare.

Always, the moment of maximum revolt comes just when things are beginning to get better, when the first liberalization sets in. When kids had had nothing at all, they had somehow accepted it. Now that life was easier, they began to riot.

Juvenile delinquency became all the rage. In Britain, teddy boys came in; they dressed like Edwardians, drainpipe pants and pointed shoes and three-quarter coats, and they wore their hair heavy with grease.

They weren't quite like any movement that had happened in earlier decades. There were so many of them and they were so aimless; they'd roam around in packs, brawling and smashing at random. A bit later, they dressed up in black leather and rode motorbikes. And still all they did was break things, win-dows and locks and bones. There was nothing else to do, and right through the fifties, the teds held command; they were the only action going. If you didn't want to join them, you had to sit indoors and vegetate.

There was something else: businessmen had never before seen teenagers as independent commercial units, as having en-tirely separate needs and tastes from the rest of the community. Now the possibilities hit them like a prophetic vision, and they moved in fast, fawning like mad.

Predictably, kids bought just about anything that was put in front of them: motorbikes, blue jeans, hair oils, ponytails, milkshakes, and, most of all, music. All you had to do was label something Teen, and they had to have it.

In music, the one snag was that the record companies had no idea what teenagers really wanted. All they could do was release noise by the ton and see what caught on best. It was only a matter of time before they struck gold.

This was solid thinking: in April, 1954, an aging country 'n' western singer called Bill Haley made a record called *Rock Around the Clock*. By 1955 it was a hit in America, and then it was a hit in Britain, and then it was a hit all over the world. And it just kept on selling; it wouldn't quit. It stayed on the charts for one solid year.

By the time it was finished, it had sold fifteen million copies. It had also started rock.

2.   *Bill Haley*

BILL HALEY was large and chubby and baby-faced. He had a kiss curl like a big C, slapped down on his forehead with grease and water, and he was paunchy. When he sang, he grinned hugely and endlessly, but his eyes didn't focus on anything. Besides, he was almost thirty, married, and the father of five children. Definitely, he was unlikely hero food.

Just the same, he was the first boss of rock. At his peak, he made a film called *Rock Around the Clock,* and when it was shown in the summer of 1956, audiences danced in the aisles, ripped up cinema seats, hit each other, and destroyed anything they could lay their hands on. In one shot, it crystallized the entire rock rebellion.

The main plot of the film was that Bill Haley grinned. He picked his guitar, and his kiss curl wobbled. He sang the title song, and the beat stoked up, and kids everywhere went berserk.

In England, the teds were small, skinny, and spotty. They'd been nourished on rationing and tended to be underfed, rat-faced. At any rate, as teenage movements go, they were the least attractive, most malicious ever, and when roused, they took out their switch-blades and stabbed each other. Because of this, the movie *Rock Around the Clock* was banned in some towns.

Up to now, the teds had been very much minority, but once they'd rioted, the press discovered them as copy and decided that they spelled full-scale revolution. For the first time, the concept of Teenager was used as news, as a major selling point, and in no time, everyone else was up on the bandwagon.

17

Churchmen offered spiritual comfort, psychologists explained, magistrates got tough, parents panicked, businessmen became rich, and rock exploded into a central issue.

Of course, teenagers weren't slow to respond. There were more riots, more knives, even a few killings. And the papers hollered harder, the panic got greater, the circle kept spinning; suddenly the generation war was open fact. It wasn't an undertone, it wasn't just a novelty any more. It really mattered. Above all, it meant money.

As for Bill Haley, he was a trouper and kept right on grinning. Born in the suburbs of Detroit, 1927, he'd started playing guitar for a dollar a night at the age of thirteen. Later, he fronted a country 'n' western group and buzzed around the Midwest, busily getting nowhere. Then he put in six years playing on a small-time radio station until finally, around 1951, he got wise, abandoned country music for good, and swung across to commercial R & B.

First, he listened hard to the biggest-selling colored blues of the time, Louis Jordan and Wynonie Harris, and copied the beat. Second, he watered down the lyrics, the sexuality, of the original and made it acceptable to white audiences. Third, he changed his group's name to the Comets ("It sounded kind of far-out, wild") and worked out some acrobatic stage routines. Then he got moving.

In 1951, under the new format, he had a minor success with *Rock the Joint*. The next year he did even better with *Crazy Man, Crazy*, and in 1954 he finally made it big with *Shake, Rattle and Roll*, which was a straight cover of Ivory Joe Hunter's big hit in the R & B charts. Later that same year he made *Rock Around the Clock*.

Musically, he was pretty dire. He was a fair country guitarist, but he wasn't remotely a singer, and his Comets sounded like they all had concrete boots. The beat was lumpish, dull. Alone of all the early rockers, Haley has no charm now, not even nostalgia value. *Rock Around the Clock* became a minor hit again in 1968, but, to me, it just sounds period bad.

Rock Around the Clock was no better and no worse than most of his work. The song was laughable, the arrangement nonexistent, but the beat was there and Haley shouted quite loud. In honesty, it was a dog—but it was also first, and that's where it won. It had no competition.

Originally, it sold as a novelty, as a joke almost. Then the press took it up, hammered it, called it anti-music, and suddenly it became a big generation symbol, a social phenomenon on its own. By the end, it was the source of an entire new music, and Haley was automatically leader. He'd been lucky, of course, but he'd been around a long time, and no one could reasonably begrudge him his break.

Soon he was featured in a film called *Blackboard Jungle,* a corny old soapbox about juvenile delinquency and generalized teen hang-ups. The opening sequence showed school kids jiving debauchedly in the playground, and Bill Haley was singing *Rock Around the Clock* on soundtrack. It all helped—the film was successful, caused fuss, helped sell records. Above all, it cemented the fiction of a uniquely teenage way of life with Bill Haley as its leader.

Through 1955 and on into 1956, he held complete control. He racked up another million seller with *See You Later Alligator* and had another monster film in *Don't Knock the Rock.* He was everything—singer, face, prophet, explorer—and no one else counted. But all the time he was on a raincheck; he was doomed. He'd jumped the gun, and he was ahead only as long as it took the rest of the field, younger, tougher, sexier, to catch him and swamp him.

Don't Knock the Rock was the signal. It was Bill Haley's film, but he lost it; he had it torn right out of his hands by Little Richard, a guaranteed genuine rock howler out of Macon, Georgia. Little Richard was the real thing. Bill Haley wasn't. Haley kept grinning, but he sounded limp by comparison, looked downright foolish.

But what really did him in was the coming of Elvis Presley. The moment Elvis cut *Heartbreak Hotel,* Haley was lost. Suddenly his audience saw him as he was—aging, married, corny, square, deeply boring—and that was that. Within a year, he couldn't get a hit to save his life. It was cruel, of course. It was also inevitable.

In early 1957, he toured England. By this time, he was already sagging on the ropes in America, but Britain hadn't yet caught on, and his arrival spelled bonanza time. He rode from Southampton to London in state on the Bill Haley Special, laid on for him by the Daily Mirror, and at Waterloo he was met by three thousand fans, many of whom had waited all day for him. He grinned. "It's wonderful to be here," he said. "I'm going to like England just fine. I only hope it likes me back." The only stroke he missed was the bit about our English policemen being wonderful.

On February 12th, he played the Dominion, Tottenham Court Road. It was the prototype of all pop concerts since. The music was drowned out by screaming, whistling, stamping, and roaring; the gallery shook so much that people below could see the floor buckling above their heads. All you could hear was the beat, the amplification, the nonstop thump. The big beat, the monster. That was all there was.

The only trouble was Haley himself. Instead of a space-age rocker, all arrogant and mean and huge, he turned out to be a dated vaudeville act. The saxophonist squealed, honked, and, blowing madly all the time, leaned over backward until his body was parallel with the floor, his head almost touching the stage. The bass player lay on his instrument, climbed up it, used it like a trampoline. Haley grinned. It was slapstick, knockabout. It was pure embarrassment. The audience was too pre-hyped to turn against it at the time, but when it was over, when the shouting and stamping had all died down, everyone finally had to face facts, and Haley was through.

It was really quite bitter. After all, he was everyone's first try at pop, and having him turn out like this was very much like getting drunk, losing one's virginity, and then waking up in an empty bed the next morning.

As for Bill Haley himself, you couldn't help feeling sorry for him. He was an amiable man and couldn't figure out what had happened to him. Admittedly, he had made a fortune, and he was assured of well-paid work for the rest of his life, but it must still have been a cruel turnaround for him.

He took it philosophically. He kept plugging away, made

new singles, toured, plastered his kiss curl down with grease water, picked guitar, and grinned at all times. In 1964, he was back in England, almost unchanged. This time nothing much was expected of him; he was seen as a historical curiosity and was received with some affection. At 37, he was attractive in his resignation. "I'm old now," he said. "But I've been around. I sure have been around." And he shook his head slowly as if he had truly seen everything there was to see.

3. *Elvis Presley*

WHAT ROCK needed to get it off the ground now was a universal hero, a symbol, a rallying point. Someone very young, private, unsharable—exclusive teenage property. Someone who could crystallize the whole movement, give it size and direction. Obviously, Bill Haley didn't measure up. Equally obviously, Elvis Presley did.

Elvis is where pop begins and ends. He's the great original, and even now, he's the image that makes all others seem shoddy. For once, the fan club spiel is almost justified: Elvis is King.

His big contribution was that he brought home just how economically powerful teenagers really could be. Before Elvis, rock had been a gesture of vague rebellion. Once he'd happened, it immediately became solid, self-contained; and then it spawned its own style in clothes and language and sex, a total independence in almost everything—all the things that are now taken for granted.

This was the major teen breakthrough, and Elvis triggered it. In this way, without even trying, he became one of the people who have radically affected the way other people think and live.

In the beginning, he was a country boy out of Tupelo, Mississippi. He was born January 8th, 1935. His twin, Jesse, died at birth. His father was a farmer, not a successful one, and when Elvis was fourteen, the family moved to Memphis. There was no work around. The Presleys lived in one room and survived. By the time he was sixteen, Elvis was a professional lawn mower. At nineteen, he did better—he became a truck driver and brought home thirty-five dollars each week.

There was nothing special about him—he was stolid, respectable, unambitious. He liked trucks. ("I used to see them drivers with their shirts off, handkerchiefs around their neck, a little cap on their head. They looked daring to me. I always dreamed of being a real wild truck driver.") He was country, naive, very religious. Beyond that, he played a bit of guitar, sang some.

Definitely, he was young for his age; he collected teddy bears, ate ritual peanut butter and mashed banana sandwiches last thing before he went to sleep each night, and loved his mother to the point of ickiness. In fact, he was cutting an amateur record of *My Happiness* as a birthday present for her when he first got discovered.

Later, he was signed to Sun Records, a local label, and went out on the small-time southern circuit, playing school dances, county fairs, and so forth.

His first record, *That's All Right*, was quite marvelous. Elvis had been exposed to a lot of different musics—colored R & B, fundamentalist revival singing, country ballads—and his singing was a mixture of all of them, an improbable stew to which he added sex. And he really was sexy. His voice sounded edgy, nervous, and it cut like a scythe; it exploded all over the place. It was anguished, immature, raw. But, above all, it was the sexiest thing that anyone had ever heard.

By May, 1955, he had a manager, Colonel Tom Parker (the title was honorary). If nothing else, Parker was a man of experience. At 49, he'd been through peepshows, carnivals, patent medicine, the Great Parker Pony Circus, and just about anything else before Elvis came along. Canny but unsophisticated, he hadn't been unsuccessful and he managed some successful country stars, but then again, he'd hardly struck gold either. On all known form, he was an unlikely revolution-maker.

Under Parker, Presley was moving up. His records were selling quietly but well around Memphis, and the girls had just begun to scream at him. His singing was as good now as it was ever going to get, and he kept moving his hips, wriggling, and every time he did that, there was some kind of riot.

Early in 1956, Elvis was signed by RCA-Victor and made a record called *Heartbreak Hotel*. It sold a million and a half straight off. By the end of six months, he'd sold eight million records, worked up to ten thousand letters a week, and raised the shrillest, most prolonged teen hysteria ever. It really was as fast, as simple and complete, as that. By the next year, he had grown into an annual twenty-million-dollar industry.

He would come out on stage riding a golden Cadillac. He wore a golden suit, and on his feet he had golden slippers. His sideburns reached down to his earlobes, and his hair, heavy with grease, came up in a great ducktail plume off his forehead. He had a lopsided grin, and he used it all the time.

When the music started, he'd begin wriggling, and he wriggled so hard that quite a few cities banned him for obscenity. "Elvis Presley is morally insane," shrieked a Baptist pastor in Des Moines, and that just about summed it up.

He was flash—he had four Cadillacs, a three-wheeled Messerschmitt, two monkeys, and too much jewelry. He built himself a house for a hundred thousand dollars, and it glowed blue and gold in the dark.

On stage, he sang hymns in between his hits. With strangers, he was invariably charming, boyish, immensely courteous. He'd smile shyly and mumble. He'd call men "sir" and women "ma'am," drop his eyes, look around frequently for approval. And, of course, this was all tremendously flattering. In these ways, he had real talent for handling people, for making himself liked.

At the center of everything was his mother. Just the same, he was an enthusiastic womanizer. Also, shy and deferential as he was, whenever he got pushed into fights by passing madmen, he'd invariably take them apart. No question, he was a very southern boy.

Always, he came back to sex. In earlier generations, singers might carry great basic sex appeal, but they'd have to cloak it under the trappings of romanticism; they'd never spell anything out. By contrast, Elvis was blatant. When those hips got moving, there was no more pretense about moonlight and hand-holding; it was hard physical fact.

With crooners, with people like Sinatra and Eddie Fisher, girls had suffered crushes, and they'd sigh, swoon, and sob gently inside their handkerchiefs. Always, they'd been romantic and quite innocent.

With rock though, it's all been down to mainline sexual fantasy. Sitting in concert halls, schoolgirls have screamed, rioted, brawled, and fainted. They've wet themselves and they've masturbaed. According to P. J. Proby, they've even ripped the legs off their chairs and mauled themselves. They've done all kinds of outrageous stuff that they'd never do any-where else, and they've been so uninhibited because there has always been a safety belt, because the pop singer himself has been unreachable, unreal, and nothing could actually happen.

In this way, it's all been sex in a vacuum: the girls have freaked themselves out, emptied themselves, and then gone back home with their boyfriends and played virgin again. As rituals go, it's not been beautiful, but it's been healthy; it's acted as a safety valve. Screaming at Elvis or the Beatles or the Rolling Stones, it's been as good as saying confession or going to an analyst.

Off-stage, Elvis read the Bible and loved his mother. "He's just like a paperback book," one of his girl fans explained. "Real sexy pictures on the cover. Only when you get inside, it's just a good story." He looked dangerous but ultimately was safe and clean. This is what young girls have always wanted from their idols, an illusion of danger, and Elvis brought a new thrill of semi-reality to the game.

With all his peacockery, his implied narcissism, he was also a major image-maker for boys. A lot of the time he sang con-ventional romantic lyrics, but some of his biggest hits were breakaways—the harshness and contempt for women in *Hound Dog* was typical.

Blue Suede Shoes was even more to the point. This had been a hit for Carl Perkins in 1956, but Elvis took it over the fol-

lowing year and gave it whole new dimensions. It was important, the idea that clothes could dominate your life. Girls and
cars and money didn't count. All that mattered were shoes,
beautiful brand-new blue suede shoes. It was the first hint at
an obsession with objects—motorbikes, clothes, and so on—
that was going to become quite central to rock.

By 1958, Elvis had ruled for two years solid, and the hysteria showed no signs at all of dying down. He'd gone into
movies: *Love Me Tender, Loving You, Jailhouse Rock*. He had
racked up twenty million-sellers. Still, he had some long-term
problems. He was already twenty-three; he couldn't go on
being a teen idol for ever. The difficulty was how to turn him
from an adolescent rebel into a respectable establishment figure
without his fans feeling cheated.

At this point, a godsend: Presley's army draft came through,
and he went on ice for two years. It meant losing a lot of
money, but Elvis took it philosophically. As for Colonel Parker,
he was delighted.

From here on in, Elvis got more and more saintly. On army
training, he was a paragon of diligence, cheerfulness, and humility. His officers praised him warmly; the press swung behind
him. Adult America was much reassured—the monster had
shown that it was only kidding.

In August, 1958, his mother took sick, had a heart attack,
and died. At the funeral, Elvis was hemmed in tight by re-
porters, jotting down every word he said, noting every last sob
and whimper. "She was the sunshine of our home," Elvis
moaned. "Good-bye, darling. We loved you. I love you. I love
you so much. I lived my whole life just for you." Next morning,
his ramblings were splashed syllable by syllable across the
papers. It was diseased, ghoulish, but it finally cemented the
new Presley image. That boy was all right.

There was even a record about it all, *New Angel Tonight*
by a certain Red River Dave. The first verse went:

> There's a new angel tonight
> Up in heaven so bright,
> The mother of Rock 'n' Roll King—

And I know she's watching down
On her boy in Army brown,
In her angel mother's heart remembering.*

When he was shipped out to Germany, Elvis was exactly everything that an all-American boy ought to be, working and playing hard, dating but not too much, visiting spastics, drawing emotional tributes from rugged G.I. buddies. He wound up a Specialist Fourth Class, a rank equivalent to corporal and worth $122 a month. The whole operation was a triumph.

By the time he came back to civilian life again, he was almost as respectable as an Andy Williams or Perry Como. Predictably, his first new record was a ballad, *It's Now or Never*, an inflated up-dating of *O Sole Mio*. Also predictably, it was his biggest seller yet, doing more than nine million world wide.

He never again went back on the road. Instead, he hid himself away in vast mansions in Hollywood and Memphis, and there he has stayed ever since. He hasn't toured in years. He lives a life of almost total privacy, kept company only by his wife, his small daughter, and twelve ex-G.I.'s, who exist to amuse him, fetch him drinks, and play touch football with him. Whatever he does, whatever fires him, he's discreet about it— nobody knows for sure what he thinks or wants to do. He gets slightly lonely, we're told. That's all.

Most of his time is spent in churning out an endless series of safe and boring musicals—*Kissin' Cousins, Clambake, Frankie and Johnnie, Harem Scarum, Girl Happy*—and each film seems worse than the one before. Elvis himself is thirty-three, paunchy, slow; his voice has lost its edge, until he now sounds a bit like Dean Martin. His songs are drab, his scripts are formula-fed, and his sets look as if they've been knocked together with two nails and a hammer. He still makes a fortune, but his singles sell patchily, and his films tend to travel the English circuits as B-features.

To be fair, he's shown recent signs of getting back into

* Words of *New Angel Tonight* by permission of Southern Music Publishing Co., Ltd., London.

business. He issued three strong singles running—*Big Boss Man, Guitar Man, U.S. Male*—and he sounded tougher, more rock, than he'd done in years. Whether this will grow into any major revival remains to be seen.

As far as his fans are concerned, he could just as well be on another planet. From time to time his gold Cadillac is sent out on tour across America, and they come to see it, touch it. His annual earnings are around ten million dollars. He has sold the best part of a hundred and fifty million records. And somehow his fans accept his absence and have come almost to like it.

The point is that he has passed beyond the edge of criticism, that he's somewhere out of reach on a plateau of showbiz untouchability. The obvious parallel is with Frank Sinatra—both of them have changed so much, have earned such astronomical money, have so dominated the entertainment worlds of their time that what they do for the rest of their lives has become largely immaterial. They have run out of challenges.

All that's left now is the image, the vision of him as he was when he was twenty-one, twenty-two, strutting and swiveling and swaggering, hanging his grin out, putting on the agony, riding on the top of his Cadillac, gold on gold, and freewheeling through everything. He was magnificent then, he really was. And his whole story has been an ultimate perfection of the Hollywood romance, an all-time saga of what happens to sexy little boys when they get fed into the sausage machine.

So Elvis now is a godhead—unseen, untouchable, more than human. The demon lover has turned into a father, an all-powerful figure who can rule a fan's life without actually having to be there. His remoteness is a positive advantage and there's no reason why it should ever end. His present slump is irrelevant. Worship is a habit that's hard to break.

4.   *Classic Rock*

ROCK 'N' ROLL was very simple music. All that mattered was the noise it made, its drive, its aggression, its newness. All that was taboo was boredom.

The lyrics were mostly nonexistent, simply slogans one step away from gibberish. This wasn't just stupidity, simple inability to write anything better. It was a kind of teen code, almost a sign language, that would make rock entirely incomprehensible to adults.

In other words, if you weren't sure about rock, you couldn't cling to its lyrics. You either had to accept its noise at face value or you had to drop out completely.

Under these rules, rock turned up a sudden flood of maniacs, wild men with pianos and guitars who would have been laughing stocks in any earlier generation but who were just right for the fifties. They were energetic, basic, outrageous. They were huge personalities, and they used music like a battering ram.

The best of them were packaged into giant barnstorming tours that trekked all around America, ninety-day marathons full of gold lamé and baggy pants and Brillcreem, wild men jumping on pianos and gigolos groveling on their knees. Orgiastic they were, true extravaganzas, and pop never again came up with anything quite so wild.

It was a great time—every month would produce someone new, someone wilder than anything that had gone before. Pop was barren territory and everything was simple every tiny gimmick was some kind of progression. Around 1960 things evened out, and much of the excitement died down. Pop has become more sophisticated, more creative, more everything. But the fifties were the time when pop was just pop, when it was really something to switch on the radio and hear what was new right that minute. Things could never be so good and simple again.

The first record I ever bought was by Little Richard; at one throw, it taught me everything I ever need to know about pop. It was Tutti Frutti, and as a summing up of what rock 'n' roll was really all about, this was nothing but masterly.

Very likely, these early years were the best that pop has yet been through. Anarchy had moved in. For thirty years you couldn't possibly make it unless you were white, sleek, nicely spoke, and phoney to your toenails—suddenly now you could be black, purple, moronic, delinquent, diseased, or almost anything on earth, and you could still clean up. Just so long as you were new, just so long as you carried excitement.

In a way, we were moving toward some kind of democracy. Under the new system, all you needed was dollar potential: earn, baby, earn. So that's what Little Richard was celebrating in *Tutti Frutti,* and he was very right.

Most of the best early rockers came out of the South: Elvis from Mississippi, Little Richard from Georgia, Buddy Holly from Texas, Jerry Lee Lewis from Louisiana, Gene Vincent from Virginia. These were the states where the living had always been meanest, where teenagers had been least catered to, and where, therefore, the rock kickback was now most frantic.

Anyhow, the South was by far the most music-conscious section in America. It always had been. It had huge traditions in R & B, country, trad, and gospel, and its music was in every way more direct, less pretentious than that up North. Mostly, it had a sledge-hammer beat and pulled no punches. Down here, rock was an obvious natural.

The only innovation was that the rockers made use of all the sources around them. Up to this time, whites had used country, Negroes had used R & B, and the two had never remotely overlapped. Now everyone incorporated anything they could lay their hands on, and it was this mix-up of black and white musics that gave southern rock its flavor.

Needless to say, this racial interaction had nothing much to do with tolerance. Black stole from white, white from black—it didn't mean they liked each other; it just meant that they accepted each other's uses. And then white kids liked playing black-sounding music because it shocked their parents, and black kids liked playing white-sounding music because it made them money. From any angle, it was strictly a fair deal all around.

Of all the great southern rockers, just about the most splendid was the aforementioned Little Richard Penniman out of Macon, Georgia, who was and still is the most exciting live performer I ever saw in my life.

He was born on Christmas Day, 1935, one of thirteen children, and had a predictably harsh childhood. At fourteen, he was singing solos with the local gospel choir. At fifteen, he was blues shouting, dancing, and selling herb tonic in a medicine show. From there, he got into a variety of groups, made a sequence of nothing records, and finally in 1955, when he was twenty, sold a million copies of *Tutti Frutti*.

He looked beautiful. He wore a baggy suit with elephant trousers, twenty-six inches at the bottoms, and he had his hair back-combed in a monstrous plume like a fountain. Then he had a little toothbrush moustache and a round, totally ecstatic face.

He played piano, and he'd stand knock-kneed at the keyboard, hammering away with two hands as if he wanted to bust the thing apart. At climactic moments, he'd lift one leg and rest it on the keys, banging away with his heel, and his trouser rims would billow like kites.

He'd scream and scream and scream. He had a freak voice, tireless, hysterical, completely indestructible, and he never in his life sang at anything lower than an enraged bull-like roar. On every phrase, he'd embroider with squeals, rasps, siren whoops. His stamina, his drive were limitless. And his songs were mostly total non-songs, nothing but bedrock twelve-bars with playroom lyrics, but still he'd put them across as if every last syllable was liquid gold. He sang with desperate belief, real religious fervor: "Good golly, Miss Molly, you sure like a ball—when you're rockin' and rollin', I can't hear your momma call." *

As a person, he was brash, fast, bombastic, a sort of proto- type Mohammed Ali ("I'm just the same as ever—loud, electri- fying, and full of personal magnetism"), and right through the middle fifties he was second only to Elvis. Most of his records sold a million each: *Long Tall Sally, Lucille, The Girl Can't Help It, Keep A Knockin', Baby Face.* They all sounded roughly the same: tuneless, lyricless, pre-neanderthal. There was a tenor sax solo in the middle somewhere and a constant smashed-up piano and Little Richard himself screaming his head off. Indi- vidually, the records didn't mean much. They were small episodes in one unending scream and only made sense when you put them all together.

But in 1957 he suddenly upped and quit. No warning—he just stopped touring, stopped making records, and went off to play piano in a Seventh Day Adventist church off Times Square.

Apparently, he'd been in a plane and a fire had broken out. Richard got down on his knees and promised that if he was spared, he'd give up the devil's music for ever and devote him- self to the gospel instead. "And God answered my prayers and stopped the fire."

So he announced that he was giving up, but his entourage thought he was crazy and laughed at him. Then Richard, in a typically flash performance, took his many rings from his fingers and flung them into the sea. Almost $20,000 worth: "I wish I'd seen the face of the man that caught those fish. A king's ransom, all courtesy of Little Richard." And he quit on the spot. At least, that's the story he tells, and it might be true. Some of his stories are.

Five years he kept it up, made no records, gave no inter- views. But in the early sixties he began to cut gospel records,

* Words of *Good Golly Miss Molly* by permission of Southern Music Publishing Co., Ltd., London.

and from there it was inevitable that he'd go back to rock again. He didn't get any further hits, but he was still a name. Several times he toured Britain, and each time he went down a storm.

The first time I saw him was in 1963, sharing a bill with the Rolling Stones, Bo Diddley, and the Everly Brothers, and he cut them all to shreds. He didn't look sane. He screamed and his eyes bulged; the veins jutted in his skull. He came down front and stripped—his jacket, tie, cuff links, his golden shirt, his huge diamond watch—right down to flesh. Then he hid inside a silk dressing gown, and all the time he roared and everyone jumped about in the aisles like it was the beginning of rock all over again.

Objectively, he didn't even do much. Anyone else that has a great stage act always has an obvious selling point: James Brown has speed, Johnnie Ray has pain, Elvis has sex. Little Richard had none of that. All he had was energy.

He howled and hammered endlessly. On *Hound Dog*, he dropped down on his knees and groveled, and still he howled. It was all gospel—"that healing music, makes the blind to see, the lame to walk, the dead rise up." He kept it up so long, so loud, it made your head whirl. Good hard rock; he murdered it and murdered us. When he was through, he smiled sweetly. "That Little Richard," he said. "Such a nice boy."

Fats Domino came from further back. In fact, he was almost pre-pop. As early as 1948, he cut a big hit called *Fat Man*, and he'd already tucked about ten smashes under his belt by the time Bill Haley came along.

At this period, he sold mostly around his home town of New Orleans and worked for a strictly Negro market. The music he peddled was a nicely relaxed line in R & B, backed by tightly knit small bands, and everything he did was casual. Fats himself wrote the songs, played piano, and sang.

When rock came in and R & B was acceptable, the fat man very quickly cashed in. He had whole strings of American hits, and by 1960 he'd sold upward of fifty million records. Fifty million is a lot of records. Officially, he's also credited with twenty-two individual million-sellers, which puts him ahead of everyone outside of Elvis and the Beatles.

Mind you, it has to be said that these figures make him sound a lot bigger than he ever was. Most of his alleged million sellers were only regional hits, and he never made much sustained impression on foreign charts. All the same, he was a solid figure. More important, he made good records.

The way he was so lazy and good humored, he was a bit like an updated Fats Waller. Most of his best songs—*Blue Monday, I'm Walkin', Blueberry Hill*—were dead simple, straight ahead, and Fats sang them as if he was even having himself a time. When he was at his best, he conjured up small-time colored dance halls on Saturday night: he played a bit and sang a bit, and everyone got lushed. Good-time music, that's all it was, and it hit the spot just right.

In his unpretentious way, he also had quite an influence on what came after him. The British jazz/blues bands in the early sixties used his understatement, his idle beat, his tight backing sound. Georgie Fame especially was a big Domino man.

Two years ago he did a Sunday night show at the Saville in London, and the audience was made up of rockers from way back when, all greased hair, drainpipes, and three-quarter coats. Fats weighed in at 225 pounds and smiled all the time. He ran through his hits, and diamonds glittered on his fingers, and he wore bright orange socks.

When he came to his finale, he went into an endless and very corny workout on *When the Saints Go Marching In*. It went on and on and on. Fats glistened and gleamed all over, his band cavorted like circus clowns, and it was all a bit embarrassing. At the end, Fats got up and started to push his piano across the stage with hard thumps of his thigh. He was past forty and not fit, and it was a very wide stage. By the time he was halfway across, he was flagging. The music rambled on, and Fats was bent almost double with effort. It was a very ludicrous situation—the rockers stormed forward at the stage, willing him on, and he kept on heaving; he wouldn't give up. And it took him maybe five minutes, but finally he did make it, and everyone cheered like mad.

Two of the rockers jumped up on stage and lifted his hands, holding them aloft like he was a winning fighter. They were big kids, and Fats, for all his weight, is quite squat. He stood shaking between them, and he looked vulnerable, almost old. Everyone was rioting. Fats streamed sweat and kept smiling, but he also looked a bit confused. Very likely, no one had gone quite that wild for him in ten years.

1495358

Like Fats Domino, Larry Williams came out of New Orleans. He started out playing piano with Lloyd Price, who was one of the biggest Negro R & B stars of the fifties and had world best-sellers with things like *I'm Gonna Get Married*, *Personality*, and biggest of all, *Stagger Lee*. But in 1957 Larry went solo, started writing songs, and became the first rock 'n' roll whistler. Straight away he turned out some of the best rock records ever.

He specialized; almost the only songs he wrote were about girls' names: *Dizzy Miss Lizzy, Short Fat Fanny, Bony Moronie*. This obsession with names was quite a central part of rock, one manifestation of the massive swing toward gibberish. Larry didn't introduce it, but he did give it new dimensions and turned it into a whole tiny anti-art form on its own. In *Bony Moronie*, which was his best, he touched true inspiration:

> "I've got a girl called Bony Moronie,
> She's as skinny as a stick of macaroni." *

As a contribution to pop history, this was all very righteous stuff but maybe less than earth-shattering, and I wouldn't give him this much space for his music alone. What gets him in is that his personality epitomized everything flash and catching about Mister Rock 'n' Roll.

Like most of the classic rockers, he didn't tour Britain until the sixties, and by this time things had very much run down for him. He'd moved on from rock to soul, but still he didn't get hits. He was almost thirty and said he felt like an old man.

* *Bony Moronie*, copyright © 1957 and 1966, Venice Music, Inc., Hollywood.

Most of the time he sat in his small hotel room and played cards with his wife, and even in decline, he was a smooth man. He wore rings on all his fingers and brushed his hair far forward like the Beatles. He had shiny silk suits and ever-present shades. And he talked a lot, with a turn of phrase that was often quite Shakespearean. In this style, he made my all-time favorite remark about rock. "In truth," he said, "it has no beginning and no end, for it is the very pulse of life itself."

Another noble rocker was Screamin' Jay Hawkins, who had been around ever since the middle forties. He wore a zebra-striped tailcoat, a turban, polka dot shoes. He began his act by emerging flaming from a coffin, and he carried a smoking skull called Henry; he shot flame from his fingertips; he screamed and bloodcurdled. At the end, he flooded the stage with thick white smoke, and when it cleared, he was gone.

"I used to lose half my audience right at the start, when I came up screaming out of my coffin," he said. "They used to run screaming down the aisles and half kill themselves scrambling out of the exits. I couldn't stop them. In the end I had to hire some boys to sit up in the gallery with a supply of shriveled-up elastic bands, and when the audience started running, my boys would drop the elastic bands onto their heads and whisper 'Worms.'"

Jay's biggest hit was the original version of *I Put a Spell on You,* and he had other triumphs with things like *The Whammy* and *Feast of the Mau Mau.* Actually, he had quite. a pleasant baritone, but on stage, he'd only screamed and ghouled. "I just torment a song," he said. "Frighten it half to death."

Then there were the Coasters, who had the most sly-sounding lead singer in the whole business, not to mention the most lugubrious bass. The lead, Carl Gardner, played the school bad boy. He sang like he had some bubble gum permanently stashed away inside his cheek, and everything he did was sneaky, pretty hip. Then he was a loudmouth, a natural-born hustler, and all the time the bass groaned and grumbled below him, the voice of his conscience speaking. The lead took no blind notice.

Mind you, they could hardly miss. For a kickoff, they had the most prolific songwriters in rock going for them: Jerry Lieber and Mike Stoller, a partnership that hustled upward of thirty million records in five years. Lieber and Stoller also wrote some of the best early Elvis hits, notably *Hound Dog* and *Jailhouse Rock,* but they were natural humorists, and Presley was just a bit straight for them. The Coasters were ideal.

Lieber and Stoller churned out stuff that was inventive, wry, and sometimes very shrewd—a running commentary on the manifold miseries of being teenage—and the delinquent talents of Carl Gardner did the rest with no sweat. Between them, they came up with some very funny records.

The format was simple: they got a fast shuffle going, reeled off the assembled lyrics, and then stuck a frantic yakety sax chorus into the middle. It was a comforting scheme of things. You always knew what was coming and could relax. So the lead snickered, the bass moaned, and everyone was happy.

Probably their most classic effort was *Yakety Yak, a* knock-down and drag-out row between a bullied teenager and his monstrous parents. The teenager, of course, is seen as martyr. He spends his whole time tidying his room, doing homework, washing, generally flogging himself.

From there they went on to further explorations of teenage hell—*Charlie Brown* ("Why's everybody always picking on me?"), *Poison Ivy,* and *Bad Blood.* Each one was perfect in its own way, but the whole style was completely geared to rock attitudes, and when times changed, they were among the first to slip.

They're still around, though, and occasionally a new single filters through. Nothing vital is changed. The lead still sounds maybe fifteen years old and carries himself as if he's just seen his geometry coach slip on a shrewdly planted banana skin.

The bass still groans. They live in a cutoff private world, and everyone is sweet sixteen for ever.

While I'm talking about Lieber and Stoller, I'd better stick in a short bit about the Drifters, who were hardly rock but who don't fit in too well any place else. Really, they were just commercialized R & B, and their major contribution was that they introduced the violin into modern pop.

Lieber and Stoller, who produced them, wrote natural hit songs for them and then used string sections to play what would normally have been the lead guitar part. It was good stuff, too, stylish, relaxed, always melodic. Over the years they came up with some beautiful things—*Under the Boardwalk, Save the Last Dance for Me, I'll Take You Where the Music's Playing, Up on the Roof,* and quite a few more.

The only comic thing about them was that their personnel changed completely every time they turned around. They ran through themselves like fire; the turnover was amazing. What's more, other groups all over America stole their name, so that you wound up with umpteen different outfits, all called the Drifters, all swearing blind that they were the original and only genuine article.

The real Drifters recorded for Atlantic and ran through such good lead singers as Clyde McPhatter and Ben E. King, both of whom later made it as soloists. No matter how many individuals came or went, they always kept the same basic sound, tight and immensely commercial. Good-time music, they were unusually polished for their time, and like everything else that Lieber and Stoller handled, they were fun.

Chuck Berry was possibly the finest of all rockers, and he's easily my own favorite pop writer. He wrote endless Teen Romance lyrics and sang them with vicious sly cynicism, and this is the clash that makes him so funny, so attractive.

His most perfect song was *You Never Can Tell,* an effort that gets a lot of its flavor from the knowledge that it was made soon after Chuck had served a hefty jail sentence for transporting a minor across a state boundary without her parents' consent. Its full lyrics went:

It was a teenage wedding and the old folks wished 'em well,
You could see that Pierre did truly love the mademoiselle,
And now the young monsieur and madame have rung the
                    chapel bell—
C'est la vie, say the old folks, it goes to show you never can tell.

They furnished off an apartment with two rooms, they were
                    all by themselves,
The coolerator was crammed with TV dinner and ginger ale,
But when Pierre found work, the little money coming worked
                    out well—
C'est la vie, say the old folks, it goes to show you never can tell.

They had a hi-fi phono, boy did they let it blast,
Seven hundred little records, all rockin', rhythm and jazz,
But when the sun went down, the record tempo of the
                    music fell—
C'est la vie, say the old folks, it goes to show you never can tell.

They bought a souped-up Jidney, was a cherry-red '53,
They drove it down to New Orleans to celebrate
                    their anniversary.
It was there where Pierre was wedded to the lovely
                    mademoiselle—
C'est la vie, say the old folks, it goes to show you never can tell.*

A jangle piano rambled away legato in the background, and
there were great swirling sax riffs, and Chuck himself more
intoned than sang, sly and smooth as always, the eternal
sixteen-year-old hustler. That was it—the Teendream myth
that's right at the heart of all pop, and *You Never Can Tell*
expressed it more exactly, more evocatively, than any of the
other fifty thousand attempts at the same theme.

Of course, this is all very naïve and undeveloped by comparison with what has come since, but then Bogart proved
thirty years ago that in mass media you don't need to be an

* Words of *You Never Can Tell* by permission of Jewel Music Publishing Co., Ltd., London.

intellectual to be great. In fact, it's a definite disadvantage if you are. What you do need is style, command, and specific image, and these are the exact things that Chuck Berry has always been overflowing with.

Basically, what it boils down to is detail. Most pop writers would have written *You Never Can Tell* as a series of generalities, and it would have been nothing. But Chuck was obsessive: he was hooked on cars, rock, and ginger ale, and he had to drag them all in. That's what makes it—the little touches like the cherry-red Jidney '53 or the coolerator. That's what gives it grip, and that, to get pretentious for a second, is what turns it into something approaching great myth.

Chuck was born in California, 1931, but grew up in St. Louis and became a hairdresser. By nature he was an operator, and he was always going to be successful. The only question was how. So he tried singing, he wrote, he made progress. In 1955, he had his first national smash with *Maybelline*, and from then on he was a natural Mister Big.

As a writer, he was something like poet laureate to the whole rock movement. He charted its habits, hobbies, and hang-ups or celebrated its triumphs or mourned its limitations, and he missed nothing. *School Days* pinned down exactly that obscure schoolkid sense of spending one's whole life listening for bells; *Johnny B. Goode*, guitar slinger, created a genuine new folk hero; and *Roll Over Beethoven* should have been adopted as the universal slogan of rock. But almost best of all was *Sweet Little Sixteen*. Nothing summed up better the twined excitement and frustration of the time:

> Sweet little sixteen, she's just got to have
> About a half a million famed autographs.
> Her wallet's filled with pictures, she gets 'em one by one,
> Becomes so excited, watch her, look at her run.
> Sweet Little Sixteen, she's got the grown-up blues
> Tight dresses and lipstick, she's sportin' high-heeled shoes.
> Oh but tomorrow morning she'll have to change her trend
> And be sweet sixteen and back in class again.

They're really rocking in Boston, in Pittsburgh, Pa.,
Deep in the heart of Texas and 'round the Frisco Bay,
All over St. Louis, way down in New Orleans,
All the cats want to dance with Sweet Little Sixteen.*

Beyond his writing, he played a very fair blues guitar,
Chicago style, and sang in a voice as waved and oily as his
hair. On stage his specialty was the duck walk, which involved
bounding across the stage on his heels, knees bent, body jack-
knifed, and guitar clamped firmly to his gut. Then he would
peep coyly over his shoulder and look like sweet little sixteen
herself, all big eyes and fluttering lids. He had a pencil moustache and the smoothness, the cool, of a steamboat gambler.
A brown-eyed, handsome man, in fact.

Then he'd do his songs for the people, so innocent, so sentimental, so greasy, and it was a very strange performance, but
it worked—he was very much like the school bad boy, the one
who's disgusting but always gets away with things.

Just when things were going so well for him, he made his
mistake with the minor and was put away. By the time he got
out again, in 1963, his kind of rock was finished. But the
British R & B boom was just getting under way, and he was
made blues hero number one by the Rolling Stones, who
started out playing almost nothing but Chuck Berry songs.
Almost as a matter of course, he landed back on his feet.

He was brought to England and made much of but turned
out to be hard to deal with. He was arrogant, rude. When he
liked to turn it on, he could be most charming, but often he
couldn't be bothered. First and last, he was amazingly mean.

There's an authenticated story that on his first British tour
he used to study the evening paper nightly and check to see if
there had been any fluctuation in rates of exchange. If there
was any deviation in his favor, no matter how small, he'd de-
mand payment in cash before he went on. On one night, this
differential came to about twenty-seven cents.

* Words of *Sweet Little Sixteen* by permission of Jewel Music Publishing Co., Ltd., London.

Still, all of that is irrelevant when you hear his records again. In any case, his hardness, his greasiness, is all part of his double-edged appeal. And when he does his duck walk, when he flirts over his shoulder and unfolds one of his best flowerpot teen epics, you know that he's one of those few people in pop that really count.

By and large, white rockers were a lot less impressive than their black counterparts. After the wildness of Little Richard, the lyricism of Chuck Berry, they sounded samey and half-hearted. As personalities, too, they were less colorful, less articulate. Mostly, they were plain boring.

The major exception was Jerry Lee Lewis, a pianist and shouter from Louisiana. He used R & B and country in about equal doses and attacked the keys in very much the same style as Little Richard, bopping them with fists, feet, elbows, and anything else that was handy. Toward the end of his act, he'd actually climb on top of the piano, hold the mike like a lance, and stay up there until the audience got hot enough to dash forward and drag him down.

His great gift was that no matter how frantic he got, his voice remained controlled and drawling country. He seemed to have a lot of time to spare, an unshakable ease, and this gave him class.

He had long yellow crinkly hair that fell forward over his eyes when he worked and a thin, slightly furtive face. He always reminded me of a weasel. And when he got steamed up, he'd sweat like mad and his face would collapse into nothing but a formless mass of heaving, contorting flesh. Still, his voice would be strong, easy. As stage acts go, it was hardly pretty, but it was definitely compelling.

After he'd rampaged through his earliest hits (the apocalyptic *Whole Lotta Shakin' Goin' On* and *Great Balls of Fire*), he did a 1958 tour of Britain and immediately plunged neck deep into trouble. He had brought his young wife with him. His very young wife, as it turned out. Her name was Myra, and Jerry Lee said she was fifteen. Later, he admitted that she was only thirteen. He also said that, at twenty-two, this was his third marriage. His first had been at fourteen ("Hell, I was too young"), his second at sixteen ("I guess I was still too young"). This second had been bigamous.

The British press duly disgraced itself. It howled blue murder, screamed babysnatcher, and finally got the tour canceled. Jerry Lee flew out in disgrace. "Hell, I'm only country," he pleaded, but no one took any notice.

Before the cancellation, he'd had time to do two concerts, but doomed by so much bad publicity, they were disasters. In the first, Jerry Lee dashed out in a red pillar box suit and smashed straight through two numbers without letup. He was brilliant, by far the best rocker Britain had then witnessed, and he half won his audience around. Then, before going into the third number, he took out a golden comb and very delicately swept his hair back out of his eyes. It was a fatal move. Someone yelled "Sissy!" at him, and from there on in it was solid murder. Finally, Jerry Lee just upped and walked off-stage. The curtain came down. Pandemonium.

All of which goes to show how superficial the rock revolt had really been. On paper, Jerry Lee's marital junketings were exactly calculated to improve his prestige, make him into an even better symbol of rebellion. In practice, it only took a fast burst of pomposity in the papers and the kids were just as appalled as their parents. And when Jerry Lee left his hotel, he was hissed and insulted and spat upon. This was just ten years ago.

Jerry Lee wasn't downcast. Arriving back in New York, he announced that his concerts had been "great, just great" and that, as he'd left, "three thousand stood and cheered."

The final irony was that the marriage worked out idyllically well. They settled down, had children. They were both intensely religious, and Myra carried a Bible with her everywhere.

In any case, he was forgiven. Through the sixties he has toured Britain often and has always brought the house down, which isn't surprising, because he has huge command and plays his audiences exactly as he likes. Recently, he's been peddling C & W rather than straight rock, and his *What Made Milwaukee Famous* reached number two on the American country charts.

There are people around who'll tell you that he's the greatest pop figure ever. I wouldn't agree, but he certainly rates. I also like his attitude. "You are either hot or cold," he says. "If you are lukewarm, the Lord will spew you out of his mouth."

Buddy Holly was really called Charles Hardin Holley and first came out of Lubbock, Texas, with broken teeth, wire glasses, and halitosis, plus every last possible kind of country southernness. He wasn't appetizing. In fact, he was an obvious loser.

On the other hand, he had a voice, he wrote natural hit songs, and what's more, he was by no means prepared to sit tight in the background and churn out smashes for other artists. He said he wanted to sit in his front room and watch his face singing to him out of the television screen. He was very firm about this. So a man called Lloyd Greenfield, a tough, no-nonsense agent, took him up and changed him into another person. Buddy had his teeth capped, his breath cleaned, his hair styled, his wire glasses exchanged for big impressive black ones, his voice toned. Then he was put into high-school sweaters and taught how to smile. Suddenly, he was all-America.

The whole saga was straight out of Stan Freberg—Holly sang lead with a group called the Crickets and promptly cut a succession of monster hits with them: *That'll Be the Day, Oh Boy, Maybe Baby*. By 1958, growing big-time, he had dumped the Crickets and gone solo, clocking up a further sequence of million-sellers on his own: *Peggy Sue, Rave On, It Doesn't Matter Any More*. He was smooth, he was clean. He had a smile straight off a toothpaste ad, and his new black glasses were major trend-setters. In every detail his career was perfect, and in February of 1959, just to round it off, he got killed in an air crash at Fargo, North Dakota. He was then twenty years old.

Long-time rock fans have always been bitterly divided about him. He wasn't a hard core rocker, being too gentle and melodic, and this eccentricity can be construed either as back-sliding or as progression. Even ten years after his death, it isn't an academic question; I have seen rock preservation meetings reduced to brawling knuckle-dusted anarchy about it. On the wall of a pub lavatory in Gateshead, there is a scrawled legend: "Buddy Holly lives and rocks in Tijuana, Mexico."

He was all adenoids—twanged them like a catapult, pro-pelled each phrase up and out on a whole tidal wave of hiccoughs and burps. As sound it was ugly, but at least it was new. It was also much copied; Adam Faith, for one, built his early career largely around his variations on it. For that matter, so did Bobby Vee.

Holly's breakthrough, in fact, was that he opened up al-ternatives to all-out hysteria. Not many white kids had the lungs or sheer hunger to copy Little Richard, but Holly was easy. All you needed was adenoids. The beat was lukewarm, the range minimal—no acrobatics or rage or effort required. You just stood up straight and mumbled. Even the obvious beaters, things like *Rave On* or *Oh Boy,* were Neapolitan flowerpots after *Tutti Frutti.*

In this way, Buddy Holly was the patron saint of all the thousands of no-talent kids who ever tried to make a million dollars. He was founder of a noble tradition.

Killed in the same air crash that took care of Holly were Ritchie Valens and the Big Bopper. Valens, at seventeen, had already made some of the direst records in pop. The Bopper, on the other hand, had made one of the all-time best: *Chantilly Lace.*

His real name was J. P. Richardson; he was a Texan disc jockey, and *Chantilly Lace* was his only hit. A fat man in his late twenties, he wore vast baggy striped suits, the jackets half-way down to his knees and the trouser seats big enough to hide an army in, and he owned a grin of purest lip-smacking lechery, a monster. *Chantilly Lace* is his testament.

He's in a phone booth, ringing some girl, and he's having to hassle like mad to get a date out of her. He sweats, he giggles, he groans. He drools, overflows himself.

You can feel him wriggling his fat shoulders in delirium, his joke suit around him like a tent, his eyes bugging and his bottom lip hanging slack: Chantilly lace and a pretty face, giggling talk, wiggling walk, pony tail hanging down, Lord, makes the world go round round round, makes him feel real loose like a long-necked goose. And all this time he's melting.

He's getting nowhere, of course, but he doesn't give up; he campaign shouts like a southern Democrat. The result doesn't matter anyhow; it's the performance that counts. "Ooh, baby," he howls. "You know what I like. You KNOW." * And when he says that, he bursts, he just disintegrates.

Apart from being so funny and good, *Chantilly Lace* was a big step: it was the first time ever that white popular music owned up to lust. Big Bopper lives.

There were also instrumentalists in classic rock, but they came a bit later. Duane Eddy played guitar man. He twanged. He was from Arizona, and he was a big country man who just stood still on stage and layed down sound like someone playing at the bottom of the Cheddar Gorge. He didn't use the top of his guitar at all; it was all solid bass, big and booming. Sensitivity wasn't the name of the game, but he made nice noise.

Apart from his own hits, he set the standard of all instrumental groups for almost five years. The Shadows copied him. So did the Ventures and just about everyone else. Eddy had his first major smash in 1958, *Rebel Rouser*, and Johnny and the Hurricanes made it the following year.

Johnny himself blew anguished sax, and the Hurricanes featured a shrill little organ. Their records were strictly novelty, small musical jokes. My favorite was *Rockin' Goose*, with Johnny pretending to be a wild goose on sax. It was one of the most ludicrous records ever made.

Gene Vincent had a bad leg. It had first been mangled when he was a child, and later it was made worse in a motor-

---

* Words of *Chantilly Lace* by permission of Southern Music Publishing Co., Ltd., London.

bike smash. Because of it, he couldn't fling himself around the stage like other rockers. He could hardly move at all.

Instead, he went through his whole act in one fixed pose. He'd dress himself entirely in black leather, right down to gauntlets and high-heeled boots, and he'd stand with one leg thrown back, the other forward and his body twisted aggressively sideways, a bit as if he was just about to start a brawl. There'd be a single spotlight on him, and he'd look agonized. He had unruly greased hair hanging in rat-tails across his forehead and a very painful mouth. The way he stood, so still, his body simultaneously thrust forward and dragged back, he looked like he was chained.

The image wasn't so very phony—he had two fast hits in 1957 (*Be Bop A Lula* and *Bluejean Bop*), and things looked good, but from then on it was all struggle. He couldn't cope. He had constant pain from his leg, and in any case, he was naturally weak, hysterical, and depressive. He went through repeated breakdowns and treatments and failed comebacks.

For a time he lived in Britain, and he was always popular there, but he couldn't cash in. He was in the 1960 car crash that killed Eddie Cochran, his closest friend, and soon afterward he faked up a story about his baby daughter having died back in America and escaped. That was virtually the end.

He's still remembered with a lot of affection. He wasn't much of a singer, but in his calmer moments, he had great gentleness and built-in innocence; he roused protective instincts in some most unlikely people. Above all, it's not possible to forget the melodramatic picture of him in his black leather, gauntlets clutching the mike, his body twisted.

He has been back in Britain several times in the last years and made sporadic comebacks without ever getting very far, but right now he has disappeared, and nobody is sure where he is or what he's doing.

The Everly Brothers started out nasty. There were two of them, Don and Phil, and they sang in high nasal voices like dentists' drills. They sounded delinquent, and when you saw them on stage, with their bony faces and sharp eyes, they looked like classic dropouts, and you might think they were really mean.

They were Kentucky boys and troupers. Their parents were long-time country singers and immediately dragged their sons in on their act. Through to their late teens, Don and Phil toured by summer, schooled by winter, and kept traveling. When they got out of high school, they turned into rockers, and very soon their parents were able to retire in comfort. In many ways, it was the classic showbiz story, the genuine Judy Garland article, but as childhoods go, it must have been pretty rough, and the Everlys were always the sharpest, most professional rockers of the lot.

Musically, they were pure country, only brought up to date a bit and given a rock bias. They'd use a fast shuffle beat, light and nervous, and throw their voices up high over the top in perfect and agonizing harmony, wild and clear and piercing. They even recorded their hits back home in Nashville, Tennessee, heart of all things country, and had publicity pictures of themselves eating ham and black-eyed peas.

They're not easy to write about, because they had no outrageousness, no major image, but from 1957 to 1961 they turned out roughly the most consistently good records around: *Wake Up Little Susie, Bird Dog, Bye Bye Love, Walk Right Back, Cathy's Clown,* and so on. They were melodic, tricky, entirely original. They introduced the idea that sound was all-important, the words and voices and backing and production all fitting to make one great booming noise. And as they went along, they lost that look of awkward delinquency, that dirty squeal in their voices, and turned into nice boys again, smooth young millionaires. They sold almost twenty million records.

But just like most of the other rockers, things began to go wrong for them at the beginning of the sixties. They had to do a service stint in the Marines, which didn't help much, and then they started to fall out with each other. Whenever they toured in England, there'd be an atmosphere of solid bitch. Don, the elder, had got married and was having trouble. The music was still as good as ever, but the background disturbance came across even on stage, and mostly their records weren't hits any more. In 1964 they did a single called *The Ferris Wheel,* and I thought it was their best ever: a marvelous careering melody line above a deepdown throb beat, a kind of Spanish-Moorish chant turned into pop terms. In England, it struggled to the edge of the top twenty and then quietly died its death.

And ultimately, there was Charlie Rich.

Rich was an ex-Georgia cotton farmer, and he was into his thirties; he had gray hair and a paunch. He looked most square, he was one natural-born ticket collector. Still, he wrote songs, played piano, and sang. And he was beautiful, he was the most mellow sound in the world. He didn't have many hits, admittedly, but he kept going right through into the sixties, and always he was classic.

His finest efforts of all were collaborations with Dallas Frazier, a songwriter. Best ever was *Mohair Sam,* made in the middle sixties, a work of genius.

And that's about where it ends: that was rock, those were the great rockers.

Looking back through what I've written, I'm struck hardest by two things—just how good the best of rock really was, and just how sadly most of its practitioners have ended up.

I suppose the trouble was only that rock was such committed music, such a very specific attitude, so tied to its time, and it wasn't possible for real rockers to ever move on. Of course this is a stock problem in any field—revolution so quickly becomes boring—but the thing about pop is that its generation cycles last five years at the very most.

Never mind: the best rock records stand up still as the most complete music that pop has yet produced. Everything about it was so defined—all you had to do was mix in the right ingredients, stir well, and you had a little rock masterwork on your hands. It was that simple, that straightahead, and finally, that satisfying.

Of course, rock wasn't ever anything like as complex, as creative, as pop is now. Does that matter? It was Superpop. On its own terms, it was quite perfect.

5.   *Highschool*

SOUTHERN rock was hard rock, Northern rock was high-school. Stan Freberg made a record that summed up Northern rock exactly. In it, he's a record-producer-cum-manager and he discovers a totally talentless kid who wants to be a rock 'n' roller. So he takes this kid and records him, standing behind him with a sharp stick to help him hit the high notes. And all that the boy has to do is sing the word *highschool* over and over again. His record is an instant hit.

Highschool wasn't a musical form; it was an attitude, and that attitude read: "We go to high school. We did rock 'n' roll. We date and go to parties and yes, we sometimes neck but no, we never pet. We also fall in love and that really burns us up. Then we pass notes in class and don't eat and even cry at night. We also drink coke, and hamburgers are really neat. We wear sneakers, short shorts, high school sweaters. The girls have pony tails and the boys are crew cut. Our parents can be kinda draggy at times, but gee whiz, they were young themselves once and they're only trying to do their best for us. Finally, we dig America. We think it's really peachy-keen."

There's a pop film that has been made maybe a hundred times over, and it is the absolute epitome of everything high-school. A girl from a nice home falls for a singer in a rock 'n' roll group. He had a mean childhood; therefore he's a bit surly and sad, but really he's a nice kid. The girl's father hears about this and orders them to break up. There is much tragedy and heartburn all around. Finally, the rock singer finds some way of convincing the father that he's all right. Everyone is happy.

In the last scene, all the kids jive while the father gently fox-trots. Everybody laughs.

Where Southern rock introduced something new to popular music—noise, violence, the mixing of R & B and country, gibberish, semi-anarchy—highschool was basically a continuation of existing white traditions. The solo singers were pretty boys, very much in the tradition of Sinatra, Eddie Fisher, or Vic Damone, and the groups sang harmony roughly in the style of the Inkspots, the Four Preps, the Hi-Los, or the Four Freshmen. All that was changed was that highschool catered solely for a teenage market and that it had no conception of quality whatsoever. It was lousy. Its concentrated badness, in fact, is what made it attractive.

Another big difference was that Southern rockers, by and large, had been their own bosses. They had business managers, but they conceived their records, worked out their stage acts, built their images all by themselves. Highschool rockers were almost always puppets.

This is where the middle-aged businessman came in. He was a manager, agent, producer, disc jockey, or general hustler. He hated pop but liked money. He was also often homosexual, and since his job lay mostly in discovering pretty young boys, this helped. He found the act he wanted and made a record. This record was then released, and either it sold or it was hyped.

Hype is a crucial word. In theory it's short for hyperbole. In practice, though, it means to promote by bribery, hustle, pressure—even honest effort if necessary—and the idea is that you leave nothing to chance. You slip some cash to radio stations, maybe some to TV producers, maybe some more to the trade press. You also throw nice parties and do all the conventional publicity strokes. Altogether, you do everything possible.

Hype has become such an integral part of pop that one hardly notices it any more. There's hardly any major pop star in the world who has never laid out some capital as insurance. From certain angles, it's justifiable: you believe in your product, and you spend money on promoting it in every possible way. You have faith. Of course, it's not ethical or even legal, but then what business is?

At any rate, the fifties were the golden age of hype. There was a huge scandal about it in 1959—the payola fuss—and a lot of people came crashing down, including Alan Freed, the deejay who'd put on the first rock shows in Cleveland back in 1951. Things have never been the same since. In the four years before the fall, however, everyone had themselves a carnival.

Highschool, in fact, is where the stock pop satire comes from—moronic groups, fat cigar-smoking agents, crooked managers, and all the rest. Things have changed, or at least they've got more complicated. In highschool, the caricature carried a lot of truth.

At the core of highschool was an unlimited assortment of faceless spotted groups. Mostly they made one big smash right off and then disappeared without trace. Sometimes they hung on for maybe a year. They hardly ever lasted longer.

The names and songs were virtually interchangeable: *Short Shorts* by the Royal Teens ("Who wears short shorts? We wear short shorts." *); *At the Hop* by Danny and the Juniors (Let's go to the hop, oh baby, let's go to the hop."); *Little Darlin* by the Diamonds; *When* by the Kalin Twins, and so on ad nauseam. Almost all of them used a bass voice like a foghorn at the bottom, an anguished falsetto over the top, and much mumbling in the middle. They cavorted and bounded and frolicked. They smiled constantly and they died cruel deaths.

The true masters of the form, the originators and still champions, were the Platters, who had a style that derived from the Inkspots. They had a good song writer going for them, a man called Buck Ram, and they made a whole streak of hits: *Only You, The Great Pretender, Twilight Time*. Their strength was that they took banality to the point where it nudged real inspiration. "Only you," they sang, "could make this change in me. For it's true—you are my destiny.† and the high tenor

---

* Words of *Short Shorts* by permission of Essex Music Ltd., London.

† Words of *Only You* by kind permission of Sherwin Music Co., London, copyright © 1954.

wailed and choked, half strangled himself in his own chords, and the bass grumbled like a volcano. They rolled soulful eyes, hammed it like mad. It got you right there. And they were all black, but the lead sang exactly like an Irish tenor. That's how confused they were.

Besides the groups, there were umpteen boys on their own, and they were interchangeable, too. Frankie Avalon, Tommy Sands, Jimmy Clanton, Jerry Keller, even Ricky Nelson—they had neat hair, they had neat voices. Sometimes they made good records and more often they made bad. Whichever, it was irrelevant. They all made money.

The most successful of them all was Paul Anka, a Canadian boy from Ottawa who wrote a song called *Diana* when he was just past fourteen years of age and then sold nine million copies of it.

In his early teens, he'd been fat and a bit isolated. So he'd written songs and flogged them around, not with much success. Then he coughed up *Diana*. He didn't stop at that either: he sold thirty million records in five years. He was number one cute teenager.

He was a showbiz natural. He had a flashy grin and much confidence. He found no difficulty in posing with nightclub managers, kissing starlets, winking at cameras, so he expanded easily from just being a singer into playing tycoon. Very fast, he was making over a million dollars a year and was reputedly America's youngest self-made millionaire.

In 1959, to celebrate, he wrote a song called *Lonely Boy:*

> I'm just a lonely boy, lonely and blue,
> and all that I want is someone like you.
> I've got everything you could dream of
> but all that I want is someone to love.*

Too bad, too tough, but he managed to keep going. Admittedly he stopped having such big hits, but he bossed a whole empire of music and production companies, and in a situation like that, who needs hits? Now he sits in Manhattan in splen-

* Words of *Lonely Boy* copyright © Sparta Music Ltd., and reprinted by permission of Hal Shaper.

dor, an institution by his middle twenties, a perfection of all American dreams. He has it made. And all because inspiration hit him at fourteen and he wrote the lines: "I'm so young and you're so old—this my darling I've been told." * *Diana:* it's the archetypal pop record, the most stereotyped highschool sound of all.

Highschool was very much a family charade. Father was played by Dick Clark, a disc jockey who looked like an all-American choirboy and who, in the late fifties, got to be just about the most powerful man in the whole industry. He was around thirty, married, with one son, and he was clean-cut as hell. He had a TV show called "American Bandstand," and on it he preached God, America, Mother, True Love, and Washing Behind Your Ears. He turned into the voice of teen conscience. What he said went.

Apart from his TV showcases, he promoted nationwide pop tours, giant ninety-day caravans which were notoriously the roughest grinds any singer could go through. The artists traveled hundreds of miles each day in buses, went without sleep, half killed themselves. Dick Clark made money. Now his TV shows have gone down a bit, but his tours still make fortunes and he is one of the very richest men in pop.

Big brother was Pat Boone from Florida, great-great-great-grandson of Daniel Boone. He started out in 1955 watering down other people's rock hits and then progressed to ballads and on to films. He was married, with very many children, and like Dick Clark, he was a preacher. Interviewed, he suggested that his own moral strength was due to having been regularly bent over the side of the bathtub and beaten when he was a child.

Musically, he was an updating of Perry Como, an ultimate in blandness, and he had thirteen million-sellers. Through the fifties, he sold more records than anyone but Elvis. "It isn't me," he explained. "It is the will of God."

Big sister was Connie Francis, a large lady from Newark, New Jersey, with a taste for sentimental ballads and a dirty

* Words of *Diana* by kind permission of Robert Mellin Ltd., London, copyright © 1957.

great vibrato. She was ideal because she inspired no sinful thoughts in anyone. Sometimes she was given good rock songs to do—*Stupid Cupid, Lipstick on Your Collar*—but she always managed to make them sound as if they'd just been sprayed with insecticide. As a sideline, she studied psychology.

Musically, highschool was a dog, but as myth and noise and comedy food, it did have its perverse attractions and sold in quite phenomenal quantities. Connie Francis, Pat Boone, Ricky Nelson, Paul Anka—these were the real superstars of the fifties. Most of all, it was an exact reflection of what white American middle-class teenagers really liked and dreamed of. Probably it was the most POP pop ever.

6. *Eddie Cochran*

EDDIE COCHRAN was pure rock.

Other people were other kinds of rock—country or high-school, hard, soft, good or bad or indifferent. Eddie Cochran was just rock. Nothing else. That's it and that's all.

There's not much known about him: he was born in Oklahoma City, October 1938, youngest of five children. His family moved to Minnesota, then to California. He grew up to be one sweet little rock 'n' roller, a nice looker, and he made records and had hits. He played good guitar and worked on sessions in Los Angeles. He wrote songs, got to be quite big, and he had hits like *Summertime Blues*, *C'mon Everybody*, *Twenty Flight Rock*, and *Something Else*. He even toured England. And on April 17, 1960, he was killed in a car crash. He was then twenty-one years old.

As a person, there's even less on him. He looked like another sub-Elvis: smooth flesh and duck-ass hair and a fast tricky grin—the full uniform. He was quiet, a bit inarticulate and aggressive, and he cared mostly about his music. He was polite to journalists, helpful even, but had nothing much to tell them. Nice kid. No twitches, tendencies, or tantrums of any kind. I was once told that he had a deep interest in toads, but I have no evidence on it. He was nothing special. He just came and went.

What made him such pure rock? In a way, it was his very facelessness, his lack of any detailed identity. With so little for anyone to go on, he seemed less a specific person than a composite of the essential rocker, a generalized fifties' blur, a bit pretty and a bit surly and a bit talented.

But he was something more than that; his songs were perfect reflections of everything that rock ever meant. They were good songs, hard and meaty, but that wasn't it. In every detail, they were so right and so totally rock.

Summertime Blues, My Way, C'Mon Everybody, a few more —there were only maybe half a dozen things that did him full justice, but among them they added up to something really heavy.

There is almost a continuous storyline running through them. Eddie is still at school and hates it. Lives at home and hates it. Works on his holidays and hates that worst of all. Still, he's a pretty ready kid, can handle himself. And he runs in some kind of gang; he's leader of the pack. Eddie Cochran, no punk or palooka of '59.

When he gets very lucky, his father gives him the car for the night, and then things are wild. Of course, after he gets back home, four in the morning, bushed and busted, he is kept in for a fortnight, but that's the name of the game: he can't win. The world rides him. When he works, he's paid chickenfeed. When he enjoys himself, he is automatically punished. Tough.

Still, when he walks down the street so nice and slow, his thumbs hooked into the belt loops of his blue jeans, his hair all plumed and whirled, the girls look up from their chewy mags, sip coke through a straw, and they think he's cute, real cute. Sure good-looking, he's something else. So, after all, he just about gets by.

You can see him: hanging around on the curb outside the poolhall, mooching along with his transistor radio held up tight against his ear, mouthing all the words but not making a sound. Real romantic visions. It's only some new version of the old American dream.

It's not as easy as it sounds. Anyone who can compress the atmosphere of a whole period into six songs, who can crystallize the way that any generation worked, must have something very unusual going for him. Pete Townshend (of the Who) is the only person who has caught the sixties in the same way, and he has had to work his ass off to do it. Cochran did it almost instinctively. For that alone, I'd rate him very high indeed.

He was the first major American rocker to do a full unaborted tour in Britain, and his impact was tremendous. He was the starting point from which British pop really began to get better.

He was a mover and writer and voice. He played his own things on guitar; he was really a musician. He sang songs that weren't just crap but did somehow get across a real and basic attitude. All of that was new. No pouncing about, no dressing-up or one-shot gimmicking: he was something solid happening. So Billy Fury saw him and woke up. Or the Beatles saw him, or the Stones, or the Who, or the Move. That's how things got started. And at that point, after the style of James Dean, Cochran got himself killed.

7.   *P. J. Proby*

THE FIRST time I met P. J. Proby, he was at his peak. He had
been in England for about a year, and immediately, he had
cleaned up, established himself as the most mesmeric stage
act we'd ever seen. So he was the biggest solo star around then,
but he was also one long streak of trouble and he was always
neck deep in hassles. He was intuitive, fast, hysterical, paranoid, generous, very funny, hugely imaginative, original, self-
obsessed, self-destructive, often impossible, just about irresist-
ible, and much more besides. Truly, he was complicated.

Anyway, I went to see him, and he was sitting in a darkened
hotel room, downing bourbon and coke by the tumblerful. He
was wearing a grubby undershirt, old white socks, and navy
blue schoolgirl's knickers. And he was tired: his hair hung all
unkempt around his shoulders, and his eyes were red, his face
swollen with lost sleep. He looked quite defeated.

When I first came in, he said nothing but only handed me
a scrap of paper covered with ragged, semi-legible hand-
writing. "That's my testament," said Proby. "Read it."

On inspection, it turned out to be something like a petition.
Crudely paraphrased, it said that ever since Proby had been
in this country, he had been systematically hounded by enemies
and fools. His name had been blackened, his life made not
worth living, his career half-wrecked. Promoters, record companies, and agents had conspired together to bring him down
and break him. Until he had finally had enough, and now he'd

decided to expose them all. Near the end, in a crucial phrase, he said: "I am an artist and should be exempt from shit."

All the curtains were drawn tight and the hotel room was full of hangers-on: Proby's hairdresser and assistant and publicists, his friends and his ladies and his unspecified sycophants. Great image: Proby himself just brooded, said nothing, and everyone else watched him.

Bongo Wolf sat next to me.

Approximately, Bongo was Proby's court jester, his most favored attendant, and he was strange. He looked like some malevolent small boy, spotty and very rounded, with crew cut and T-shirt and resident snicker. Then he used thick-lensed glasses and had blank eyes behind them.

His great passions were for werewolves, comics, dirty jokes, bongos, and P. J. Proby. When he spoke, he whined, and when he whined, he also snickered. Mostly, he seemed about ten years old.

On this afternoon, Bongo looked over my shoulder at the testament and framed the words as I read them. "Would you believe it?" he said. "He wrote it all himself."

Very suddenly, Proby began to talk at me and then didn't stop for maybe two hours. He told me many things, all about his life and his soul and his many agonies, and he made everything epic, everything wild and somehow magnificent. The way he told it, his life was a composite of Jesus Christ, Judy Garland, and Errol Flynn.

According to the saga, he was born in Texas, real name James Marcus Smith, and his father had been a very rich man, a much respected citizen. His earliest years were filled with happiness, but it didn't last. His parents' marriage broke up, and after the divorce, Proby was sent to military college, which trained and disciplined him to be a man, and then he changed his name to Jet Powers, became a singer, and went west to Hollywood. He wrote songs and hustled, waited for breaks to happen and, around this time, got married. So he and his young bride used to sit in their window when the evening came, looking down into the street below, and they'd dream about the way it'd be when he finally made it, when his name was big in lights. That's exactly the way Proby told it: young love, first love, filled with deep devotion.

Later, some of his songs were made into hits, and he moved up. He was a Hollywood face. And Jack Good planned to stage a musical of Othello, Proby playing Iago to Muhammed Ali's Moor. That was really something.

But then, just as the time of his ultimate triumph was approaching, he quarreled with his true love, and he was all capsized again. He came to England and, of course, became a superstar, but he wasn't happy; he never could be. He was hollow inside.

Picture him: a man crucified, a genius destroyed, a beautiful animal caged—he told me all of that, and when he was finished, he lapsed into silence and stared at the floor, drank more bourbon. Finally, he raised his head, looked at me, and flashed me his first smile. Pure malice. "How's that?" he said. "Did I break your fucking heart?"

(Being halfway honest for once, I have to say that there are many people around who'll tell you entirely different versions of the Proby trauma, and they'll all swear blind that theirs is the only right one. Myself, I'd say that mine is as possible as any other and I stick by it).

At any rate, I was just eighteen when Proby hit me with this, and I was never so impressed by anything in my life. The darkened room, the bourbon, the knickers, the fat Texan drawl —this was true heroism and it made me shake. I never grew out of it, either. At first sight, Proby was installed as my ultimate pop obsession, my real idol, and he's stayed that way ever since.

On stage, he was quite magnificent.

He'd stand behind a curtain and extend one toe, and all his little girls screamed. Then he'd draw it back again, then he'd extend it again, then he'd draw it back again. He might continue this for five full minutes, getting slightly bolder, even flashing his ankle, and then he'd suddenly bound out like some puppy St. Bernard. He wore blue velvet all over, loose jerkin to hide his paunch and skintight pants, and he had his hair tied back in a bow, and he wore buckled shoes, and he was camp as hell. Simply, he was outrageous.

He'd stand quite still, and then he'd turn around; he'd mince across the stage like some impossible drag-queen, and then he'd stop dead again; he'd grind his groin like a really filthy burlesque stripper, and then he'd flounce across to the wings like an overweight ballet dancer, and then he'd come back all coy and demure like a small ribboned girl, and then he'd snarl, and then he'd pout, and then he'd start the whole thing over again. He'd sing a ballad and he'd agonize; he'd raise one hand, he'd let fall an invisible rose. Or he'd sing soul, and he'd scream, grind, go berserk. Then he'd make a monologue, and he'd explain how he was mistreated, conspired against, and how his only friends in the world were his fans, his little girls. Then he'd be camp again, and he'd flaunt one hand on his hip, and his lashes fluttered like fans. Well, it could all have been horribly embarrassing; it very nearly was, but he had a great voice, he owned real presence, and somehow he brazened it out. The way he explained it, he'd taken all his movements, all his faces, from different girls. You could well believe it. Whatever, he kept going for a full hour, and he screamed himself voiceless; he sweated till he was slimy all over like a toad, till he was quite hideous, and still he piled on intensity, agony, outrage. "Am I clean?" he'd squeal. "Am I clean? Am I spotless? Am I pure?"

When he was done, when he'd quite destroyed himself, he'd stagger off blindly into the wings and collapse, semi-conscious, in his dressing room. He'd just lie there for maybe twenty minutes without moving, and Bongo Wolf would watch over him, quietly reading his comic. Then Proby would rise up refreshed, and he'd bound out through the stage door and into his waiting limousine, surrounded and protected at all times by his entourage, and then the whole circus would roll back to London.

Wild camp, marvelous image: P. J. Proby lay back exhausted in his cushions, the Sun King, his hair like drenched rope, his mouth full of bourbon, and everyone entertained him. No medieval warlord ever had it better.

The strange thing was, he was talented. He had no right to be but he was. Specifically, he had giant range and perfect control, and he was a flawless mimic: he could turn himself into anyone from Billy Eckstine to Frankie Valli, Gene Pitney to James Brown. And he was a voice. As a straight ballad singer, he entirely outclassed Sinatra or Tony Bennett or any of them, but he'd distort his diction, exaggerate, melodramatize, until the whole thing turned into a subtle burlesque of the original slop.

On songs like *My Prayer* or *When I Fall In Love*, he'd be so almost straight that you'd really be fooled, and then, just when you'd be nicely lulled, he'd suddenly slip in something sneaky and capsize you. Always, it was neatly done, never crude. So his version of *Somewhere* and *I Apologize* and *If I Loved You* were strange little classics, almost surreal, and their great flavor was that you never knew just how you were meant to take them.

Anyhow, soon after that first time I met him, things started going very wrong indeed. *Somewhere* made number three, and he landed his first headlining tour, always a major milestone but, on the first night, he split his velvet trousers from knee to crotch. On the second night, he did exactly the same. On the third night, he did it one time too often and the curtain came down and he was flung off the tour, banned by the cinema circuit, banned from TV, hammered by the press, much insulted by the industry, and enthusiastically kicked in the teeth by almost everyone.

Really, that was the end: he did have other hits, he did hang on, but he was cut off from the most crucial outlets and he got progressively cornered. More, he was never forgiven. (Of course, Proby himself has always sworn blind that the trouser-splitting was purely accidental and, myself, I'd say that it's possible that nothing was ever deliberately planned. In other words, Proby just bought some tight trousers, dubious at the seams, and let fate ride. Either way, I wouldn't like to bet on it.)

Even in decline, he hardly walked small.

The thinking was always simple: Proby was a face, a Hollywood star, and he lived like one. He owed it not only to himself but to his fans and, most vital, to his image. At any rate that's the way he figured it; accordingly, he kept up a lush household in Chelsea and supported his full entourage and spent fortunes in discotheques and hired twenty-piece P. J. Proby Orchestras to back him and just kept right on drinking bourbon. By the end of two years, he was some $175,000 in debt and smashed.

He went to America for a year, had a couple more marriages, tried raising horses, failed, and came back home to London. This was early 1968, and by now he was officially bankrupt and his liver was shot, but he smiled smiles, looked angelic, and said most solemnly that he was an entirely re-formed character. On his first comeback gig, he was heckled and ridden. Immediately, he exploded in a rash of four-letter words, and the curtain came down. And everyone was happy —nothing had changed.

Whatever else, he has proved himself resilient. His greatest gift has been that he's always been able to convince everyone around him, myself included, that he is a genius. And just so long as that gift survives, he can't ever be written off and he can't ever starve. He can always find someone to pay his bills and love him and launch him one more time.

Well, I suppose I've given him more space than he deserves, and really, I have no justification except that I dig him so much. Along with Muhammed Ali, he is the great doomed romantic showman of our time, the Rasputin or Hearst or Jelly Roll Morton, and I'm left with two central images of him.

The first is a portrait of him (the work, he once told me, of "an Italian old master", and it shows him all in velvet, angelic-faced, walking on the clouds.

The second is of him recording his entry for a San Remo festival, and the Italian composer has flown over to supervise. The Italian is a caricature composer, all twirled moustachios and rapturous eyes, and Proby, who isn't entirely sober, is a classic Proby figure, all stubble and blear. And they're standing alone in the middle of a vast studio floor, and Proby is singing. He doesn't know a word of Italian, he has no idea what he's saying, and still he spreads his arms, throws his head way back, and soars. He'd break your heart. Such pain, such yearning, such terrible passion—the composer has never heard anything like it and he's drooling.

At the end of the take, the Italian flings his arms full around Proby's neck and hugs him. Proby beams. "Mr. Proby," says the composer, "how do you do it?"

"Maestro," says Proby. "I don't do. I am."

The Beatles

na Turner (left) the wildest and sexiest female singer in rock. She tours with her
usband Ike, laying down an archetypal soul roadshow, very sweaty indeed. More im-
ortant, she made a few classic singles with Phil Spector, including *River Deep—
ountain High,* one of the best pop records yet made. Little Richard (above) the frantic
e, was one of the original fifties rockers, the most torrid of the lot. Since the late
ies, he has alternated rock with gospel singing and has rather faded out. Still, he
d Tina Turner are as exciting as rock gets.

s Presley, the King (top left): raw and sexy in the mid-fifties and (bottom left) ᵴsent-day, desexed and degutted. Either way, he's still godlike. Cliff Richard (mid-) started out as an English imitation of Elvis but subsided into schmaltz. P. J. Proby tᵗom) was massively talented but self-destructive. Jerry Lee Lewis (above) a classic ᵉer.

The Rolling Stones (above) have been the toughest, most evil and most talented of c
hard rock groups. Frequently, they're misguided, self-destructive, or just plain dumb b
Mick Jagger (center) is an explosion, the natural sixties Elvis and, if they handle them
selves right, the Stones could still wind up more important than even the Beatles. B
Dylan (right) made lyrics count in pop. During the early sixties, it was Dylan who to
folk out of the coffee houses and put it across to a mass public. Later, he got heav
involved with pop and it was his synthesis of folk and rock that stopped pop from bei
just a noise and developed its current pretensions as an art-form. These days, Dyl
himself has become a recluse but his influence remains huge and there's no one
progressive rock who hasn't been changed by him.

Styles change, the basics stay the same: pop lives off exhibitionism. Johnnie Ray (left) the Nabob of Sob, a prerock singer who had many big hits in the early fifties, used to weep on stage and is still a performer of agonized intensity. Pete Townshend (above) lead guitarist and songwriter with The Who. As naturally talented as any writer that English rock has produced *(Substitute, My Generation, Tattoo)*, is also celebrated for smashing his guitar against his amplifiers.

Phil Spector (far left) came out of Brooklyn in the late fifties. He was the first pop tycoon who was the same age as his audience, the first to grow his hair long and wear outrageous clothes, the first to bring any kind of intellectual concepts into pop, the first to bother about quality. Frank Zappa (left) is the most anarchic of all the new West Coast intellectuals in rock—he runs, writes for, and sings with the Mothers of Invention and his stuff is full-scale pop staire, surreal American nightmare; in them the encrusted cliches of Tin Pan Alley are turned back savagely against themselves and used to lampoon the whole American lifestyle. The result is Dada in pop, sometimes sharp, sometimes pompous. Meanwhile, Diana Ross and the Supremes (below) are everything that Zappa mangles. Originally a typical Tamla Motown group, peddling no-nonsense commercial R & B, they've become increasingly sugared and now sing in plush white nightclubs, cover themselves in sequins and giggle in chorus. Even now, though, they're still capable of occasional brilliances (Love Child).

Three generations in blues—Fats Domino (below) was an R & B singer/pianist/song writer from New Orleans, dead simple but perfect in himself, who started having hits as early as 1948 and racked up twenty-two worldwide million sellers, without ever being quite as big as that would suggest. Right through the late fifties, Ray Charles (centre right) was the best R & B singer going, a blind gospel-based shouter of great power and a strong jazz pianist, and his influence on young white singers was immense. Later he got bogged down with strings, angelic choirs and cornball country balladry and were never quite so good again. Otis Redding (far right) caught on big during the mid-sixties but was always more popular with whites than with the mass black public. His premature death in an air crash, 1968, has made him a fashionable myth hero and, accordingly, his talents have been exaggerated.

For more than a decade now, James Brown has bossed R & B, and his stage a
remains the most theatrical in pop. A beautiful dancer and monotonously hysteric
singer, his records get boring. Live, though, he stirs his audience into real frenzie
quasi-religious ecstasies.

8.   Britain

BRITISH POP in the fifties was pure farce.

Nobody could sing and nobody could write, and in any case, nobody gave a damn. All anyone ever had to do to get himself a hit was to bend over in the right place at the right time.

The industry survived in a state of perpetual self-hyped hysteria, screaming itself hoarse about nothing in particular. There was much assorted greed, schnidery, and lunacy. Trousers dropped like ninepins. Sammy Glick would have had the time of his life.

Before this, in the early fifties, the biggest stars were people like Dickie Valentine and Anne Shelton and Joan Regan, automatons all. Mostly they had come up through dance bands, and once they had established themselves, they were safe for life. Nothing changed from year to year. The stuff they sang was just as maudlin and meaningless as its American counterpart. Worse, they didn't even have that certain flair and style that made Sinatra or Como or Tony Bennett halfway bearable. They didn't have anything.

At this time, records weren't too important. The really big money was in stage performances and sheet music sales; accordingly, the business was controlled by agents and publishers. Especially publishers. They had a long-term agreement with the B.B.C. by which they paid fixed rates to get songs plugged. In return, the B.B.C. insured that at least half of every popular music program was made up of songs that had been paid for. This was polite phraseology for payola.

What it meant was that nothing got hard-sell plugging unless the few major publishers willed it. Effectively, this was monopoly, and until the system was abolished in the middle fifties, it wasn't possible to have a hit song without falling meekly in line.

In these years the industry was structured around the massed publishing offices of Denmark Street, England's Tin Pan Alley. The men in control were mostly middle-aged, and they ran slow businesses, very cautious. If they had to be cut-throat, they were always sentimental with it, and many of them did truly believe that they were turning out quality. They tended to be married, with children. They had great sense of tradition. If you asked them, they'd probably tell you that there was no biz like showbiz.

Rock knocked all of that on the head. Records took over as the main focus of interest, and because of this, publishers found themselves increasingly fazed by managers, producers, engineers.

Denmark Street still thrives, of course. Publishers get a cut every time their records are played on the radio, and they make deals, get rich, as they have always done. But they don't hold control any more; they have no monopoly. No one interviews them on TV, no one fawns. They buy their new Rolls, and no one is even interested.

Rock brought in operators who were younger, faster, tougher, cleverer, nastier. More complicated and more neurotic. In every way, more interesting. They were young hustlers who had probably been hanging around in some other trade, films or journalism or crime, and immediately saw rock as a gold-mine dream come true. Sometimes they genuinely liked pop and sometimes they didn't. Either way, they cleaned up.

Most of them were homosexual. They'd see some pretty young boy singing in a pub, take a liking to him, and sign him up. They'd bed him and then they'd probably very quickly get bored with him.

The boy would fade and disappear again. Or, every now and then, he would turn out to be a stayer after all, and he'd somehow keep himself afloat. It was this scrabbling, this desperate jockeying for favor, that made the fifties such black comedy.

I haven't brought this up purely as a tidbit: the managerial queerness of this time has had an indirect but strong and lasting effect on teen life in general.

What happened was that managers decided what their protégés should wear on stage, and not surprisingly, they went for effeminacy, for flash and flamboyance. They chose things that would previously have been worn only by exhibitionist queens. Then the singers went out in all this outrageous tat, and some of them were successful, and their styles were copied. Private sexual fantasy turned into minor public cult. From there, things snowballed like mad, and by the early sixties, the movement had been enshrined in Carnaby Street. So now millions of kids all over the country are wearing pure homosexual regalia as a matter of course, and nobody gives it a second thought.

Of course that's a simplification, and there were many other factors at work in the swing toward flamboyance. Still, early managers have a lot to answer for.

The first attempt at a major British rocker was Tommy Steele, and a sad flop he turned out to be. Launched in 1956, he was eighteen years old, came from Bermondsey, and had been a merchant seaman. He had a lot of curly blonde hair and a grin as deep and wide as the Grand Canyon.

He was discovered singing in a Soho coffee bar, the 2 I's, by a man called John Kennedy, a New Zealander in his late twenties. Kennedy had been around in a variety of trades and had flair, invention, and a fast mouth.

Anyhow, he did a good job on Tommy Steele. He started him out as one more poor man's Presley but ballyhooed him with more energy, more imagination, than anyone was used to. He swept aside obstacles like so much kindling, wouldn't slow up for anything. He was a truly obsessive man and barnstormed Tommy through to number one in six months flat.

Give him credit: Tommy did his best to live up to the spiel.

On stage he squirmed and wriggled in all the right places, strummed his guitar till his fingers went numb, snarled animal, generally did the whole bit. Still, he wasn't really cut out for it. The trouble was, he wasn't evil enough. He was amiable, perky. Almost sweet, and that wasn't any good to anyone.

As it turned out, he was natural showbiz. He had instant charm going for him; he was photographed with his mother, and he kept right on flashing that bottomless grin. He was all hair and teeth. Adults took one look at him and weren't remotely fooled—the boy was all right. So he moved on from rock as fast as he could and turned to ballads, comic recitations, novelties. He played Shakespeare at the Old Vic and studied tap dancing and squeezed himself into evening dress. He even combed his hair.

Naturally, teenagers were much disillusioned and switched allegiance. It didn't matter: he was an all-around family entertainer now, that mythical beast, and he couldn't miss. He sang and danced and quipped. He was much loved by everyone. And he was that all-time showbiz cliché, the lovable Cockney, always merry and bright.

Compare his saga with the Elvis story and you have the precise difference between the great American and the great British entertainment epics. Elvis became God. Tommy Steele made it to the London Palladium.

Terry Dene was next in line. He wasn't talented; he had smooth features, and he sang rock without giving it any personal flavor at all. What happened to him sums up the fifties very well.

He had bad nerves. He'd come from roughly the same background as Tommy Steele, had emerged out of the Elephant & Castle, but he wasn't anything like as brash or self-assured; he wasn't remotely tough. He was plain petrified in fact.

He had a round face, unformed, childish, and he always looked as if he was on the point of bursting into tears. Very often he did just that, which made him ideal maternity food for those who liked it but poisoned him for just about everyone else. No question, the boy was cuddly.

All the time he had troubles. He wasn't much of a singer and often got the bird. This upset him. He'd brood until he got out of control, and then he'd have some form of breakdown. He'd be told to take a rest, and he'd return glowing, earnestly promising reform. Things would go all right for a bit, but inevitably he'd slip back. Then the cycle would begin again.

He didn't even get many hits. Factually, he was never more than a minor success, but the press found him fascinating—his breakdowns and comebacks, his almost weekly crises—and they plugged him like mad. This way, even by pop standards, he grew into a figure out of all proportion to anything he'd ever done.

In July 1958, aged nineteen, he married a singer called Edna Savage, a few years older than himself, and it was the fuss wedding of that year. The papers picked it up as a signal that even rockers were human, were capable of finer feelings, and ran it huge. The whole industry glowed with reflected pride. Terry Dene wept with happiness.

Predictably, it didn't work out. Edna Savage quickly got disgruntled and threatened to leave, reasons not disclosed. Just when things were coming to a head, Terry got his draft notice.

The press yelled bonanza again. The comparisons with Elvis were most lavishly drawn, the image of pretty young rocker giving up a fortune and selflessly marching away to fight for king and country was nudged home with a bulldozer. Terry himself was quiet and dignified. Edna Savage was proud of him; his mother was proud of him. For one week, he was a hero.

As Rifleman 23604106, he smiled for cameras, waved for weeping fans. He kissed Edna Savage good-by and flashed a thumbs-up sign. A few hours later, though, having realized exactly what he was taking on, he burst into tears and collapsed. "It was grim, man, just grim," he said. "I was standing up there with my tin tray, having my bit of food plonked down in front of me like all the others. The thought of me in that little bed with fifteen other blokes around—I felt real sick."

Two months on, he got his medical discharge and made his ritual comeback. This time it didn't work. Edna Savage left him and nobody was proud of him any more. His records didn't sell. "This time I'm older, sadder, and much wiser," he promised, but no one believed him. He retired and came back, retired and came back again. He had a couple of years in badly paid tours in cockroach halls, and everything was rough. Finally, he dropped out of sight.

That wasn't all: a couple of years later, he was seen standing on a Soho street corner, preaching the gospel with the Salvation Army. What he preached was repent your sins; change your way before it's too late. Nobody much stopped to hear him.

He looked much older, grayer, a small seedy man with a cancelled face. But he said he was happy and fulfilled. He didn't want publicity; he wouldn't give interviews. For some reason, he didn't trust the press.

What's more, he stuck it out; he didn't break down. He went on the road, and as far as I know, he's still out there, preaching as he goes.

Tommy Steele and Terry Dene were the heavies. Wee Willie Harris, Vince Taylor, and Screaming Lord Sutch added slapstick.

Wee Willie had his hair dyed flaming pink and wore a polka dot bow tie like elephant's ears. Also baggy candy-striped Big Bopper suits and neon shoes. All set off by an unchanging idiot grin.

Vince Taylor was black leather and chains, the final rocker. High boots and studs and black greasy hair. He did all right in England and then cleaned up in France, where British rejects always go over big. The sixties finished him. Last thing I heard about him, he had turned mystic and hung out in a big room in Soho with a gaggle of disciples. He saw himself as prophet. In his big room, there were two telephones. One he used for ordinary calls. The other was his hotline to God.

Screaming Lord Sutch was nobody's idea of a genius musician either. He didn't need to be, because he was a tireless self-publicist instead. Basing himself very much on the antics of Screamin' Jay Hawkins, he pulled all the standard stunts of the time—clambered out of coffins or dressed up like a cave-man. What made him a standout was his persistence.

His gift was that, whenever he looked like fading, he always managed some stroke. He stood for Parliament, got engaged, grew his hair long, tried some new form of fancy dress, hustled like mad. As stunts they were lousy, but they were also endless, and their cumulative effect wasn't resistible.

He had real staying power. He has never had hits, but he's outlasted everyone and still goes out for good money now. He's an institution. These days he has transformed himself into Lord Caesar Sutch and rides on stage in a chariot. Why the change? "You have to move with the times," says Sutch.

In all this chaos and foolishness, the only man who had any remote awareness of what was really happening was a TV producer called Jack Good. Everyone else saw pop as a one-shot craze and rushed to cash in on it fast before sanity returned and everything returned to normal. By contrast, Good realized it clearly as a major phenomenon.

I suppose he was the first pop intellectual. He'd been to Oxbridge, had letters after his name, and could spell words of more than two syllables. More, he knew that pop was going to boss the entertainment industry from here on in, that it was the product of real social change rather than publicity hype, that its possibilities were just about limitless.

As a producer, he was responsible for "Six Five Special," "Oh Boy," and the other major rock TV shows of the fifties. In the sixties, he emigrated to America and produced "Shindig," their best pop showcase ever.

He sent P. J. Proby to Britain in 1964. He dreamed up a musical version of *Othello,* Muhammed Ali to take the title part and Proby himself to play Iago. He even made a great record called *I Sold My Heart to the Junkman,* by Lyn Cornell, an English version of an American hit, out-of-tune and hopeless but quite amazingly exciting, a little joke masterpiece. In every job he tried, he did something good.

I can remember hearing him interviewed on the radio once, sometime in the late fifties. He said that Elvis Presley was a genius and that he'd go down as one of the major artistic figures of our century. Even now that would hardly go unchallenged. In its time, it was total anarchy. And his willingness to be outrageous, to shoot his mouth off blind at a schnide, skeptical audience was a big help in getting rid of rock's built-in inferiority complex.

The next figure to come along was Larry Parnes, who was a very big-time manager indeed and sold pop in bulk. He handled whole battalions of singers and gave them marvelous technicolor names—Billy Fury, Cuddly Duddley, Marty Wilde, Vince Eager, Johnny Gentle, Dickie Pride, Duffy Power, and so forth.

Parnes was the perfect fifties' manager—meaning that he was shrewd, fast-witted, and had natural publicity flair—but didn't go further. He had limited imagination, didn't plan years ahead, and didn't bother his head too much about art or progression. Instead, he made money and avoided stupid mistakes. He was a good businessman.

His first major property was Marty Wilde, who tried hard, had many hits, and was a thoroughly likable man but didn't have the magnetism to bring him right through. Billy Fury was different.

Fury was the closest that Britain ever got to producing a genuine rocker, someone almost in the class of Eddie Cochran. For one, he was a face: high cheekbones and moody little eyes and a comma of hair drooping down on his forehead. For two, he was a mover: he rolled his hips like he almost meant it.

Fury was one prong of the triumvirate that dominated British pop from about 1959 until the Beatles first broke through in 1963. The other two were Cliff Richard and Adam Faith. Of the three, Fury was the most exciting, Faith the most intelligent, Richard the most competent. What they had in common was that they were all articulate, smooth, composed. In every way, they were presentable. They had tidy smiles and noncommittal accents and nice manners. They tended not to make fools of themselves in public. Among them, they made pop singing almost respectable.

Cliff was easily the most successful. His great secret was that he was like some magic slate, a pad on which almost anyone could scrawl their fantasies and rub them out and try again. He was the nice boy that girls could be proud to date, the perfect son that mothers could be proud to raise, the good guy that schoolboys could be proud to have as a friend, the earnest youth that intellectuals could be proud to patronize, the perfect flesh that homosexuals could be proud to buy drinks for, the showbiz smile that hipsters could be proud to despise, and so on. It was a format that Tommy Steele had used first and that the Beatles were later to perfect. It is the classic British way of making it: be a clean white wall and let everyone write graffiti on you.

Just the same, for all the shining purity of his image, he was never exactly innocent. At the time when he got his first hit, 1958, he was seventeen and had already hung out a lot around Soho. By any standards, he was adult for his age, very cool and knowing indeed. Probably that's why he never let himself be conned or mismanaged. Whenever it counted, he was always shrewd.

He started out as one more computerized rocker, one more sexy mover and sub-Elvis rebel, but this wasn't ever his natural style. He wasn't butch enough for it; he didn't even hint at rape. Instead, he sang in tune and showed many toothpaste teeth. He was sleek, glossy. Most important, he was amazingly scrubbed; he radiated a kind of glowing cleanness that ordinary mortals couldn't even hope for. With all that going for him, rock was out. He was born to sing ballads.

His first ballad hit, *Living Doll*, was by far the most influential British single of the whole decade. It was cute and sweet and bouncy. It was tuneful and ingenuous. Even better, it was dead easy to copy, and it killed rock stone dead.

Britons hadn't ever really been capable of solid rock anyhow. It was an essentially American knack, and no one else could quite get it off. *Living Doll* was a different matter. Suddenly you didn't have to go berserk, rape microphones, jump on pianos, pretend to be King Kong. All you had to do now was murmur gently and clean your fingernails.

It was the British equivalent of highschool, and it was des-perate. In months, it took over completely. No rage, no farce, no ugliness left. We had mass-produced faces with mass-produced voices on mass-produced songs. It was as bad as the pre-rock early fifties all over again. That's mostly why the Beatles were hailed as such messiahs when they first started.

It has to be said that Cliff at least did it well. He was un-assuming, he worked hard, and he came to be very professional. He was insipid and syrupy, but he wasn't nauseous. And he was genuinely a very amiable person, modest and thoughtful and essentially decent. He doted on his mother, was considerate toward his fans, and so on. These aren't very exciting virtues, and he did always seem too good to be true, but that was hardly his fault.

His peak was probably *The Young Ones,* a 1962 musical that epitomized the entire Mister Clean movement. The scene where he sang the title song said it all. He's on a beach and he looks at his girl, flashes those white teeth at her, and looks soulful. Cue for a song. All around them teenagers are frolick-ing, and every last one is fit and keen and happy: a master race. No one is old and no one is black and no one has bad breath. Darling, we're the young ones, and one day we'll have young ones of our own. So he smiles and she smiles. Everybody smiles.

The Young Ones came out right at the peak of the Harold Macmillan period, just before things started going wrong for him, and it reflected the extraordinary smugness and optimism of that time perfectly: the British never had it so good. It was all too utopian to last, of course, and the post-Profumo return to national reality brought Cliff down just as surely as it did Macmillan.

Cliff didn't crash. He remained easily our most popular solo singer and his records went on selling and his films were box-office. It was just that he stopped being the center; he stopped echoing the predominant teenage mood. Everywhere there was a sense that times were turning tough again, that not all life was a fairy tale, and the need now was for something earthy, something halfway honest. Something, in fact, like the Beatles.

When Beatlemania did finally shut him down, though, Cliff took it well. He praised the Beatles' records, refused to bitch back when they were rude about him, held on to his dignity at all times. He just slid neatly into the background and looked benign. After all, he made upwards of a hundred thousand pounds a year and could afford to be kind.

Then, in the mid-sixties, he began to make mutterings about religion. He had lunches with bishops at the Atheneum, studied scripture between shows, and finally appeared on the platform at a Billy Graham crusade. He led choirs in hymn singing.

This wasn't entirely unexpected; he'd had lurid teenage times but had got increasingly puritan toward himself, worried and self-doubting, and he wasn't happy at all. Religion was the obvious way out.

Predictably, he got accused of using God as a spare publicist. This was almost certainly unfair. At any rate, he has stuck at it; he lay preaches, raises money for charity, turns out religious propaganda—lives the part in every way. And to be fair, he isn't pushy about it. At 28, he is rich and secure, he has kept his fans, he even seems happy. He is loathed by hippies everywhere as an ultimate of middle-class conformity, but I shouldn't think it worries him much. In his own terms, he is a thoroughly successful man.

So, all right, British pop in the fifties: it got better as it went along, I suppose, but it was still pretty lousy. There's one image that expresses it all, and it's not my own but comes from George Melly's book *Owning Up*.

Melly, at this period, was a blues singer with Mick Mulligan's band and was due to appear on a TV show. Also on the bill were two infant rock prodigies of the time, Jackie Dennis and Laurie London. Dennis was sixteen and wore a kilt on stage; London was even a bit younger. And when Melly came across them, before the show, they were having a pier-six showdown about who should get top billing. They were kicking and screaming, tearing each other's hair out, scratching each other's eyes out. Two brats brawling in a sandpit while their handlers looked on lovingly. That was the fifties in one.

9. *America 1960+*

1960 WAS probably the worst year that rock has been through. Everyone had gone to the moon. Elvis had been penned off in the army and came back to appall us with ballads; Little Richard had got religion, Chuck Berry was in jail, Buddy Holly was dead. Very soon, Eddie Cochran was killed in his car crash. It was a wholesale plague, a wipe-out.

Why didn't rock sustain? Not easy to answer. Partly it was because the vintage rockers were so ill-fated. Partly it was because they weren't flexible—they did what they did perfectly but couldn't progress. But mostly it was because pop is by nature ephemeral; it must change constantly to keep alive, and not even the very best things can hold.

New people came up to replace the gone heroes, of course, but they weren't in the same class: certainly they weren't flat-out rockers. Hard rock was done. What had replaced it was a continuation of highschool, a further spate of pretty nothing boys and pretty nothing songs. Most of them were just as forgettable as their predecessors: Brian Hyland, Jerry Keller, Johnny Tillotson, and a bit later, Bobby Vinton. Bobby Vee was not much better but was given good songs like *Rubber Ball* and *Take Good Care of My Baby*. The only standouts were Neil Sedaka and Dion Di Mucci, two of the most under-rated figures in the whole of rock.

There's not much to be said about them, beyond how good they were and what lasting records they made. Sedaka came from Brooklyn and trained as a classical pianist. Then he knocked off songs for Connie Francis, Clyde Macphatter, Laverne Baker. Then he began to make records of his own. Almost without exception, they were classics.

He was quite some writer. He'd start out steadily, build up gradually, and then, when he snapped into the chorus, the hook, there'd be a real explosion. It isn't possible to explain it right, but he'd come out with a sudden aching, pulling figure that made me catch my breath and count. It had nothing to do with words; it was purely musical. Something would burst.

His best sides were *Breaking Up Is Hard To Do* and *Oh Carol* and *Happy Birthday Sweet Sixteen*. Ten years later they still make me gasp every time I play them.

Dion was simpler. He was just given some hit songs and he did them well: *Little Diane, Runaround Sue, Ruby Baby, The Wanderer*. He was a format singer, meaning that all his singles sounded alike, which was fine by me. They were a bit like catch songs, everyone singing different riffs and chasing each other, and this gave them a curious circular feel. Comforting. His best was *Little Diane*: "I should knock you down and slap your face—bad girls like you are a disgrace." *

He went through a long bad patch in the middle sixties but made one beautiful record in 1967, *Mr. Moving Man*. Then, out of nowhere, he walked off with a 1968 smash hit in *Abraham, Martin, and John*.

Neither Dion nor Sedaka was strictly a rocker, but they were in direct line of descent. That's how they came to be so good—they had drive, guts, when everything that surrounded them was jellyfish, damp and flabby.

Why had everything gone so dead? Really, it was a failure of imagination, a simple inability to think things out from basics.

When rock had come along, it had changed everything; it had seemed the complete answer, and the industry had got used to the idea that what you had to do was, say, imitate Elvis, change his format slightly, add a mandolin, take away

* Words of *Little Diane* reproduced by permission of Spanka Music, Ltd., London.

a triangle, and you were automatically made. And they weren't far wrong.

But each imitation was a small emasculation of the one before; each rehash took things further and further away from the original hub. Pop ended up as a copy of a copy of a copy. Teenagers got bored, records sold less. In the end, there was just nothing left, and that was 1960.

1960 was the gap between two separate generations, the changeover, and the reason it was so bad was really that pop moves in very specific generation cycles: there is one breakthrough, followed by maybe three years of great excitement, followed by three years of stagnation, followed by a fresh breakthrough. Each cycle takes roughly seven years to run its course, and 1960 was the stagnant trough between.

Seven years seems nothing but it's really surprisingly much. After all, one rock generation really only lasts four years, the time it takes to get from eleven to fifteen and from fifteen to nineteen, and a seven-year cycle means that a whole generation gets skipped.

Why does it work like that? Probably because seventeen-year-olds are up too close to things; they don't see straight. When someone like Elvis first explodes, they buy his records and copy his looks, but it goes no deeper; it's only imitation.

With fourteen-year-olds, however, it becomes a big part of growing up: Elvis is their great adolescent hero; he's central. They buy their first suits and have their first sex and promote their first hangovers with him in the background. And then they have five years in which they distance him, get him into perspective and absorb him deeply. So when they come to do their own thing, they don't ape him but use him to form their answers.

Roughly, that's why 1960 was bad, and in the same way, that's why 1963 came on so good.

Also, Tin Pan Alley was back in the catbird seat. As soon as record sales began to fall, the music publishing world gleefully decided that hard rock was finished, and they shut out everything that wasn't highschool. Instead of yakety saxes and greasebox basses, the big black sounds of classic rock, we all got stuck with Disneyland.

Tin Pan Alley, of course, saw this as a clean-up campaign, a repudiation of all that sinful jass music, a return to decency. Ironically, though, 1959–60 was the ultimate golden age of hype —the only way to make kids accept such crap was by flat-out payola, and so the swing back to godliness turned into the dirtiest period that pop has been through.

Also, this was the time of the "beach party" movies, made by American International and starring such worthies as Tommy Sands, Frankie Avalon, Annette Funicello (ex-Mickey Mouse Club Mouseketeer), and Fabian.

These epics never changed—there were always a lot of clean-cut bodies in bikinis and/or briefs, a few bad jokes, a few songs, half a dozen assorted faces in the leads, and a lot of water. Seen in retrospect, they're camp and they're true Pop Art; they say more about Campbell Soup cans than Andy Warhol ever did. As 1960 teenage entertainment, though, they were killers.

All of this, the whole 1960 bit, was epitomized by Fabian. His real name was Fabiano Forte, and he came from Philadelphia. When he was thirteen, he was signed up by two local record men and computerized.

To start with, he had the basic requirements: olive flesh, duck-ass hairstyle, conveyor-belt features. He had the required passing resemblance to Elvis Presley. On top of this, his management did the full Professor Higgins bit. They had him groomed, had him taught to speak nice, had his voice trained. Made him round and flawless like a billiard ball.

One small snag: he couldn't sing. He ran through voice teachers the way old-time Hollywood stars ran through wives. What did that matter? His management launched the biggest publicity campaign ever, besieged the trade papers for weeks on end, howled him from the rooftops. Fabian himself only stood still and sparkled.

Once the snowball had got started, it was hardly stoppable. In no time, Fabian was going out for twelve thousand dollars a

night, and then he sold a million of a record called *Tiger,* and
then he was into movies. Not just crap movies either; he was
in *North to Alaska* with John Wayne. Later, he got married
and was duly mobbed. And all the time he could hardly sing a
note. That's highschool. So, all right, he's less than mister big
these days but what should he care? He's rich. He made it.

Outside of the prevalent highschool pulp, however, there
were three originals from this time: Roy Orbison, Del Shannon,
and Gene Pitney. They had a lot in common. For a start, they
weren't amateurs.

They had good strong voices, and none of them did much
cavorting on stage; they just stood up straight and did their
thing without fuss. Then they were songwriters, businessmen,
and they were built to last. They were shrewd. Among them,
they added up to the first major onset of professionalism.

Of the three of them, Orbison was easily the most impressive. No question, he wasn't a likely looking pop star, but he
could cut just the same. He had a pudgy, pasty face, very
white and sickly. Then he was chronically short-sighted and had
to wear glasses as thick as lemonade bottles. No Mr. Universe.
But he had a classic voice, perfectly controlled from mumble
through to full-blooded yell, and he approached his songs like
operatic arias.

Usually he set off almost conversationally, then broke into
tortured tempo, got gradually more fevered, more tragic, and
finally wound up in frantic howls of anguish. It was a formalized pattern, used on almost all his best records, and he
had it by heart. He never missed a trick.

If your nerves were bad, the unbroken agony of it all might
get a bit oppressive after a time. But if you were suckered by
schmaltz, Orbison was the very best brew going. Whatever, he
attracted great regiments of fans, and they've stayed endlessly
loyal to him. Outside of Elvis, he has probably the most un-
questioningly devoted following in the world.

Not that he has stuck exclusively to ballads. In his time, he's
rocked harder and longer than most, but he always sounds as if
he wants to slow things down, and even at his toughest he's

likely to launch himself into sudden spasms of bug-eyed operatics.

Orbison was born in Texas, 1936, and by his teens, he was writing country 'n' western. In the fifties, he was on to rock and wrote *Claudette*, a million-seller for the Everlys. So by the time he recorded *Only the Lonely* in 1960 and finally made it big, he'd been ten years in the business. An old pro, battle-hardened. That's how he came to last so well.

He was a quiet man, not flash or imposing, not outstanding in any way. He was polite and amiable. When he wasn't touring, he stayed home in Texas with Claudette, who was his wife, and they played motorbikes together. Finally, she had an accident and was killed. Wasting no time, Orbison put out a record called *Too Soon to Know,* very much based on her death, and it was a big European hit for him. Well, he's in pop to sell records, isn't he? You couldn't expect him not to cash in on such an obvious hit situation, could you? Anyhow, as Orbison himself pointed out, almost anyone else in the business would have done exactly the same.

Never mind, he's still a pretty good performer. The last time I saw him was at the 1966 New Musical Express poll winners' concert, and he shared the bill with the Beatles, the Rolling Stones, the Walker Brothers, Cliff Richard, the Shadows, Dusty Springfield, the Who, and umpteen others, the full flower of British pop. With hardly any exceptions, he cut them to pieces.

He wore something like an out-of-work flamenco dancer's outfit: high-waisted trousers and boots and a tatty little jerkin. Then his puff-pastry face and those impenetrable tinted glasses. All the time he was on stage he didn't move an inch, didn't even nod his head. He just stamped his foot, stood his ground, and belted.

Why was he good? It was something to do with presence. Everyone else was frantic, ran themselves crazy trying to whip up reaction. Orbison just commanded: the big O. He sang nothing that hadn't been a major hit for him—*Running Scared, Pretty Woman, In Dreams*—and he banged it out so solid, so impossibly confident, that he made everything that had gone before seem panicky. He'd been around, had twenty years behind him. Almost on his own, he knew what it was all about.

Orbison is based in Nashville, Tennessee. Basically, it's the center of country music, but it handles a lot of pop as well; it carries more recording sessions than anywhere else outside New York. Almost everyone works there—Elvis Presley, the Everlys, Joe Tex, even Bob Dylan—and then the straight country 'n' western acts, Johnny Cash and Chet Atkins, George Jones and Buck Owens and Hank Snow.

It's a strange city, filled to overflowing with guitar pickers by the thousand, all scuffling, and at its highest levels the music community there has formed itself into some kind of unofficial club, managers and publishers and artists. To get accepted into this, you have to be very big indeed, you have to be a monster, but once you've made it, you're in for life and you're looked after; you're just about guaranteed work for as long as you can walk. You're in an an oligarchy and you can never fall. Roy Orbison is in this league.

Del Shannon was built along the same lines, meaning that he had a lumberjack voice and never budged. Not as operatic as Orbison, he just wound himself up until he roared, and then he gradually got louder and louder and louder, climaxing with a frantic falsetto shriek. All it took was a lot of lung power and one sharpened stick. Simple but effective.

He has always been one of my heavy heroes—the way he charges head-on at his songs like some angered bull, mauls and destroys them, bangs them against the board until they're shattered. Over the early sixties he turned out long streaks of world-wide hits and wrote them himself: *Runaway, Hats Off to Larry, Two Kinds of Teardrops, Swiss Maid, So Long Baby.* There was no craft to them, no pretense at quality. It was all sound.

On stage, there was the same appeal. Shannon was pretty sawed-off, and he wore his big guitar slung high across his chest so that he had to hunch to get at it. That made him look aggressive, and he stood square and howled. Beautiful songs, beautiful noise. Pure pop. The backing pounding along like a

cavalry charge, all organ and percussion, and Del himself bull-
dozing through everything. He could have knocked down brick
walls, that man; he could have demolished skyscrapers.

There wasn't much more to him. He was originally an out-
of-town boy from Grand Rapids, Michigan, but he turned into
very much the spruced, smooth-voiced young businessman,
shaved and manicured, toting a smile like a slot machine. That
didn't matter; he sang like someone else entirely, and it was
his records I cared about. Raunchy might be the word I need.

If Del Shannon looked like some kind of budding executive,
Gene Pitney came on like a full-blown tycoon, which was exactly what he was. He was of Polish extraction, and money
interested him deeply. Deals—they lit him up like neon.

The one time I met him, he was in his hotel room, and he
was talking business on the long-distance telephone. Shirt torn
open at the neck, tie twisted, sweat marks under his armpits:
classic Hollywood image. As he talked, he moved one hand in
small upward circles, as if he was trying to conjure up something tangible out of the air. Like banknotes. So I stood like
one lemon, waiting to get noticed, and he looked straight
through me. I wouldn't say he was ignoring me. I'd really say
that he didn't know there was anyone else in the room.

Ballads were his meat. Tearjerkers, monstrous flowerpots
that made Roy Orbison's songs sound like Woody Woodpecker
symphonies in comparison. And he had a big voice, a fine
range, and most professional projection, but he chose to sing
in a whine like an electric saw. Cutting, needling, excruciating.
It has given me more real pain than any other voice I've ever
heard. I can't be objective about it: it nags me like toothache.

Still, he's sharp. He has never looked remotely like slipping.
His judgments have been cautious, unadventurous, but always
accurate. And, even forgetting England and America, he has
huge followings in Europe, in the Far East, in Australasia—
almost everywhere. He commutes endlessly. He makes deals,
cuts hits, accrues, amasses. Truly, Gene Pitney is a man of our
times.

On stage, he looks small and has a schoolboy's face, round

and unused, his hair slicked flat across his skull. He stands still in a single spotlight, all lost and lonely, one hand in his pocket, the other extended toward his audience, and he wades through heartbreak ballad after heartbreak ballad. Between numbers he sits on a stool and reads out sentimental letters from his fans. His audience hushes for him as if he was making a funeral oration. Then he sings more ballads, and he looks sad as hell, trapped inside his spotlight, and everyone feels sorry for him. Mothers adore him.

It's all a bit like a recital; he carries himself like an updated Richard Tauber. Everyone is miserable. When he completes a song, he looks down and stares stonily at his feet. You almost expect him to let drop a rose. Anyhow, his control is remarkable; he never drops a stitch. By the time he's through, even those who hate him as much as I do feel like we've been swimming in a cement mixer.

Most important of all, there were the Four Seasons.

In pop terms, the Seasons were freaks: they were four bodies of ill-assorted shapes and sizes, all getting on a bit, and they looked like bank clerks, accountants, floor managers— they looked like anything on earth, but they never looked like any pop group.

As it happened, they weren't only pop; they were the most POP pop ever. I mean, if I had to explain pop to anyone in one throw, I'd just play them a Four Season record—*Sherry, Rag Doll, Big Girls Don't Cry, Let's Hang On,* or *Dodie.*

The thing was, they had a lead singer called Frankie Valli, and he had the most piercing falsetto ever, a monster, an excruciating screech, and whenever he really let it go, he'd shatter plate glass windows all across the city. It was the ultimate deterrent, and it was also beautiful; it was a thing of true wonder. It would scream out of your hi-fi like some insane air-raid siren, and it deafened you, destroyed you, turned you blind. So you'd stumble and shake in the sheer wildness of it. You'd be tripped out on sound alone.

They had two ultra-shrewd hustlers behind them, Bob Crewe and Bob Gaudio, producers and writers who kept them fed with natural hit songs. From 1961, they've peddled a string of American smashes; they've never looked like slipping. Almost every time they walk in the studio, they cut some major classic. Altogether, they've probably turned out more mind-snappers than any other group in the world.

There's not much to say on them, they're not analyzable. They're perfect, that's all.

Then there was Brenda Lee, who didn't make sense. Just five feet tall, she looked like an all-time peak in highschool teenybop. She wore wide party dresses with frilly petticoats underneath, and she had an unformed elfin face, hugely grinning at all times. She chewed gum, read comics. Had outbursts of adolescent spots and pimples. Wore high heels and nylons on big nights out. For Chrissake, she was even her school cheerleader.

She came from Atlanta, Georgia, a real Southern girl, and she was making hits by the time she was eleven: Little Miss Dynamite. Right through her teens, she alternated singing and going to school. Her songs were just what you'd expect, bouncy little routines, halfway between rock and country. The thing that didn't make sense about her was her voice, which was freakish, making her sound thirty at least, and was also most sexual, knowing, very world-weary indeed. By the time she was seventeen, she had a ballad style along the lines of Edith Piaf, as used and bravura as that.

She could be magnificent. She conjured up real three-in-the-morning visions: ashtrays full of butts and lipstick smears on the coffee cups, small rancid rooms, offhand desperation. Then she'd come out and she'd be like some kewpie doll, all sheen and varnish and eyes that really roll. It was this woman/child contradiction that made her happen.

When she grew up, the greatest part of her appeal inevitably fell away. She got married and had a child. Still, she looked amazingly innocent; she wore the same bobbysoxer uniform as ever, but it just wasn't the same thing. So her records stopped being hits.

Her voice hasn't changed, still feels like bad whiskey. Sometimes she puts out new singles; they're not good songs, not well produced or anything, but herself, she cuts through it like a laser. If only she didn't look so precisely like Little Orphan Annie.

In any case, she made no difference. Nor did Del Shannon or Dion or Orbison or Neil Sedaka. 1960 meant doldrums just the same.

The point is that pop doesn't work around good records or pretty voices or cute people—those are only details. Really, it happens off superheroes and superdollars, off hyped mass hysteria and even deep-down social change, off short-term collective insanities. People just aren't relevant.

10.   *The Twist*

"I'M NOT easily shocked but the Twist shocked me . . . half Negroid, half Manhattan, and when you see it on its native heath, wholly frightening. . . . I can't believe that London will ever go to quite these extremes. . . . the essence of the Twist, the curious perverted heart of it, is that you dance it alone": Beverley Nichols reporting from New York in January 1962.

It's strange the way the Twist got so fussed about. Realistically, it was the least sexual dance craze in forty years. With old faithfuls like the jitterbug and the jive, after all, the girls spun like tops and everyone got fast flashes of panties. With the Twist, you got nothing. Just Chubby Checker telling you to imagine that you'd had a bath and were toweling your back. Approximately as carnal as cornflakes.

Well, pop was now sunk neck-deep in pigshit and needed something violent, something quick, to pull it out again. Never mind if it be real or phony, straight or hyped, just so long as it could hit. And it happened that there wasn't anything real available at the time, so hyped it had to be.

And the Twist was lying around. Most often it would have been a scraped grade-C fad, maximum span of six months. Another hula hoop. But 1961 was parched, was really desperate. So first Chubby Checker had a hit record. Second, New York smart society decided that the Twist was cute and started to hang out in the Peppermint Lounge. Third, the gossip columnists jumped aboard. Fourth, the whole industry started hyping. And fifth, madness set in.

At this point, enter something like Beverly Nichols on a white horse, and suddenly you get visions of kids copulating on dance floors, mass national debauch, and the breakdown of all known moral standards—the collapse of Western civilization. Strong stuff: that's the way the money grows. So now you finally have a story, a phenomenon. All right, so nobody really gives a damn and nobody ever will. That isn't quite the point.

The Twist wasn't even new. Hank Ballard, who had been around on the R & B scene ever since the early fifties, wrote the original song in 1958 and had a specialized hit with it. Dance-craze records have always been a stable part of the Negro market, and nobody paid much attention.

Two years on, Chubby Checker re-recorded it and got himself a national breakout. Checker was Ernest Evans from Philadelphia and had been a chicken-plucker. He looked something like a young Fats Domino, and he played it up; he even bowdlerized the fat man's name (Fats Domino = Chubby Checker: do you dig?). Truthfully, he wasn't much talented, but he was shrewd: he found himself with a hit on his hands and he hammered it. He twisted like a maniac. Demonstrated it on television, diagrammed it in the papers. Lost thirty-five pounds in a year just pretending to towel his back. So the Twist seemed almost fun, and it caught on. Journalists satirized it gently, how ludicrous and freak it was. The Peppermint Lounge, just off Times Square, hired a group called Joey Dee and the Starliters, and they played Twist all night every night. Chubby Checker cut *Let's Twist Again*. Even Elvis had a number one twist song, *Rock-A-Hula-Baby*. This was all getting to mean big business.

Here's where something odd happened. New York socialites, truly smart people, started to haunt the Peppermint Lounge. Elsa Maxwell and Greta Garbo and Judy Garland, Noel Coward and Tennesee Williams, the Duke of Bedford. Everyone, as they say, who was anyone. All of them twisting like there was no tomorrow and looking very foolish indeed. Inside weeks, you had to spray twenty-dollar bills like confetti even to catch a glimpse of the dance floor.

This was only odd because no jetsetter had ever shown any remote interest in pop before. Not a flicker. In the fifties, it had seemed hip to like the more refined end of modern jazz—Miles

Davis, the Modern Jazz Quartet, even Thelonious Monk. But not rock and roll music. Anything but that. The thing to be was cool and there was nothing cool in pop. Certainly not in fat Negro chicken-pluckers from Philadelphia.

But the sixties were something different, and it was suddenly fashionable to be frantic again. It was like the twenties, the Scott Fitzgerald thing, the Charleston, all that dazzle and fevered decadence. So pop was permissible. Amusing. Jackie Kennedy was rumored to twist. In London, Margot Fonteyn shook it down in public. In Paris, so did Jean Cocteau.

This is where it started, the hysterical adulation of pop singers by the rich and trendy all over the world. It became hip to know Joey Dee, hipper to know Checker. Huge status to be publicly snubbed by Phil Spector. A bit later it was paradise to be entirely ignored by the Beatles. And by 1966, Mick Jagger was the most wanted guest in the world, the final face, the ultimate. For one pout of his red lips, any millionairess hostess going would have promised away her life.

Why pop? Because the yen was all for youth and beauty, and if nothing else, pop was always young, always beautiful. Because pop made its money for itself. Because it spoke so coarse ("common as dirt, darlings, isn't he divine?"). Because it was what's happening, babydoll. What more reason does anyone need?

Out of this arose a whole new superclass, and how did you qualify? You only had to be a face. And what was a face? Roughly, it was when you walked into any snob restaurant anywhere and everyone sensed you come in behind them and automatically turned around. You were young, flash, international. *Vogue* said you were Now. Exactly, you were the beautiful people. Names: Terence Stamp and David Bailey and Jean Shrimpton and Terry Donovan, Rudolph Nureyev or Margot Fonteyn, Andy Warhol, Baby Jane Holzer, Justin de Villeneuve. Twiggy. Not Truman Capote or Norman Mailer or Elsa Maxwell or even Marlon Brando. But definitely not. This was a most exclusive league. Muhammed Ali was its patron saint. Princess Margaret and Anthony Armstrong-Jones were its recognized monarchs. Most super of all superstars.

Anyhow, once the faces had showed at the Peppermint Lounge, the Twist ballooned almost instantaneously from a fad into an industry. The papers pissed themselves. Big money got invested. Very quickly, there were Chubby Checker T-shirts and jeans and ties, Chubby Checker dolls. Or Twist skirts and Twist raincoats and Twist nighties. Conveyor-belt Twist movies. Ballrooms had their biggest boom in decades. Everyone cleaned up. And the insanity was that, even now, nobody really cared. Try finding one truly hooked twister and you'd have had quite some search. No competition, the Twist was the most total hype ever.

The one thing remotely interesting about it, as Beverley Nichols pointed out, was that you danced it alone. Suddenly, dancing hadn't anything to do with romance any more, nothing to do with companionship or fun. Instead, it became pure exhibitionism, a free platform for sexual display, and down among the teenybops, that passed for kicks.

Certainly, the Twist's appeal had nothing to do with its music, which was always drab as hell; its cuteness was simply that it allowed kids to do something that would have got their faces slapped for them in any earlier generation; namely, to stand up in public and promote their ass. And all right, so it looked foolish, but it felt illicit; that was the full equation.

The Twist itself didn't last long. Well, it wasn't really meant to. In any case, it was replaced by other dances, other campaigns, and the same people went on making money. In the absence of any dominant individuals, dance-crazes bossed pop right up until the Beatles broke. There was the Hully Gully, the Madison, the Fly, the Pony, the Popeye, the Mashed Potato, the Dog, the Monkey. A bit later, the Slop and the Waddle and the Frug. The Jerk and the Block. Right on into these last years and the Boogaloo, the Philly Skate, the Sanctification, the Beulah Wig. The inspired Funky Broadway. That's not all. Endless and interchangeable steps. Go to a club one week; go back the next, and everyone is moving different. There are kids who devote all their lives from sixteen to twenty-one in mastering dances that nobody else is up to yet. It's a full-time career. More than a career—an art almost. At the least, a vocation.

Dancing was a focus. So was radio. Between them, they made up the hard center of early sixties' American teen romance. They bossed.

Millions of kids up in front of their bedroom mirrors, getting hip to the Pony with the Good Guys on Station WMCA. Or out in the park on the Hully Gully from the All-Americans on WABC. Or sipping coke through Murray the K's Monkey on 1010 WINS. That's the way the fantasy went. It was a self-contained cycle, twenty-four hours each day, deejays spieling like maniacs all across the nation, and music splintering and feet shuffling, butts twitching by the megaton. It didn't ever have to end; it needed no improving. It was perfection.

Radio was a big surprise comeback. Television had completely taken over in the forties, the fifties, but now steam was huge all over again. Not to be listened to, not like before TV, but as an endless burble background for teenage daydream. It was all music, no speech and no interruptions allowed—kids didn't like talk; they flipped dials fast to another station. So the only way a deejay could survive was to develop a spiel so fast, so smooth, that it became music on its own. No message, no sense to impart. It was pure noise: "So hit me one time, that's a groove, that's nice, baby, ooh mammy-o, lay it down, sock it to me, John, George, Paul, and Ringo, Fab Four, babydoll, it's what's happening, baby, and bam bam bam—" starting as a rumble and rising gradually to an unending Hitlerian scream. It was like electricity, it was like glass. It was just there.

Murray the K was king jockey. Of all deejays ever made, he spieled hardest, fastest, loudest, and longest. Hustled the biggest deals and pulled the biggest strokes. In his hysteria and unflagging speed, in his total shamelessness, in his haste to cash in and equal haste to later opt out, he entirely epitomized the phase.

He wasn't hip or heroic in the least, but he won out on brashness alone. He was in his late thirties, a sturdily built businessman, and he wore Stingy Brim straw hats, tight pants, lurid shirts. He could have been a successful insurance salesman from Ohio going berserk on Hawaiian vacation. But still he talked blind streaks and never ran out of wind.

His catch phrase was "It's what's happening"; he used it all the time. And he rocked in his seat, he roared and hollered, pounded, went purple in the face, but he never once stumbled in his spiel. Never ever. He was surrounded by tapes: commercials, one-shot interviews, trains, cavalry charges, explosions, weirdbeard laughs, end of the world screams. In between, he even played records. Everything was impetus. Murray the K, wham bam thankyou mam. Interminable shows like roller-coaster rides: he's what's happening.

He outstayed all rivals, beat them blind when it came to cunning. In the very early sixties, he was unchallenged top dog, and then naturally, because American deejays hardly ever last, he began to flag. By early 1964, he was definitely on the slide.

Right then the Beatles flew in for their first American tour. At this moment, they were at their utmost peak; they had the top five records on the American charts, and they were the hottest properties ever. And when they touched down at Kennedy Airport, they went straight into press conference, there to be interviewed by the cream of the nation's journalists. And, strangely, by Murray the K.

It wasn't ever a fair contest. The journalists huddled together and fired questions. But Murray the K somehow wriggled through their legs and got right to the Beatles' feet, crouched there and just about crawled up them. Stingy Brim hat, maniac leer, and his stick mike pushing upward, ever upward. His mouth shooting questions all the time. And he stole it, he broke it up. He turned a formal occasion into farce. So Paul McCartney looked down at him. "Murray the K," said Paul, "cut out the crap."

Immortality: the nation's pressmen got routine, Murray the K got exclusives. "Cut out the crap." That's all. Nirvana. Quite possibly, it was the scoop of the century.

From there, he hounded the Beatles like Charlie Chan. He roomed with George Harrison and taped his thoughts just before going to sleep, just after waking. Dubbed himself the Fifth Beatle and got away with it, because who could resist such nerve, who could fail to be secretly impressed? So Murray came back to New York with a mountain of exclusive tapes and played them endlessly. Sample—Murray the K; "What's happening, baby?"

Ringo Starr: "You're what's happening, baby."

Murray the K: "You're happening, too, baby."

Ringo Starr: "O.K., we're both happening, baby."

By the end of the tour, Murray was right back on top again and stayed that way. He made one hundred and fifty thousand dollars a year. Sold Murray the K T-shirts and hosted albums of Murray the K's Golden Gassers. And his resourcefulness is such that he might never end. He summed it up himself. "I'm not riding the Beatles' coattails," he told Tom Wolfe once. "If they go, I'm going to be ready for the next person that comes along."

Crude stuff, maybe, but it was something; at least it was action. It wasn't 1960 and blankness. Everyone was up and running again. We were back to rock.

11. *Spectorsound*

SO PHIL SPECTOR is in some plush nightclub and he's dancing with his wife and he's doing no harm to anyone. He's around twenty-two years old and he is five foot seven, 125 pounds, and he has long ratty hair hanging all down his shoulders, and he has a high-pitched mincing voice, and he's wearing totally outrageous clothes. At this time, in the early sixties, he is a freak. But he has made about twenty straight hit records and earned two million dollars, and he's the hottest thing in the whole of pop. And he dances with his wife and minds his own business.

Suddenly he feels something tugging his hair from behind, and he turns round and there is this large man. The man starts calling him filthy names, terrible dirt, right in front of Spector's wife. The man is an animal, and he keeps tugging Spector's hair. Spector stops him. "I'm going to tell you this one time, that's all," says Spector. "Don't ever try that again." And he fixes the man with terrible eyes; he burns him, assassinates him with one look.

So what happens? So the man reaches out and knocks Spector halfway across the room.

"I mean, I've studied karate for years," said Spector later. "I could literally kill a guy like that."

Spector was born in the Bronx, and his father died when he was nine. So his mother took him out west to California, teen paradise, and he grew up small, runtish, with bad hair and unhealthy skin. But he was clever, he was really talented, and he had imagination. So when he was about seventeen, he wrote a song called *To Know Him Is to Love Him* and formed a group called the Teddy Bears, and the record sold around two and a half million copies across the world.

The title? Spector remembered it off his father's tombstone: TO KNOW HIM WAS TO LOVE HIM. That was typical.

This was in 1958; two years later he was a major producer at Atlantic Records, and very soon afterward he had his own label, Philles Records, and was cutting huge hit records every time he walked into the studio. *He's a Rebel* and *Da Doo Ron Ron* and *Then He Kissed Me* by the Crystals, *Be My Baby* and *Baby, I Love You* by the Ronettes, *Zip-A-Dee-Doo-Dah* by Bob B. Soxx and the Bluejeans, *Wait Till My Baby Gets Home* by Darlene Love—every one a beautiful noise and every one a monster smash.

He was a real breakthrough. Before him, it might have been allowed for kids to turn into stars and get their names in the papers, but they never managed, produced, or hyped; they were never in control. Pop was still overwhelmingly a middle-aged industry. Then Spector came through and knocked all that down.

He was a tycoon: he gave orders, made things happen, was responsible to nobody but himself. What's more, he was disgustingly successful. On nothing but energy and knowledge of what records were about. At one throw he destroyed forever the concept that pop took experience, that you had to be a long-time businessman. And he showed up the business as slow and flabby and hopeless, an industrial joke. For this revelation, the middlemen—distributors and pluggers and hypers and publishers—never forgave him.

But he was more important than that. What he really spelled was huge good news for losers. There he was, seventeen years old, skinny and ugly and poor, neurotic as hell. A true dropout. And he was hopelessly maladjusted for any life he was ever likely to get: he wasn't tough and butch and boorish; he wasn't one of the boys. He thought that most Americans were animals, and he became agonized at the very first hint that he was being crowded. Simply, he wasn't equipped.

So he went into pop and became a millionaire. Just like that. From start to finish in five years. Insulated himself against everything that he loathed. Grew his hair long and wore fancy dress and adopted a falsetto. Was outrageous in every way possible. Then not only did he get away with it, but he even became famous for it; he was celebrated. So, all right, he was talented, very talented indeed. Just the same, he'd done something extraordinary.

Except, of course, that he was dancing in a nightclub once and a large man knocked him halfway across the room. It's not so easy, that's America. Then he had to hire bodyguards. Even with two million dollars, he still couldn't get left in peace.

Anyhow, Phil Spector was the first man to see pop as the new natural refuge of the outsider. The place you could make money and cut yourself off from filth and also express whatever you wanted without having to waste half your lifetime looking for breaks. The way he saw things, America was sick and pop was healthy. It was uncharted territory, and its potential was endless. It was teenage property. In all these ways, he was an important signpost for the hippies that followed him.

Otherwise, though, he wasn't so much in any dada/beat/-hippie tradition as pop bowdlerization of Oscar Wilde. Meaning that he was sharp and bitchy, fastidious, vulnerable, and a culture snob, that he had great style, and that you always felt he was doomed. He even looked rather like Wilde; he had exactly that kind of ostentation.

His most persistent image of himself was paranoid—creative Phil Spector hemmed in by cigar-chewing fatties, beautiful Phil among the uglies, groovy Phil versus hair-tugging America. His records were his best revenge.

They were dirty great explosions, guerrilla grenades. They were the loudest pop records ever made.

Spector himself was a prodigy, knew more about the actual mechanics of recording than any other producer before or since. Most producers say what they want and their engineers provide it, but Spector ran it all, understood every last insignificant dial or switch in his control box and bossed it. So what he did, simply, was to assemble all of the noise in the world and then ride it.

He was demonic. He'd take one good song and add one good group, and then he'd blow it all up sky-high into a huge

mock-symphony, bloated and bombasted into Wagnerian pro-
portions. Magnificent, chaotic din: he'd import maybe three
pianos, five percussion, entire battalions of strings. Drums and
bass underneath like volcanoes exploding. Tambourines by the
hundredweight. And he looked down from his box and hurled
thunderbolts. Added noise upon noise, explosion on top of explosion. Until it wasn't the song that counted, the voices, nothing like that—only the sound, Spectorsound, and the impetus.
Momentum, lurching and crushing and bursting, and it couldn't
possibly be stopped.

That's my image of him: he's up and burning in his box, his
long hair wet, his ratty little face collapsing, and under him,
there's impossible sound; but he drives it, he keeps adding to
it, and still he can't ever make it finally loud enough. So when
you bought Phil Spector records, you were buying no throw-
aways but huge frantic outpourings of spite and paranoia, rage
and frustration and visioned apocalypse. And if you were teenage, you probably felt exactly the same way, and you loved it.
That's how Spector came to make two million clear at the age
of twenty-two.

At any rate, everything was good to him for a time, but
then he wasn't cut out for serenity; it wasn't his style, and he
couldn't hold. For one, he'd made it; he'd achieved everything
possible, and what in hell did he do next? For two, the Beatles
came along, early 1964, and wiped him out.

Spector had been number-one pop phenomenon in America,
and now the Beatles replaced him. He wasn't the youngest, the
newest, the wildest any more. He was definitely last year's
model. Life was drooping. Stung, he made his best throw yet,
You've Lost That Lovin' Feeling by the Righteous Brothers,
and it was also a world monster. It was also endlessly brilliant.

Still, he wasn't made happier. He was more capricious,
petulant, foolish all the time. He was afraid and had premo-
nitions (there's a famous story about how he stopped a plane
just before takeoff and wouldn't fly in it because he felt something creepy about it, something wiggy). And he had always
been hooked on image, but now he was getting quite obsessive:
he plunged his whole office into darkness, and when anyone
went to do business with him, all they could see was his shape

in the gloom, all they heard was his voice squeaking out of nothing. It worked, of course; it had great effect, but it was an obvious failure tactic just the same.

Early in 1966, he made his best cut, *River Deep—Mountain High* by Ike and Tina Turner, and it flopped. Very possibly, it was the best pop record of all.

It was total brainstorm. Spector was louder, wilder, more murderous than he'd ever been, and Tina Turner matched him, big earth woman, one scream of infinite force. At one time, there's an instrumental chorus and everything thunders, crashes, gets ready for final dissolution. Tina snarls and wails in the background. Then she screams once, short and half-strangled, and everything goes bang. That's the way the world will end.

In England it made number two, but what's England? In America it bombed. Spector was destroyed. He wrote off American record buyers as finally moronic and stomped off into the California desert to make art movies. Nothing much came of this. After about a year rumors came filtering through that he was about to make a comeback. He made one more record with Ike and Tina, *I'll Never Need More Than This,* and it duly bombed. After that, nothing.

Presumably, he will return. What else can he do? He has made money, but he has spent a lot. He hasn't taken root in movies. He has made hit records, but they're history. Most of all, he's only approaching his late twenties and has his life to fill in.

It's been quite a melancholy little story. Poor little rich boy perhaps, but still a sad saga. After all, he had real talent; he was one of those very few who've genuinely had what it takes. Spector and Elvis and Charlie Rich. John Lennon and Pete Townshend. P. J. Proby. Then who?

His big stumbling block has been the problem that every major pop success faces and hardly anyone solves: when you've made your million, when you've cut your monsters, when your peak has just been passed, what happens next? What about the next fifty years before you die?

12. *California*

CALIFORNIA is teen heaven. It is the place that pop was created for. Chuck Berry did a song about it called *The Promised Land,* and like always, he knew what he was talking about.

This California is hugely enlarged reality, verges on complete fantasy. In pop, it is the joob-joob land far beyond the sea, where age is suspended at twenty-five and school is outlawed and coke flows free from public fountains and the perfect cosmic wave unfurls endlessly at Malibu. The home of the lotus eaters. That's what it is for, kids who live in gray cities, tenement blocks, and it keeps raining and they know this can't be right; there must be something better. California is the something better.

No drag lives there but only sun, sun, sun. Surf in the morning, hot rod later, and maybe a barbecue at night—isn't that the way life should be? Surf City, two girls for every boy. Drive-ins and Muscle Beach Party. California dreaming: that's what Chuck Berry meant.

To fit these fantasies, Californian pop has always been like comic strips, continuing images of sand and sea and sun, everything drawn bright and clean and simple.

It hasn't ever properly grown out of highschool. As late as the middle sixties, West Coast heroes were still pictured sitting in class all term, passing sly notes to the school iceberg. At night they went to drive-ins and necked. On weekends they bombed up and down the coastline in their hot rods. Eddie Cochran would have understood it perfectly. And when summer came and school was out, they went down on the beaches, surfed, barbecued steaks, and danced barefoot in the sand.

117

That's when they also fell in love, happily or unhappily, and they stayed that way till fall. Then they went back to school and started all over again.

It was a tightly limited world, very compact, very safe, and there are people around who see it as a vision of hell, but I'm not one of them.

Anyhow, it was a storyline that never seemed to run out of steam, and from 1960 on, which was about the time that California developed a specific pop identity, separate from all other highschool, it was variously used by the Beach Boys, Jan and Dean, the Hondas and the Ripchords and the Rivingtons, Ronnie and the Daytonas, Dick Dale, and umpteen others. The market was inexhaustible. All you had to do was throw in the right dream words, wipe-out and woody and custom machine, and you were home. Californians bought you out of patriotism, and everyone else bought you for escape. The more golden your visions, the more sun-tanned your sound, the better you sold. It was almost that simple.

Musically, as well as emotionally, it was all updated highschool, big bass voice at the bottom and careening falsetto up above. All that was new was the efficiency with which it was done.

Californian pop tended to be competent. Almost professional. Sometimes it used quite complex arrangements, lines interweaving, voices unexpectedly juxtaposed, even a bit of half-baked counterpoint. More, nearly everyone sang in tune. As pop, it was light and flexible and fast. Vastly attractive. And it was perfected by the Beach Boys.

In the first place, the Beach Boys were three brothers, Brian and Dennis and Carl Wilson, and one cousin, Mike Love, rounded out by a local boy soprano called David Marks. All five of them lived in Hawthorne, California, and went to school and surfed.

This was the beginning of the sixties, and surfing was everything; it was the maximum West Coast cult. It had been a major world sea sport ever since the war, a bottomless box of myths and remembered afternoon heroics, a sunshine pool-shoot, but it had been mostly adult, mostly the property of hairy athletes in their mid-twenties. Now, by the early sixties, schoolboys had finally got wise to it, and they were altogether hooked.

It was understandable hysteria—imagine yourself riding waves, everyone watching you, girls gawking, and you have this one small board under your feet, that's all, but still you swoop and soar, fly free, and nothing can bring you down. You walk the water. And so fast—what speed, what poise, what godlike splendor. No wonder bikinis pop. No wonder your class-mates turn their heads away (boy, were their faces ever red?!). And at the end, you tuck your surfboard under your arm like some briefcase and walk up the beach so cool and easy, not looking to left nor right, not even caring. Still the greatest. Then you lie down in the sand and starlets cluster to feel your muscles. That's surf fantasy. No more peacock sport was ever invented.

Anyway, the Wilsons surfed like everyone else, and Dennis, who was a light golden color, who was good-looking and fit and always made out with girls, was very smart at it. But Carl and Brian were overweight and weren't so hot. Carl was the youngest and even-tempered by nature, and he didn't mind too much. But Brian was the eldest, the most intelligent, the most talented, and he didn't like fatness one bit.

Around 1962, the Wilsons formed themselves into a group—their father was a long-time songwriter, and it was almost inevitable that they'd get involved with pop—and Brian, being the cleverest, became their writer. What he wrote about was surf.

Amazingly, this was the first time that any specifically surf music had been written, the first time that California was given its own pop identity. Out of nowhere, though, Wilson wrote songs with titles like *Noble Surfer, Surfin' Safari*, and *The Lonely Sea*, and they were wild.

He worked out a loose-limbed group sound and added his own falsetto. Then he stuck in some lazy twang guitar and rounded it all out with jumped-up Four Freshman harmonies. No sweat, he'd created a bona fide surf music out of nothing. More, he had invented California.

In 1963 he adapted Chuck Berry's *Sweet Little Sixteen* and

called it *Surfin' U.S.A.* This was the great surf anthem: the clincher, a hymn of unlimited praise. He did *Surf City* for Jan and Dean, and it was a national number one. So surf was suddenly American big business, and Brian Wilson ruled it.

It made sense. Maybe he did have flab problems, maybe he wasn't Mister Surfing Universe—but he wrote the songs, did the real work, and Dennis just sat at the back playing drums. Other kids surfed much better, but no daddy Brian Wilson articulated it all, made pop poetry from it, got rich off it. Inside very few years he could afford to hide his belly inside the Rolls Royce he'd bought from Brian Epstein.

Very quickly he expanded from surf to hot rod, the other major West Coast obsession, and then further into generalized pop. He handled things well, kept progressing all the time. By the time any fad burned out, the Beach Boys were inevitably long long gone.

His car songs were beautiful. Hot rods brought out a huge sentimental streak in him, and he wrote real flowerpots. When his cars won out, he celebrated them like monster heroes, and when they broke down, he mourned them like dying lovers. His great maudlin falsetto quavered and ached, the harmonies behind him went dirge-like.

There was no subject too soap-opera for him to take on. He churned out *A Young Man Is Gone,* an ode to the departed James Dean, and *Spirit of America* and *Be True to Your School*. At the same time he did some fine rejoicings, full of energy and imagination: *Shut Down, 409, Little Deuce Coupe.* Fine rock and roll music but brought up to date, kept moving and not left to atrophy. Best of all was *I Get Around.*

What Brian Wilson was doing now was making genuine pop art. Not camp word-plays on pop, but the real thing. He was taking the potential heroics that surrounded him and, not being arty, not being coy in the least, turning them into live music.

Simply, he'd taken highschool and raised it to completely new levels; he'd turned it into real myth, and as far as I'm concerned, this was his best period.

Personally, he wasn't easy. He was arrogant, solitary, and

very self-involved. He understood well that he *was* the Beach Boys, that the rest of the group were virtually only his assistants, and he wasn't too gentle about it. Also, everyone told him how clever he was, how talented, and he believed them. He began to see himself as an artist.

By now, he had established the Beach Boys as the most successful group going, and he was tired. He had all the songs to write, all the decisions to make; at the same time, he was on the road, traveling and losing sleep, huddling in cockroach dressing rooms—generally hustling himself half to death. Then, from late 1964 he was under pressure from Beatlemania, and the Beach Boys went through a bad slump, their records selling less. So he thought he needed time to reflect, space to stretch in, and he decided he'd stop touring. He'd stay home in California and write masterworks instead. As for the rest of the group, they could go right on touring and earning. That's what he thought and, no arguments allowed, that's what he did.

Since that time, he has been increasingly withdrawn, brooding, hermitic. He has developed strong mystic traits, runs in no gangs. Occasionally he is to be seen in the back of some limousine, cruising around Hollywood, bleary and unshaven, huddled way tight into himself. Most secret and enigmatic: a pop Howard Hughes.

In the meantime, the Beach Boys keep touring, keep working hard, and their man looks after them. He writes their songs, works out the arrangements, puts on backing track, looks after every last detail for them. Sometimes he allows them into the studio with him and gets them to add their voices. Sometimes he doesn't give them as much as that—he does the voices himself, lead and falsetto and all the harmonies. Whatever, it all revolves around him; the Beach Boys simply accept what he hands them.

It's hardly a flattering position for them to be in, but they can't really complain. After all, none of them is brilliant in his own right, and Brian Wilson has done well by them: they're rich and famous and they've had a good run. So they take it and keep going. Truthfully, they haven't much choice.

Musically, Brian Wilson has traveled a long way, most of

it backward. As he has become more and more a recluse, so he has gotten increasingly hooked on the concept of Wilson as genius. No more surfboards and hot rods, no more amateur myth-making. Instead, he has emerged as a full-blown solemn romantic, turning out successions of near tone-poems, fragile pools of sound, very limpid. Small choirs running through mock-fugues, rambling boy sopranos. Sad songs about loneliness and heartache. Sad songs even about happiness. Sometimes it works and then it's exquisite: *Caroline No, Here Today, Don't Talk (Put Your Head on My Shouder)*. More often it's just sloppy.

On *Heroes and Villains*, for instance, he worked nine months and came up with a product lasting a couple of hours or so. The record company took one small snippet from it and released it as a single. Net result: a medium hit, a medium record, not bad by any means, but certainly not in the same class as the stuff he'd once knocked out on a lazy afternoon.

It wasn't so hard to understand what had gone wrong. When the Beach Boys started out, pop wasn't too complicated; it was mostly a knack, a certain game to be mastered. Either you could do the trick or you couldn't. Brian Wilson could do it perfectly. The way he wrote car songs, so simple and obvious but still so improbable, it was something like the way Muhammed Ali fights, Elvis moves, Brigitte Bardot looks sexy. That's rating him too high, but it isn't grotesque. By any standards, he had instincts, strange talents, and you couldn't explain them.

Later on, though, after he stopped touring, he wasn't doing tricks any more; he was playing no inspired games. He was being an artist.

This was fine: it was good that he should progress, that he should attempt to go beyond his depth. But he took himself too solemnly; he was mildly megalomaniac about it all. Almost, he was ashamed of pop. He got snob. Running so fast and precious, his hat got away from his head.

This wasn't his only problem. His other trouble was that, like all talented and intelligent pop writers, he found himself stuck in an entirely phony position. Understandably, writers want to grow up and progress. But their crucial audience, the people who finally buy their records, are maybe sixteen years old and by no means hooked on experiment. Pop is always teen music. People in their twenties may be interested, may think it smart to name-drop, but basically they aren't consumers. They don't spend. So you have stalemate: the writers aren't allowed to go forward, don't want to stand still, can't go back. They're wedged from all sides. Their big failing is only that they're too intelligent. If they were robots, things would be forever simple.

Given all this, how can pop ever move? How can it be adult and still sell? How can it make itself understood to teenagers and not be stagnant? Probably it's the most urgent dilemma in the industry, and I'm not sure there's any real answer.

Brian Wilson is hardly a loser. He still writes big hit records, and the Beach Boys still go out for fortunes. But that's not the whole object: he has real talent going, and it isn't working itself out right. The pace has gone off him: off-hand, I'd lay money that *I Get Around* will be the best record he'll ever make. Partly that's his fault, partly it's pop's, partly it's nobody's. Whatever, it's a waste.

California pop, in general, happened mostly in Los Angeles and Hollywood (San Francisco, at this time, still thought that pop was vulgar), and a whole new breed of West Coast hustlers was emerging—managers and artists and producers, hypers of all kinds—and they were sharp; they took California over.

These weren't the beautiful people. They were hard nuts one and all, redolent schnides, and they got very rich very quick. Hardly lovable, but they did understand pop; they made good records, and they made things happen. No time wasted, they turned California into the most hip center in world pop.

Almost invariably, they were obsessed by image. They spent the most part of their lives competing for cool, racking up points in some undefined but desperate struggle for gloss. How did they sit and how did they move and how did they speak? How did they pull? Who did they sleep with? How did they look when Phil Spector walked in? How was their high? Did they sweat? Was the TV in their car black-and-white or color? The battlegrounds were endless and the competition deadly. Blow your cool just once and you were gone.

You can't really play image unless you're well surrounded at all times, stooged and bodyguarded, set off like some precious stone, things arranged and people hit and cigarettes lit for you. You must do nothing yourself. Just sit there and project. Just ooze out cool. And because of this, Hollywood produced hangers-on even more abject, more agonized than other places. It was the bottom.

Hollywood is always like that. Losers by their thousands: once they'd have been around movies and now they used pop, the true Pat Hobbys of their time. Promotion men, all toupee and seersucker suit. Publicists and pushers and just bodies. The Rolling Stones got them quite right: "I'm sitting here thinking just how sharp I am—I'm an under-assistant West Coast promo man." *

Most of these aforesaid hustlers were pretty boring, but not Nick Venet. He had managed the Beach Boys once but hadn't quite kept it, had made definitely erratic progress from there on in. Still, he always kept going. He made some surfing records, did records with Timi Yuro, produced and directed a documentary on Mississippi peace marches. Really, he was an amazing stayer, the kind of man who's always around, never beaten. And he gets into this book only because he survived longer off nothing than anyone else in pop history.

Dark and florid and flash inside camel-hair coats, he looked the eternal operator, a B-feature heavy, and he talked entirely in declamations, slogans, odd little sayings. I had lunch with him once. "I'm known as the Gutsy Greek," he told me. "I got where I am by hustle, bustle, and elbow grease." Everything he said was ornate, an attempted proverb: "Even stopped clocks are right two times a day" or "The music is the maestro" or "When the Gusty Greek strike, he never miss." I was most impressed, liked him enormously. "Baby," he said, "unto thine

---

* Words of *West Coast Promotion Man* by permission of Mirage Music Ltd., London.

own self be true." With advice like that, how could I possibly miss?

The center of California hip was Lou Adler. He managed Johnny Rivers and Jan and Dean (later he also discovered Barry McGuire, P.F. Sloan, and the Mamas and the Papas, but they belong in another chapter). He owned Dunhill Records, too, the most astronomic of all independent West Coast labels. And he was a millionaire.

Jan and Dean had a streak of surf and hot rod hits, mostly written by Brian Wilson, and acted as something like Adler's lieutenants, his Rosencrantz and Guildenstern. They weren't notably talented, but they were pure California, all clean and golden, and they were given hit songs to record.

Johnny Rivers was a small roughneck from Louisiana, and he was America's first major discotheque star. Discos were an early sixties' development, an improvement on big impersonal concert halls. The idea was that you had an intimate nightclub atmosphere and played mostly records, with only occasional live acts. First and last, discotheque records had to be dancing records, and that's just what Rivers turned out.

He played Hollywood's Whisky A Go-Go and laid down a most solid beat—nothing fancy, just four-square all the way. Sang old classic rockers like Chuck Berry's *Maybelline* and Willie Dixon's *The Seventh Son*. Chalked up hit after hit. Never smiled once.

He epitomized the Hollywood cool. Slouching and shrugging and looking mean, he gave me the toughest interview I ever did in my life. Every question I asked, he answered by grunting. High grunt for Yes, low grunt for No. And all the time I was there, he looked straight past me at Lou Adler, and Adler looked back at him, both of them expressionless. This wasn't being moronic, this was being cool. This was image.

After some time he left the room and came back with shades on. Nothing changed much, nothing improved. When I left, he did shake hands with me and moved his mouth. "I'm Johnny Rivers," he said. "Who are you?"

Adler himself was a very successful man and a very tough one. Tough and cool and clever. From the whole Californian image race, he emerged as the runaway winner, a walkover. If you were a would-be face and you got accepted on his team, you were making out fine.

The nucleus of this team was his contracted product—Jan, Dean, and Johnny Rivers. Brian Wilson, whenever he came out of hiding, tended to string along. Then a few lesser lights to make up the numbers and fawn.

They were perfectionist. They were the most rigid of all possible societies. Every last detail was studied, checked and rechecked. No clumsiness, no fractional uncool allowed. Mistakes simply didn't happen. No one laughed out loud, no one waved their arms, nobody ever made fools of themselves. Everyone was watchful. The etiquette was crippling.

I have a photograph of the Adler team in London. They have tried to get into a hotel restaurant and have been told that they can't sit down without ties. So they're all sitting around a corner table—Adler, Johnny Rivers, and assorted flunkies and girls—and the men are wearing T-shirts, flash jackets, and so forth, but they're also wearing completely incongruous ties, old school models supplied by the restaurant. They look quite ridiculous. But they're not smiling, they're deadpan. They see nothing remotely funny. Well, that's California cool entirely summed up.

Obviously, this was all a long way from the original 1960 dream. Wasn't innocent or highschool whatever. Just the same, California has remained the great pop utopia: let's all go to San Francisco.

The semi-illusion still survives that West Coast life is somehow essentially freer than anywhere else. If I ever get there, the dream goes, I'll live in a penthouse and drive Cadillacs and spend my money without thinking. More, I'll develop perfect flashing teeth and my body will go a light golden color. I'll become oddly fascinating. And I'll even be able to adopt slouching Brando cool without being ludicrous.

The California promise, then, is that you won't be a person any more, not just a slow and boring human being like all other humans, but you'll be somehow magnificent. Overnight, you'll be transformed into something heroic.

13.   *Soul*

IN ITS simplest terms, soul was only updated rhythm 'n' blues, a rehash of the same old format that has dominated Negro music for the past thirty years, and the only thing new about it was that it had been gingered with a big fat shot of gospel.

In the thirties and forties, big city blacks used their music mostly in first-degree escape. If they lived in the ghetto, if they were poor and badly housed and hopeless, they could at least look flash on Saturday night and shake down to Cab Calloway or Chick Webb, Stick McGhee or Louis Jordan, Wyonie "Mr. Blues" Harris, or whoever else happened to be big at that particular time. Then the musicians fitted themselves sensibly to the situation; they kept things light and flip and sexy, and if they had sense, they did nothing to remind their audience of what was really going on outside the dance hall.

Good-time music, loose and amiable; by comparison, gospel was purest poison. It was archaic, primitive, and determinedly down-home. It reminded northern Negroes of everything they most wanted to forget. Older generations liked it all right, but their kids, hip and sharpshooting, got embarrassed by it and thought it was somehow Uncle Tom.

With the fifties and the upsurge of some kind of organized Negro militancy, things began to change. The black public was no longer so keen to ignore its past; instead of being something vaguely shameful, gospel came to be seen as a real part of the black tradition, private black property. Also, its flat-out emotionalism was an exact expression of the new rage and aggression in Negro life.

So around the middle fifties, Negro pop started grafting gospel feel onto the existing R & B styles. The beat didn't change, neither did the subject matter, but everything dug deeper, more passionate, and everyone sweated. That was soul.

Soul has always been bossed by James Brown. Born 1928, he was a hysterical blues screamer out of Atlanta, Georgia. Very down-home: he had got his training in a southern gospel quartet and used the same technique when he turned to pop.

It's just about impossible to overestimate how big a figure he's been. For more than ten years now, he has crisscrossed America in endless ninety-day barnstormers, and in that time he has gone far beyond being just a singer. Really, he's the final symbol of everything that Negroes can do, of the money they can make, the style they can achieve, the arrogance they can get away with. More even than Muhammed Ali, James Brown has been the outlaw, the Stagger Lee of his time.

Beyond having had maybe fifty straight American hits, he has a show that's made up of a twenty-one piece band, four drummers, a boy and a girl singer, Elsie TV Mama, and anyone else he feels like hiring. He owns three music companies, five record companies. When he goes out on tour, he sends out a team of interior decorators ahead of him to redesign all the hotel rooms that he'll have to stay in. In these ways he's a sultan, an unreachable, and whites simply don't come into it.

He's a small man, rather ugly, but he is a beautiful dancer and he has a freak voice, hysterical and piercing and quite unnaturally loud. Little Richard, Arthur Brown, John Lennon, P.J. Proby—they're all whisperers by comparison. Basically what he does is to set up some very simple pattern, one deep-down riff, and then he hammers it, hits it over and over, calling a phrase and having his band answer it, building on infinite repetition, piling it on until the tension gets to be almost physically painful. It's the call-and-response gospel thing, the same old preach, only hyped into line with the sixties.

His stage act lasts one full hour, and all that time he's doing nothing but working up panic, hammering and hitting, shrieking, falling to his knees in fake anguish like some cryman Negro Johnny Ray, striding the stage on bandy legs like some dwarfish Negro Groucho Marx. And his band grinds on behind him and his dancers pirouette and his drummers lay about him. Then he goes into some dancing, a faster Mick Jagger, tight black pants and legs like propeller shafts, and he's only beautiful.

On *Prisoner of Love* he walks away from the mike and calls the title in the darkness. Very thin and distant, repeating just these three words over and over. And then he comes back into the light, up to the mike, and he lets out a series of screams, mad anguished shrieks that last ten seconds each. Probably they're the loudest sounds you've ever heard any human being make, and physically, you can't not be moved by them. That's the way he works on you. That's the way he hurts you and beats you up.

Right at the end of his hour, on *Please, Please, Please*, he pretends to collapse and is hustled off-stage by an attendant, his shoulders covered by a blue cloak. When he gets into the wings, he suddenly breaks loose and rushes back to the mike, screams a few more bars and falls down again. This time a red cloak gets used. He goes through silver and gold and leopard spots. Never gets off until his fifth attempt.

It's terrible ham, of course, so calculated and precise that Brown fines his musicians each time they make a mistake, even each time their shoes aren't brightly polished enough. But under all its gimmickry, it's sexual and menacing and genuinely meant. It is also a black show, an Apollo show, and no white man could ever fully join in with it. More than anything, that's what has made him so crucial.

He's such a tycoon. Besides all of his companies, he has organized his musicians into something like a cooperative society: they pay in a part of their wages and hold shares in the organization and, among them, own real estate and businesses and so forth. When anyone opts out, Brown has him replaced by someone unknown and struggling, someone who really needs the break. Uncle James—everyone gets looked after.

Talking to white journalists, he is withdrawn. Not mean or boorish, but always guarded. He can be helpful, most courteous, but he doesn't stretch out. Why should he? He has no need of us. We don't count.

Next in line was Ray Charles.

If James Brown got the soul train moving in the Negro market, Charles was responsible for breaking it around the world, and at his vocal peak he has always made his rivals look straight silly.

Born in Georgia in 1932, blinded at six, orphaned by fifteen, he had it hard in every way possible and took a long time to get going. Well on into his twenties, he sold himself as a carbon Nat King Cole and hicked from town to town with a trio, playing a bit of piano, singing the good old good ones. Settling himself down for a lifetime of safe mediocrity.

But around 1953, for no good reason that he or anybody else has ever explained, he just suddenly upped and quit. Threw Nat Cole out the window and hit for himself. What he changed into was purest gospel. The real thing and no padding allowed.

He got himself a big band that could play the blues, hired a solid tenorman called Fathead Newman, added a girl group called the Raelets, and topped it all up with his own new voice, which was curdled and hurt and quite magnificent. Raw, very agonized. Crabbed and ugly and unmusical, but it carried a kickback like a mule. All you could say: it sounded right.

Anyhow, he was very successful. He sold massively among Negroes, gradually built up a following among whites, and by 1960 had emerged as a definite world force. Remember: this was the dead time, the phase when rock 'n' roll had run out of steam and the charts were dominated by the detergent inanities of Frankie Avalon and Connie Francis. Pop was sicker than at any time before or since; coming when it did, a record like Charles' 1959 hit, *What'd I Say?*, was pulverizing. So strong, so fierce, so sexy. Simply so real. More than just a one-time smash, it was a rallying point, a trampoline from which pop began to bounce back.

Apart from anything else he was a musician, good on piano and adequate on alto sax, and this was something almost entirely unknown in pop. He did albums of just instrumentals. He took solos. He recorded with Milt Jackson, the great MJQ vibist, and wasn't disgraced even then.

All of this seemed so extraordinary at the time that his publicists promptly dubbed him the Genius, and what's more, many people believed it. Coming after Pat Boone or Fabian, who was to argue?

He was in no pop tradition; more he was in the line of doomed jazz heroes: Billie Holliday, Thelonious Monk, Charlie Parker. He was black and blind, reportedly very neurotic, and as such, he appealed not so much to any mainline pop crowd as to students and schoolboys and teen rebels of all shades. Kids like myself who were snob, who thought that pop was nice but maybe a bit banal and Ray Charles was the real thing, smashed and tortured, the soul cry of an oppressed people. So if you thought yourself at all hip, you automatically worshiped him. Beat poets and jazzmen and hipsters everywhere preached him as messiah: Allen Ginsberg, Jack Kerouac, Charlie Mingus. In those times, he was hip status symbol number one.

He had great presence. He'd grope his way out on stage, wave into the blackness around him—and then you couldn't look away from him. You just watched him all the time. Not that he did anything—he only sat and played. Still, he was mesmeric, he had it.

And his voice, when it soared, it chilled you and you sweated. He twisted you and hurt you. The first time I saw him, he stretched me so tight that I threw up. All right, I was sixteen at the time and very romantic. All the same, I didn't spew for just anyone.

Of course, it was too good to last—he signed up with the giant commercial complex of ABC-Paramount and promptly had all his natural force smothered in great wads of candy floss. In 1962, he committed virtual hara-kiri by cutting a slop country 'n' western ballad, *I Can't Stop Loving You,* complete with strings and background choir. Predictably, it sold upward of two million and was followed by sundry other abortions in the same style. But apart from being lousy, they were bad long-term commercial policy, alienating him from his blues public and leaving him without any stable following.

The next step was to put him in a movie called *Ballad in*

Blue, a backdated weepie in which he played himself as an all-time caricature of the folksy, lovable, cornbread-and-mo-lasses nigger, and the softening-up process was complete.

Subsequently, things have gone a bit hard by him—he's been arrested a few times on drug charges and has also had various periods in asylums and sanatoriums. As a blind man, his taste for driving fast cars has been a bit alarming, and he gives the impression of being an entirely balled-up person. When he's given his head, he can still outsing anyone, and some of his last records have been brilliant again. But it's a bit late now, and hits have been hard to come by.

Ray Charles, in many ways, goes down as a black Elvis Presley, a great natural vitality strangled and aborted by the mechanics of showbiz. That's too melodramatic an image but it isn't untrue. Charles could have been anything and wound up almost nothing.

Sam Cooke had charm.

He came from Chicago, son of a minister, and he spent years touring with a gospel group called the Soul Stirrers. When he finally went solo, he sang soul gently, melodically. Sometimes he softened down so much that he was hardly soul at all, he was straight pop. Watered down or not, he was sweet without being sickly, and he wrote some fine songs: *You Send Me, Cupid, Bring It on Home to Me, Having a Party.*

He was infinitely professional. He'd been through the small-time American nightclub bit and knew his business backward. When he toured Britain in 1962 with Little Richard and Jet Harris, he got up against solid rocker audiences and they wanted to hate him. Every night he'd go out cold and work his ass off, keep right on pushing until they finally broke, and absolutely without fail, wind up slaying them. By the time he got through, they'd all be up on their feet and waving white handkerchiefs at him. Very corny, of course. But still it took some getting and he got it. He never missed once.

Off-stage, he was sharp, self-confident, fast on his feet. He was a close friend of Muhammed Ali, among the first into the ring to congratulate him when he first beat Sonny Liston. In every way he was smart. Too smart for his own good, in fact, because a woman shot him in a hotel, December 1964, and he died.

The word *soul* originally came out of modern jazz. Negro musicians like Charlie Mingus, Cannonball Adderley, Les Mc-Cann, and Bobby Timmons reacted violently against the West Coast cool, white and gutless, that had bossed jazz through the fifties, and by 1960 they had taken things right back to the roots again. Amens, built-in funk, straightahead twelve-bars—all the tricks of down-home or gospel got dragged back in. Black blues, black musicians, black traditions showed in the titles: *Better Git It in Your Soul, Work Song, Wednesday Night Prayer Meeting, Moanin'*.

Somewhere along the line the word soul got used, sounded right, and stuck. In no time it had become the most overused cliché in the whole range of popular music. It has stayed that way ever since.

Jazz soul got copied by pop. All the riffs and patterns and catchwords of a thousand commercial hits were first used by jazzmen. Very often jazz and pop were indistinguishable anyhow: didn't Ray Charles play jazz? Didn't the Adderley Brothers flirt with pop? And which was Jimmy Smith, where did Brother Jack McDuff belong? The easiest answer was that they were sometimes jazz, sometimes pop, and mostly a bit of both. Really, the distinctions didn't matter much.

Across the past decade, pop or jazz, soul has become progressively stylized, even formal, and now tends to be as ritualized as some religious festival.

In pop, groups are mostly northern; solo acts are mostly down-home. The groups wear silk suits, comb their straightened hair into quiffs, concentrate obsessively on synchronized hand gestures; soloists sweat hard, yell themselves hoarse, and are usually fast, tricky dancers. Groups and soloists alike indulge in standardized bouts of dialogue with their audience ("Is everybody all right?" "Yeah." "Let me hear you say Yeah."

"Yeah." "No, let me hear you say Yeah louder." "YEAH.").
Everyone grins a lot. In these ways, soul is as crisp and pat as
a recorded message.

What makes all of this such a bring-down is the total lack
of any real involvement. Most soul singers come on like windup
dolls; they almost sleepwalk, and they smirk, leer, and grimace
like so many nigger minstrels. They don't act like people, and
they don't treat their audiences like people either. It's all de-
pressingly Tom.

Now if soul really has become Uncle Tom, it's largely
traceable back to the Tamla Motown and Atlantic record com-
bines, the first soul companies to wake up to the obvious propo-
sition that since white kids have more spending money to waste
than black ones, they're a vital market. In the light of this
discovery, the music has been made gradually less harsh, less
racial, and more accessible to half-baked white taste.

The worst offender like this has probably been Tamla Motown, which is a pity because it has also dug up a lot of very
heavy talent and turned out some really marvelous music.
Apart from anything else, it has been one of the most romantic
success stories in pop.

In 1959 Berry Gordy, Jr., a Detroit songwriter and ex-auto-
assembly-line worker, launched Gordy Records on a loan of
seven hundred dollars. This was fair enough: there are hundreds of small-time colored labels all across the States, turning
out minor local hits and just ticking over. They don't make
fortunes, but they usually don't go broke either. They survive.

But Berry Gordy somehow exploded. He wrote some good
songs, little beauties, and turned them into national hits by
sustained flat-out hustle. Then he formed two more labels,
Tamla Records and Motown Records; he wrote some more
songs, had some more hits, and by now he was a snowball.
In 1961 he got his first million-sellers, the Marvellettes' *Please
Mister Postman* and the Miracles' *Shop Around.* So suddenly
he was an industry.

From there he just exploded like mad. Signed the Supremes,
the Temptations, Little Stevie Wonder, Marvin Gaye, Mary

Wells, Martha Reeves and the Vandellas, the Velvelettes, the Four Tops, Brenda Holloway, the Contours, and sundry others, all of whom clocked up monster hits for him. Unearthed two writing machines, Smokey Robinson and Holland/Dozier/Holland. Anyway, by 1964 he was selling upward of twelve million records each year. Five years, out of nowhere, and now he bossed the first real shrine of soul. He'd been running fast.

The format was, and still is, simple: the songs are all written with one obvious hookline, to be repeated and hammered home ad nauseam; the beat is kept heavy, and the individual voices stay secondary to the over-all sound. The rhythm sections are invariably magnificent, the singers strong and professional. Most times, the records sound as though they've been put together by computer, but just every so often, a little more trouble is taken, and then a classic pop record comes out.

At its worst Tamla has always churned out good noise for dancing, and at its best it has been superb. At its norm it has put out more slick, well-made, commercial foot food than any other company in the world.

The one drag is that once he's broken an act in the soul market, Gordy invariably converts them into cabaret turns. Puts them into the white nightclub circuit and has them make like family entertainers. Which is fine for the acts themselves, because they make more money, but a bit rough on their long-time followers, because the music turns lousy.

Of course, I'm being too prissy: pop is a business first and last. It has always been full of false messiahs, and bring-down is an essential part of the game.

I'm not going to go into any detailed analyses of the individual Motown acts. Most of them are excellent, but they're also largely interchangeable. The Supremes are the best looking, the most astronomically successful ("America's Sweethearts"), and Diana Ross, their lead singer, has the sexiest voice. The Temptations have the best sound and are almost my favorites. The Four Tops are the most passionate, and Stevie Wonder is the most exceptional. Gladys Knight sings the best blues. Brenda Holloway is the most underused. So on and so on.

They all have regular, almost automatic, hits; if anyone

should happen to miss out three or four times running, then everyone thinks a bit straighter, works a bit harder next time out, and a giant is made.

The only real standouts are Smokey Robinson and the Miracles, who have been around almost longest of all. Smokey is lovely. He sings lead in a perfect woman's soprano, not a falsetto shriek or anything so vulgar, but a finely controlled warble, full of its own small subtleties. Pop's first female impersonator, original prima donna.

The Miracles grunt away in the background, and Smokey is everything. Most of his best songs, like *Ooh Baby, Baby, Tracks of My Tears,* and *I Second That Emotion,* are begging letters for love, and he pleads, he sobs, he keens. Torments of one teenage girl-child, operatic agonies—his voice breaks, bends, and trembles on every last note. Sometimes it's a cry of pure pain and sometimes it's only a sigh. Either way, it would like to break your heart. So high and soft and busted. Such fractured sound: *Ooh Baby, Baby* is likely the most lung-pumping ballad in pop.

How could I criticize him? He only has to open his mouth and I'm melted. Strictly, he's my man.

Still on Motown, I really can't dismiss the Supremes in one line. They have, after all, been the most consistently triumphant American act of the last five years. Every time they walk in the studio, they sell a million.

First and last, they're professional. They sing the right notes, smile the right smiles, and move like three synchronized robots. They're lookers, politely sexy, and they open their big eyes for all the people, show their teeth, even wriggle their shoulders. Pink tongues and false eyelashes: they're cute.

They paraphrase the whole Motown saga. In the start, they were rough and noisy and they made good commercial soul music, but when they got to be successful, they cooled it; now they play only white nightclubs and sing standards, film songs, blockbusters out of musicals. They're clean. They give the politest, blankest, most boring interviews in the world, real showbiz stuff about being glad to be back in our wonderful country again and aren't London policemen just gorgeous?

So what about black power? What about it, indeed—they gently steer the conversation back to clothes and show you their brand new mink.

Atlantic Records, Tamla's major rival, pre-dates pop.

It's run by the Ertegun Brothers, Ahmet and Nesuhi, and it has been going for upward of twenty years now. In that time it has always been the most perceptive, tasteful, and committed label around.

Over two decades it has pushed Joe Turner, Stick McGhee, the Clovers, Ruth Brown, Ray Charles, Laverne Baker, the Drifters, the Coasters, Solomon Burke, Wilson Pickett, Aretha Franklin, and whole regiments besides. Everything that has been new and worth shoving. And not only pop but much good jazz: Charlie Mingus and The MJQ, John Coltrane and Arnette Coleman, often when rival companies were still running scared of them. It's not a record that any other combine could even approach.

The Erteguns are clever men, civilized and urbane, even sophisticated. Not obvious hustlers by any means. Ahmet, who has been the more dominant, looks like a Turkish diplomat— he has a billiard-ball skull, a goatee, a squeaky voice—and he comes on like an all-time playboy. Inside the image, he has shrewdness and staying power. Not long ago he sold Atlantic to Warner Brothers for twenty million dollars, and that just about rounded everything off.

Again, there's not much point in going into any individual breakdowns; Atlantic's major strength has always been its professionalism, and the Erteguns have invariably used the best writers, producers, engineers, or sessionmen going at any given time.

The most cosmic singles have probably been *Drinkin' Wine Spo-Dee-O-Dee* by Stick McGhee and his Buddies (1947), and *Hello Stranger* by Barbara Lewis (1962). Outside of that, it's been brilliant.

Their ablest lieutenant has been Jerry Wexler, about whom there's not much to say except that he's probably played producer on more great records than anyone else in the industry.

Another of their associates who rates a mention is the late Bert Berns, who wrote such enduring stuff as *Twist and Shout, Hang On Sloopy, Here Comes the Night,* and *I Don't Want to Go on Without You.* He wasn't owned by Atlantic, but he did a lot of work for them; I bring him in only because I never met anyone who understood pop so well. Who agreed so much with me, that is.

He was a typical American recordman, canny and tough and flash, always money-conscious; he wasn't a beautiful person, but he was intelligent and articulate and he made some good lines.

One time, in my innocence, I asked him what pop was about. We were sitting in some restaurant, and straight off, Berns swung round at our table and yelled the one word: "Waiter!"

Immediately, three waiters burst out of the wings at a canter and dashed to our table. Berns asked for a match and was faced by a sudden wall of flame, by three flickering hands. When the waiters left, Berns looked at me and wasn't even smug about it. "Wouldn't you say?" he asked. "That's what pop's about."

Aretha Franklin has been a different class.

Of all the many people in this book, she's the only talent I can rave about without making reservations of any kind.

Simply, she's magnificent. She's infinitely the best voice that pop has produced.

Really, she's the newest in the great line of Ma Rainey, Bessie Smith, Mahalia Jackson, Dinah Washington—big women, classic women, and they've all had voices of infinite strength and command. And they've none of them messed about. They've just stood up and hollered. Foghorn lungs that could shatter plate glass windows at twenty paces, no microphones required. Simple white dresses and slaughterhouse shoulders. Big legs and big breasts and big hands. There's been nothing remotely girlish about any of them, but they've all been marvelous women.

Aretha herself is nothing new. In the first place, she led the choir in her father's church. New Bethel Baptist, flat-out gospel, and she used to be a happening all to herself. Then she turned secular, and things didn't go so well any more. She was lumbered with nothing songs, third-rate producers; not much progress got made. Not that she starved: she played nightclubs and built herself a tidy reputation. Still, she wasn't an explosion. Not the way she should have been.

She wasn't finally signed to Atlantic until 1967, but since then everything has come together fast. Almost every single she's made has done a million. And it has been so easy, so straightahead: Jerry Wexler, her new producer, has thrown out all clutter, all fuss and bombast, and has only let her voice ride free, blazing like a six-gun, so fierce and bossy and bottomless that it doesn't seem possible.

She has repose. Massive certainty—she has an infinite sweep in her phrasing, great size, a crippling ferocity—and she hits even mediocre songs so hard that they're smashed, gouged, entirely annihilated, and then renewed. Given some crap to sing, she lays into it like mad and simply tears it to pieces, scattering strings and brass and angelic choirs like some avenging thunderclap. And where her rivals panic and have to climax each number in strangled hysteria, she doesn't move, but unrolls one steady steamroller progression from first chorus through to last. From an opening of monumental queenly calm right through to final apocalyptic breakup, it's Aretha roaring and whooping and snarling like a Holy Roller. She's some amazing natural force, not stoppable, and she rips through brick walls like candyfloss, destroys skyscrapers, tramples the city underfoot. But when she's quite finished, she only smiles slightly and doesn't sweat, doesn't even perspire.

More than anyone else in pop, it's irrelevant what she's like offstage or what she eats for breakfast or who she takes to bed. She's only music. She is a talent that's hardly possible, and she exists to be wondered at.

Her only possible rival is Tina Turner, whom I've already mentioned when I was talking about Phil Spector. On *River Deep*, she came across as a voice of vast potential, a hurricane, but she must have been Svengalied by Spector, because she's never been quite so good again. Usually, she wallows in exactly that kind of strangled hysteria that Aretha disdains, and it becomes boring; she wastes herself.

Never mind, she's sexy. She's a great big woman with long black hair right down her back and a beautiful snarling animal face and a truly cosmic ass. Not pretty but sexual as hell. And her energy is endless; she flings herself about the stage like some maniac, and her hair flays her flesh and her butt, always her butt. Then the sweat rolls off her in sheets and her lips peel back from her teeth and she's quite murderous.

All this time, Ike Turner, her husband, plays guitar behind her and looks mean, a neat little man with a goatee and sad cynical eyes. He looks like some elegant black magician, so calm and sinister, and Tina his spell, his servant possessed by spirits.

I remember seeing them in a London club one time, and I was standing right under the stage. So Tina started whirling and pounding and screaming, melting by the minute, and suddenly she came thundering down on me like an avalanche, backside first, all that flesh shaking and leaping in my face. And I reared back in self-defense—all the front rows did—and then someone fell over and we all immediately collapsed in a heap, struggling and cursing, thrashing about like fish in a bucket.

When I looked up again, Tina was still shaking above us, her butt was still exploding, and she looked down on us in triumph. So sassy, so smug and evil. She'd used her ass as a bowling ball and she'd scored a strike. Smart woman: her flesh dissolving and her hair all flying and her big man-eater teeth flashing.

Outside of Tamla and Atlantic there are other major American soul labels, notably Chess, Bell, and Minit. And there are maybe five hundred minors. If you like soul music, they're all fine, and if you don't, they're boring. There's not much more I could say on them.

The thing about soul is that a quite astonishing number of American Negroes are good at it. They tend to have naturally strong voices, and they sing in tune, keep time, and are loud. Usually they have no individuality whatever, but they're at least competent. So they come streaming out of the South in their thousands and hassle. Their records seldom make the national charts, but they're still regional R & B sellers, and money gets made just the same. Huge complicated networks of labels and artists and radio stations all across America—it's a self-contained business within pop and is independent of all trends outside itself.

Because the supply of singers is so limitless, colored labels can afford to get tough, and they do. In fact, they're probably the most fascist corporations in the whole industry.

The bargain they make is that they'll get an artist a hit; they'll start him off, but they won't pay him royalties, nothing like that, and they'll sit tight on all profits. All they do is give him a ladder: they get him known, and he can then make money out of live shows. And if he doesn't accept that, he can drop dead. No sweat. Plenty more back on the farm.

The thing is very circular: the company robs the artist, and the artist underpays his musicians, and the musicians take it out on the road manager, and the road manager kicks the dog, and then the dog bites the boss of the company, Mister Big. Is everybody happy, you bet your life we are.

Of course, there's sometimes trouble. Maybe the artist accepts the bargain at first, chalks up hits, gets himself established, and then turns difficult. The companies don't like that. They even hate it. So they're likely to beat him up. Or at least they'll make sure that his career gets squashed flat.

But if his mind stays straight, if he isn't foolish, then everyone gets on fine. It's rational: except for pro football or boxing, soul is usually the only chance that southern Negroes have of escape. The companies give them that chance. In return, they want only humility.

That's sick but that's showbiz.

The only other label I'm going to waste space on is Stax-Volt, which is Memphis based and has a roster including the deceased Otis Redding, Sam and Dave, Eddie Floyd, Carla

Thomas, Arthur Conley, plus sundries. It is also the heart of the sweat-and-Tom syndrome and has much to answer for.

The basis of Stax is its house rhythm section, Booker T and the M.G.s, and they're the best engine room around; they make everything burst. Booker T. Jones plays organ and Steve Cropper plays guitar and Duck Dunn plays bass and Al Jackson plays drums. That Memphis soul stew. They're all tremendous.

On top of this you get singers, and they're almost all clockwork. Or they're caricatures of the black man, prancing and hamming and beaming all over their big shine faces: why did de chicken cross de road? They just beg to be patronized, the way they jiggle like puppets and leer so humble and churn out the dialogue ("Say Yeah, say YEAH"). That's not soul, that's sweating Al Jolson: the Black and White Minstrel Show goes pop.

White kids love it. They think it's cute. And so soul singers everywhere have to tag along, have to grind the same charades. Then it's so simple for whites to dismiss blacks as clowns, lovable but stupid, essentially inferior. Maybe unwittingly, that's what Stax is promoting. There's a lot of militant Black Power in soul. In the light of this, I'd like to think that the Stax shows are fierce ironies, masked insults. But somehow I don't believe it.

The biggest Stax seller yet has been Otis Redding, and there are plenty of people around who'll tell you that he was a genius. He was from Macon, Georgia, and started out very much in the style of Macon's other chosen son, Little Richard. All huff and puff and sharp sticks.

In the early sixties he went on a soul kick and was very good at it. He had a fine anguished sound, clues-drenched, full of attractive little tricks and mannerisms, and his early hits were most convincing: *Mr. Pitiful, Respect, I've Been Loving You Too Long*. Meaty stuff, full of guts, and he seemed as if he really meant it.

In person, he wasn't so hot: paunchy, baggy-trousered, white-socked, and ham as hell. He stomped about the stage on his heels, waved his arms, grinned, sweated. He sang well and used good songs. But he was monotonous; he approached every number the same, and all those mannerisms that had once been cute were now very stale indeed. Face it, he was typical soul, a bit Tom. Still, he wasn't bad. He just didn't slay me.

He was very popular with white kids, with hippies especially, and he played along with them, making small folksy speeches on Soul and Love and Brotherhood. At the 1967 Monterey Festival, the great Love happening, he was the only soul singer to show. Others stayed away because it was a white event and because they were expected to appear unpaid, a condition entirely counter to the whole spirit of Negro entertainment. Otis himself hesitated but finally turned up. And he did himself a lot of good; he became the hero of the whole bonanza.

He was worshiped. Well, after all, he was black. And not just brown black, northern black, but a real rich Georgia black.

He made good records and sang nice and was perfectly fine. But he wasn't the greatest soul artist in the world, not nearly, and that's what the hippies thought he was. Aretha Franklin, James Brown, Smokey, Tina Turner—they were all, in their different manners, more impressive performers, but none of them sued for white favor with quite such persistence, and Otis won out.

Just as he was at his peak and had won an English poll for World's Best Male Singer, he was killed in a plane crash, along with his backing band. He was said to be only twenty-six. Maybe it was true.

Just before he died, he'd cut a record called *Dock of the Bay,* and it was his best, his least fake work in ages, more thoughtful and more felt again. So, the signs were he would have improved.

Myself, I've always much preferred Joe Tex to any of the Stax crowd. He's a soul Chuck Berry, a true baddy. Or he's all very big-hearted and avuncular on top, but way down deep, he's sly. He stands a lot of watching.

He comes from Baytown, Texas, and he's been around a whole long time. Nobody is quite sure exactly how long, but he

certainly had years of scrabbling, hassling, and surviving before
he ever got a hit. Maybe a full decade. And now that he's
finally made it, he's hanging on like a limpet. He is notoriously
hard, wary, and he does nothing, wouldn't even spit unless he
got paid for it. Even by money-mad soul standards, he's
outstanding.

He writes his own material, halfway between country and
the blues, softer and subtler than most soul, and according to
his hand-outs, he makes "songs of kindness, compassion, and
humility." Maybe so, but such kindness I could easily live
without. Like for instance *I Believe I'm Gonna Make It*, his
Vietnam song:

> When I got your letter, baby,
> I was in a foxhole on my knees, oh yes I was,
> And your letter brought me so much strength
> (Tell you what I did baby, you won't believe it)
> I raised up and got me two more enemies.*

He's a great one for handing out advice. The way he poses
himself is as benevolent Uncle Joseph, forefinger wagging and
head shaking in quizzical puzzlement at the boundless foolishness of man. And his songs are folksy little sermons, things like
Lying's Just a Habit, John or *Hold What You've Got* or *Don't
Make Your Children Pay*.

He has a cunning voice, real back-country Texas, and he's
hugely smug. Most of all, he enjoys doing spoken monologues,
extended debates on the state of the world. Or more particu-
larly, on man's responsibility to woman. All of this he delivers
in a very humble mumble. Impressive: Uriah Heep is quite
outclassed.

Still, he's lovable.

All right, he's a monster, an obvious con man, but he has
great greasy charm, much wit and inventiveness, and it just
isn't possible to hold out against him. He's so transparent about
it all; in *Don't Make Your Children Pay*, for one, it turns out

* Words of *I Believe I'm Gonna Make It* by Joe Tex by permission
of London Tree Music Ltd., London.

that he's against starving our children, not on any moral grounds, but because we might need them some day and it wouldn't do to have them hate us then. Investment and repayment. Self-interest right along the line. And he's funny, he really is, and he obviously enjoys himself. So his records turn into good clean dirt and you can't resent them. You keep trying to disapprove, but your principles slip. That's how you're corrupted.

Finally, in this chapter I have to say something about B.B. King, who has nothing much to do with soul, who is hardly pop at all but has been a major figure just the same. Most simply, he's the blues.

He's a tubby man in middle age, and he plays maybe the best blues guitar in the world. Originally, he comes out of a Mississippi plantation and is Bukka White's cousin. And there's no hyped-up gospel about him, no commrecial sixties' hysteria; he plays pure blues, the real thing, and makes no compromises with anything.

Even though he's from the South, what he peddles now is northern big city stuff, tough and cynical. He uses organ, trumpet, and tenor behind him, a small rough-edged band, and he only sings a bit, plays a bit. His voice is harsh, mean-sounding, and his guitar wings way over the top, simultaneously brutal and incredibly delicate. So he sells nothing to a white audience, but among Negroes he's one of the genuine giants and has been for the last fifteen years.

His songs are mean and humorous and boastful. Very full of B. B. King's importance. And he trusts nobody, he rates women very low indeed and takes no jive, no mess.

His music is mostly simple twelve-bars, straight ahead, and he doesn't ever change. Just the blues, only the hard blues. You learn him off by heart, it's so casual, so static; it only works because he's just naturally riveting, because he can play some chorus you've heard a hundred times before and somehow make it new again. He's heavy.

The biggest influence he's had, outside of other black blues guitarists his own age, has been among the young intellectual whites: Eric Clapton, Mike Bloomfield, Peter Green. The way they see him, he's the last hero of a long romantic tradition, and they revere him just as much as trad jazzmen once worshiped Bunk Johnson. They're truly in awe of him. Not, of course, that he's much interested: he has his own black public, he has owned them for two decades now, and earnest white cults are so much jam. All he does is play the blues.

Inevitably, this chapter has been a bit of a ramble: I've had to cover quite a long period, a range of styles, a variety of approaches, and still make them seem as if they had something in common.

The odd thing about soul up to here is that, having started out as a great return to roots and reality, having brought some desperately needed guts into pop during the early sixties, it has grown into something even more phony than the stuff it replaced. It is exciting or sexual or even moving, but does it reflect a new black pride, does it, hell! It is commercial. It is professionally servile. And all the impulses that created it in the first place have long since been forgotten. Now it's only a sleepwalking factory. That's what happens to all pop.

14. The Beatles

NEXT COME the Fab Four, the Moptop Mersey Marvels, and this is the bit I've been dreading. I mean, what is there possibly left to say on them?

In the beginning, I should say, the Beatles were the Quarrymen, and then they were the Silver Beatles, and there were five of them: John Lennon, Stuart Sutcliffe, Paul McCartney, George Harrison, and Pete Best. All of them came from working-class or lower-middle-class backgrounds in Liverpool, and the only ones with any pretensions to anything were Paul McCartney, who had racked up five "0" levels, and Stuart Sutcliffe, who painted.

The heavies at this time were Sutcliffe and John Lennon, who were at Art School together.

Sutcliffe was something like an embryo James Dean, very beautiful looking, and he wore shades even in the dark: he was natural image. Of all the Beatles at this stage he was the most sophisticated and the most articulate; Eduardo Paolozzi, the painter, who taught him for a time, says that he was very talented indeed.

As for Lennon, he was a roughneck. His father, who was a seaman, had left home when Lennon was still a small child; his mother had died, and he'd been brought up by his Aunt Mimi. And by the time he got to Art School, he'd grown into a professional hard-nut, big-mouthed and flash, notorious for his great skill as a thiever; and he rampaged through Liverpool like some wounded buffalo, smashing everything that got in his way. He wrote songs with Paul McCartney. He had hefty intellectual discussions with Sutcliffe. He was rude to almost everyone, loud and callous and brutally funny; his put-downs could kill. A lot of people noticed him.

The Beatles, at this time, were still total Teds: they wore greasy hair and leather jackets and winkle pickers; they jeered and got into fights and were barred from pubs. Mostly, they're remembered as thugs.

The music they played then was souped-up rock, much influenced by Eddie Cochran and Buddy Holly, not notably original, and they were less than an explosion. In 1960 they managed a tour of Scotland with Johnny Gentle, one of the lesser figures in the Larry Parnes stable, but mostly they alternated between random gigs in Liverpool and seasons at the Star Club in Hamburg, where they played murderous hours each night and halfway starved to death.

At this point, Stuart Sutcliffe left the group to concentrate on his painting and, soon afterwards, died of a brain tumor. He was twenty-one. Meanwhile, the Beatles had begun to move up a bit—they'd made some records in Germany, bad records but records just the same, and they'd built themselves a solid following, both in Germany and at home. And musically, they'd become competent and they had their own sound, a crossbreed between classic rock and commercial R & B; they were raw, deafening, a bit crude, but they were really exciting. At least, unlike any other British act ever, they didn't ape America but sounded what they were—working-class Liverpool, dirty-mouthed and scruffy, unfake—and that's what gave them their strength; that's what made Brian Epstein want to manage them.

Epstein was the eldest son in a successful Jewish business family, and he ran a Liverpool record store. In his early twenties he'd wanted to be an actor and he'd gone to the Royal Academy of Dramatic Art, but now, approaching thirty, he'd resigned himself to being a businessman. Intelligent and loyal and neurotic, painfully sensitive, he was nobody's picture of a hustler, but he was civilized, basically honest, and he had capital. So he asked the Beatles to let him be manager and they agreed.

Soon after this, Pete Best, the drummer, got flung out and

was replaced by Ringo Starr. Best had laid down a loud and clumsy beat, quite effective, but he'd been less sharp, less clever, less flexible than the other Beatles and they'd got bored with him; they wanted him out. Characteristically, though, they saddled Epstein with the job of telling him.

Ringo Starr's real name was Richard Starkey, and he'd been playing with Rory Storme and the Hurricanes, Liverpool's top group of that time. Actually, he wasn't too much of a drummer, and he had rough times at the hands of vengeful Pete Best fans; he was given a fierce baptism, and the Beatles themselves mostly ignored him—he didn't belong. But he had his own defenses, a great offhand resilience and a deadpan humor, and he survived.

Meanwhile, Epstein acted like a manager. Privately he had huge inhibitions about hustling, but he fought them down and sweated. The Beatles roasted him any time he showed signs of flagging (Lennon in particular was merciless), so Epstein had demos made and touted them around the record companies; he pleaded and spieled and harangued. And having first been turned down by Dick Rowe at Decca, the King Dagobert of pop, he finally got a contract with E.M.I. and everything began.

From there on in, it was fast and straight ahead: the first single, *Love Me Do,* made the thirty; the second, *Please Please Me,* made number one; the third, *From Me To You,* also made number one (louder), and the fourth, *She Loves You,* made the biggest hit that any British artist had ever cut. All of them were written by Lennon and McCartney.

By spring of 1963, they had taken over from Cliff Richard in Britain, and by autumn they were a national obsession. At the beginning of 1964, given the most frantic hype ever, they broke out in America and stole the first five places solid on the chart. That summer, they released their first movie, *Hard Day's Night,* and it smashed, and that just about rounded things out. Altogether, it had taken two years from first big push to last.

At the end of all this, they had become unarguably the largest phenomenon that pop had ever coughed up, and even more remarkably, they've hardly slid since. To the time of writing, they have sold upward of two hundred million records, and they're coming up for their twentieth straight number-one.

Beyond that, they had made millions of dollars for themselves and many more millions of dollars for their government; in reward, they were all given the M.B.E. for their contributions to the export drive. This was a clincher—assorted retired majors and jumped-up clerks sent their own medals back in protest, but everyone else was delighted. That's how respectable pop had become, and it was the Beatles who'd made it like that.

One side effect of Beatlemania was that there was a hysterical boom in Liverpudlia. Two days after *Please Please Me* had crashed number one, the collected managers and agents of Britain hit Merseyside like a plague, and they didn't leave again until every last able-bodied guitar picker in town had been hijacked. They were pure Hollywood, straight out of Mad Magazine—smoked cigars, drove limousines, waved shiny contracts, and conned everyone blind. They slavered greed from their throats, lust from their nostrils, hype from their eyeballs, and inside six months they'd run the city clean. Nobody left but women, children, and crips. Total wipe-out.

In the first wave alone, there were the Searchers, Gerry and the Pacemakers, Billy J. Kramer and the Dakotas, the Mojos, the Swinging Blue Jeans, the Undertakers, Tommy Quickly, the Merseybeats, and the Big Three. Without exception, they had a few fast hits and then, without exception, they blew up.

Liverpool is a strange town; it gets obsessed by everything it does. It's a seaport made up of different races, a city full of neighborhoods, full of gangs, and outside of Glasgow it's the rawest, most passionate place in Britain.

It has a certain black style of its own, a private strength and humor and awareness, real violence, and it is also grim, very much so. After the pubs close down, everyone stands out on corners and watches what happens and has nowhere much to go. Clubs are small, sweaty, and dumb. Kids don't move by themselves or they get nutted by the guerrillas. This is America in England: a night out ends almost inevitably with a punch on the nose.

In such an atmosphere, hungry and physical, pop could

hardly miss. It exploded. It took over completely, it turned everyone fanatic, and by the early sixties there were upward of 350 groups around, more getting born each day. Almost always, they were musically dire, quite dreadful, but that wasn't the point—they were loud, crude, energetic, and they weren't faked.

Of course in the normal run of things, almost none of them would ever have happened, but this was no normal run; the Beatles had smashed, Liverpool was a national obsession, and suddenly they couldn't lose.

Quality wasn't remotely relevant here—all they had to do was open wide, let those lush scouse accents out, and they were home in one; they had walkovers. In this way, the charts got filled with musical assassination. But it was a fierce time; at least it was rowdy, and nobody was bored.

Individually, nobody came to much: the Searchers were the most melodic, the Swinging Blue Jeans the most frantic, the Merseybeats somehow the most archetypal. Outside of that, nothing.

But with the Beatles, beyond their music itself, their greatest strengths were clarity of image and the way they balanced. It's a truism that no pop format is any good unless it can be expressed in one sentence, but the Beatles went beyond that; they could each be said in one word: Lennon was the brutal one, McCartney was the pretty one, Ringo Starr was the lovable one, Harrison was the balancer. And if Lennon was tactless, McCartney was a natural diplomat. And if Harrison was dim, Lennon was very clever. And if Starr was clownish, Harrison was almost somber. And if McCartney was arty, Starr was basic. Round and round in circles, no loose ends left over, and it all made for a comforting sense of completeness.

Completeness, in fact, was what the Beatles were all about. They were always perfectly self-contained, independent, as if the world was split cleanly into two races, the Beatles and everyone else, and they seemed to live off nobody but themselves.

There is a film of their first American press conference that expresses this perfectly. Hundreds of newsmen question them, close in and batter and hassle them, but the Beatles aren't reached. They answer politely, they make jokes, they're most charming—but they're never remotely involved, they're private. They have their own club going, and really, they aren't reachable. They are, after all, the Beatles.

Throughout this, they are very subtly playing image both ways—they are anti-stars and superstars both. They use Liverpool accents; they're being consciously working-class and non-showbiz and anti-pretension, but in their own way they're distancing themselves, building up mystique for all they're worth. With every question that gets thrown at them they spell it out more clearly: we are ordinary, modest, no-nonsense, unsentimental, and entirely superhuman.

For some reason, such built-in arrogance hardly ever misses —it's the same equation that the inherited rich sometimes have, the way that they can be charming, gentle, humble as hell, and still you know you can't ever get to them; they're protected, and they function only among themselves. They're in their own league and you're insulted; you sneer but you're hooked and, kid, would you ever like in.

This is the superstar format, the only one really works, and the Beatles had it exactly; they were a whole new aristocracy in themselves. They'd have been huge anyway, they'd have come through on their music and their prettyness alone, but it was this self-sufficiency, this calm acceptance of their own superiority, that made them so special.

Among them, the four of them being so complementary, they managed to appeal to almost everyone. Lennon, for instance, trapped the intellectuals. He started writing books and knocked out two regulation slim volumes, *In His Own Write* and *Spaniard in the Works*, stories, poems, doodled drawings, and assorted oddments. Mostly they were exercises in sick, sadistic little sagas of deformity and death, written in a style halfway between Lewis Carroll and Spike Milligan.

Predictably, the critics took it all with great solemnity, and Lennon was set up as cultural cocktail food; he got tagged as an instinctive poet of the proletariat, the twisted voice of the underdog. He himself said that he only wrote for fun, to pass time, but no matter; he was turned into a heavy Hampstead cult.

Meanwhile, he sat around in discotheques and tore everyone to pieces. He was married and had a son. He lived in a big suburban mansion in Weybridge, and he was vicious, crass, impossible—but he wasn't stupid. He was sharp as a scythe; he was a villain, and his head was crooked; he wrote songs as if he was suffocating. Still, he was powerful and he generated a real sense of claustrophobia; he had great command of irony, and he owned one of the best pop voices ever, rasped and smashed and brooding, always fierce. Painful and obsessive, his best songs have been no fun whatever, but they've been strong: *I Am the Walrus, A Day in the Life, Happiness Is a Warm Gun,* and most racked of all, *Strawberry Fields Forever.*

On stage, he played monster and made small girls wet their panties. He'd hunch up over the mike, very tight because he couldn't see an inch without his glasses on, and he'd make faces, stick his tongue out, be offensive in every way possible. On *Twist and Shout* he'd rant his way into total incoherence, half rupture himself. He'd grind like a cement mixer, and microbops loved every last dirty word of him. No doubt, the boy had talents.

Paul McCartney played Dick Diver. He was stylish, charming, always elegant, and whenever he looked at you, he had this strange way of making you feel as if you were genuinely the only person in the world that mattered. Of course he'd then turn away and do exactly the same thing with the next in line, but just by that flash, while it lasted, you were warmed and seduced and won over for always.

He was a bit hooked on culture: he went to all the right plays, read the right books, covered the right exhibitions; he even went through a stage when he started diluting his accent. No chance—Lennon brought him down off that very fast indeed. Still, he educated himself in trends of all kinds, and when he was done, he emerged as a full-blown romantic, vastly sentimental, and he wrote many sad songs about many sad things, songs so soft and sweet that grandmothers everywhere bought them by the millions.

In their different styles, then, both Lennon and McCartney had gotten arty and their music changed. In the first place, their work had been brash, raucous, and the lyrics very basic: *She Loves You, Thank You Girl, I Saw Her Standing There.* Good stuff, strong and aggressive, but limited. From about 1964 on, though, they got hooked on the words of Bob Dylan, and their lyrics, which had always been strictly literal, now became odder, quirkier, more surreal. Message and meaning: suddenly it was creative artist time.

My own feeling is that Lennon has heavy talent and that McCartney really hasn't. He's melodic, pleasant, inventive, but he's too much syrup.

Still, they do make a partnership: Lennon's toughness plays off well against McCartney's romanticism; Lennon's verbal flair is complemented by McCartney's knack of knocking out instantly attractive melody lines. They add up.

Of course, when McCartney runs loose with string quartets, some horribly mawkish things can happen—*Yesterday, She's Leaving Home*—but he has a certain saving humor, and he's usually just about walked the line.

At any rate, he looks sweet, and Jane Asher, his steady actress girl friend, also looks sweet, and between them they make a couple much loved by mothers and female columnists everywhere. More than anyone, he made the Beatles respectable at the start, and he's kept them that way, no matter what routines they've gotten involved in. Even when he confesses to taking acid or bangs on about meditation, he invariably looks so innocent, acts so cute, that he gets indulged; he's always forgiven. Also, not to be overlooked, he is pretty and girls scream at him.

More than any of the others, though, Ringo Starr came to sum up the Beatles.

America made him. In England, he was always a bit peripheral; he always sat at the back and kept his mouth shut, but when the Beatles hit New York, they were treated very much like some new line in cuddly toys, long-haired and hilarious, and Ringo stole it.

Big-nosed and dog-eyed, he had a look of perpetual bewilderment and said hardly anything: "I haven't got a smiling mouth or a talking face." He only bumbled, came on like some pop Harry Langdon, and women in millions ached to mother him. In fairness, it has to be said that this was not his fault—he looked that way by nature and couldn't change.

Every now and then, out of deep silence, he'd emerge with some really classic line. No verbal gymnastics like Lennon, not even a joke—just one flat line, so mumbled and understated as to be almost nonexistent.

My own favorite was his summing-up of his life as a Beatle: "I go to John's place to play with his toys, and sometimes he comes down here to play with mine."

He's solid. When he got married, he chose no model, no starlet, but a girl from Liverpool, a hairdresser's assistant. He'd known and gone steady with her for years. Or when all the Beatles went meditating in India with the Maharishi, he said that it reminded him of Butlins and came home early.

Really, he summarizes everything that's best in the English character: stability, tolerance, lack of pretension, humor, a certain built-in cool. He knows he's not a drummer and he doesn't care. He doesn't care about much, in fact; he only sits at home and plays records, watches television, shoots pool. Simply, he passes time.

He is hooked on Westerns, and he loves new gadgets, and he spends a lot of his time just playing. He sits with his wife and his children. Well, he's slightly bored at times because he has nothing much to do any more, but he isn't much bothered, and quite genuinely, he would make out all right if the Beatles went broke on him and he had to get a nothing job again. No matter what, he keeps moving.

George Harrison is more problematic.

To begin with, he wasn't much more than a catcher, a trampoline for the others to bounce off. On stage, he'd set himself a little way back from the mike and play along without smiling. He hardly moved, and he'd look cut off, vaguely bored.

His big moment used to be when he and Paul McCartney would suddenly bear down hard on the mike together, and cheeks almost touching, they'd shake their heads like mad. This gesture, with its strong flit undertones, used to provoke more screams than almost anything else. But when it was over, Harrison never followed it up; he only dropped back and looked bored again.

In interviews, too, he was less than impressive. He was slower than the rest, less imaginative, and he tended to plod a bit. In every way, he was overshadowed by Lennon/McCartney.

At this stage, his most publicized interest was money, and he got very tight with Epstein, who used to explain the complexities of Beatle finance to him. Epstein, who worshiped the Beatles and was greatly afraid of losing touch with them, loved this and used to speak of Harrison as his favorite son.

Still, as Lennon/McCartney got increasingly arty, Harrison was stung and he began chasing. He went on a heavy intellectual streak himself. First up, he got interested in Indian music and took lessons on sitar from Ravi Shankar. Second, he was to be seen flitting in and out of London airport wearing beads and baggy white trousers. Third, he started writing Indian-style songs, all curry powder and souvenirs from the Taj Mahal, most fake, very solemn. And finally, he went up a mountain with the Maharishi Mahesh Yogi, guru to the stars, and came down again a convinced mystic. From here on, he was a philosopher, a sage, and his interviews were stuffed full of dictums, parables, and eternal paradoxes. Sitting crosslegged in Virginia Water, he hid his face behind a beard, a moustache, and two Rasputin eyes and was almost unrecognizable as George Harrison, guitar-picker.

Ringo apart, all of the Beatles went through heavy changes. In 1963, they'd epitomized everything that was antipretension: they'd been tough and funny and cool, merciless to outsiders, and they'd had the most murderous eyes for pomposity of any kind. That was one of their greatest attractions, their total lack of crapola, and even after they'd made it so huge, they didn't lose out. Well, maybe they read more books, went to more theaters, and so forth, but basically they stayed as hard as ever. Paul McCartney wrote a few sentimental ballads, Harrison learned sitar, Lennon put smoked windows on his Rolls—but the wit was still dry, the put-downs fierce, the lack of sellout total.

It wasn't until the release of *Rubber Soul*, Christmas 1965, that the cool first began to crack. Musically, this was the subtlest and most complex thing they'd done, and lots of it was excellent—*Drive My Car* and *Girl* and *You Won't See Me* —but there were also danger signals; the beat had softened, and the lyrics showed traces of fake significance. One song at least, *The Word*, was utter foolishness, and hardly anything had the raw energy of their earlier work; there was nothing as good as *I Saw Her Standing There* or *I'm a Loser*. Simply, the Beatles were softening up.

The next album, *Revolver*, was further on down the same line. Again there was a big step forward in ingenuity, and again there was a big step back in guts. *Eleanor Rigby* was clever but essentially sloppy. Harrison's *Love You To* wasn't even clever. And there was *Tomorrow Never Knows*, musically brilliant and lyrically bullshit.

What had happened? In general, it was probably the inevitable effect of having so much guff written about them— they got told they were geniuses so often, they finally believed it and began to act as such. In particular, it was acid.

In the context of this book, it doesn't matter much whether acid was good or bad for them. All that counts is that it greatly changed them. Right then, they quit being just a rock group, Liverpool roughnecks with long hair and guitars and fast mouths, and they turned into mystics, would-be saints.

Soon after he'd owned up to using acid, early summer 1967, I did an interview with Paul McCartney. No put-downs, no jokes, no frivolity whatever—he was most solemn, and his eyes focused somewhere far beyond the back of my head. "God is in everything," he said. "People who are hungry, who are sick and dying, should try to show love."

Having gone through acid, the next inevitable step was that the Beatles went into meditation: George Harrison climbed his mountain with the Maharishi, and soon the others had swung behind him; they'd renounced acid and devoted themselves to lives of total spirituality.

Undoubtedly, all of this was a major triumph for Harrison. It must have been sweet indeed to have Lennon and McCartney follow his lead, and he made the most of it; he came out on TV and looked beautific and scattered dictums like chaff. "This is going to last all our lives," he said, and he sat crosslegged on the floor.

Inevitably, being so successful, he'd been the butt of much schnidery within the industry, and generally he'd been rated pretty low. Paraphrased, the party line was that he was really less than averagely shrewd as a businessman but he'd gotten lucky one time, very lucky, and he'd happened to be hanging around as the Beatles came by.

Also, beyond incompetence, he was said to be weak, vain, and maudlin. Most of this was true. Just the same, he mattered.

The main thing about him was that he wasn't moronic; he wasn't even entirely fascist. He wasn't much criminal, and he didn't have people beaten up, and he didn't automatically scrabble on his knees each time someone dropped sixpence in a darkened discotheque. More, he read books and went to theaters and understood long words. No use denying it: he was intelligent.

By the conventions of British management, this was all eccentric to the edge of insanity, and it changed things, it set new standards. After Epstein, managers became greatly humanized: they weren't necessarily any more honest, but they were less thuggish, altogether less primitive, and sometimes they even liked pop itself.

Beyond the Beatles, of course, Epstein handled whole Liverpudlian armies: Gerry and the Pacemakers, Billy J. Kramer, Cilla Black, the Fourmost, Tommy Quickly. In the beginning, around 1963–64, these were all hugely successful but desperately light on talent and, Cilla excepted, they floundered. Still, in failure, Epstein always stayed remarkably loyal to them, never kicked them out, never let them starve. Partly this was due to injured pride, but partly it was conscience, principle, integrity—the whole bit. Whatever else, he wasn't a shit.

Just how much did the Beatles really owe him? Well, he was no Svengali, no alchemist, and obviously they would have happened without him. He wasn't greatly imaginative; he pulled no outrageous strokes for them, but he was steady, painstaking, and he didn't flag. Occasionally, his inexperience betrayed him into raw deals, but taken overall, he worked well for them.

Most important, he was a mother figure—he cared for them, reassured them, agonized on them, nagged them, even wept for them. He needed them. Even toward the end, when they'd outgrown management and would no longer take orders from anyone, he was always there, always available, devoted and doggy as ever. He could always be fallen back upon. And, most of the time, his advice was good and they took it rightly. After all, in all the time he managed them, they never once made fools of themselves. Since he died, they've done practically nothing else.

His major problem was anticlimax.

Having managed the Beatles, having helped make maybe the biggest entertainment phenomenon of this century, he still had to get on with managing people like Billy J. Kramer. And he'd been a lonely, neurotic man at the best of times, but in his last two years he got quite frantic: he financed bad plays that flopped, promoted tours, sponsored a bullfighter called Henry Higgins, turned the Saville Theatre into a would-be pop shrine, and kept thrashing about for new diversions to keep himself amused. Nothing worked. Everything bored him.

Already, in the last days of Epstein's life, the Maharishi had been taking his place as resident mother, as adviser and comforter-in-chief, and now the guru had the field all to himself. Like I said earlier on, meditation was a logical progression from acid, just because it did the exact same things for you as acid did, except that acid love was artificially induced and nirvana was natural. And so, when the Beatles jumped, half the hip end of pop followed dutifully behind them—Donovan and the Beach Boys and Mick Jagger, Eric Burdon and the Doors—and the Maharishi's Indian headquarters got all clogged up with hair and hippie beads.

As for the guru himself, he cut a pretty wretched figure; he did nothing much but giggle, and by spring 1968 the Beatles had wised up to him and they quit. Within one week, wouldn't you know it, there wasn't a single self-confessed meditator left anywhere in rock.

Meanwhile, Christmas 1967, they'd showed *Magical Mystery Tour*, their first self-produced film, and it was bad, a total artistic disaster. It was the first real failure they'd ever had, but it still made profits and hardly weakened them at all. That's just how secure they'd become—they were establishment, institutionalized, and nothing could touch them.

More important, they launched Apple. In the beginning, this was conceived as a huge artistic and business complex covering records and films, merchandising and electronics and music publishing, TV and literature, plus any other assorted media that might arise; it was going to straddle the world in one vast benevolent network, handing out alms to anyone and everyone that deserved them. Young poets that couldn't get published, musicians and designers and inventors, unrecognized talents every one—they were to come straight to Apple, and the Beatles would review their cases in person; the Beatles would help.

Inevitably, such saintliness was short-lived; the Beatles promptly found themselves beseiged by massed no-talents and maniacs and charlatans, bummers of all descriptions, and they began to cut back fast. Within a year, the whole utopian structure had boiled down to not much more than one indie record label, no better and no worse than any other.

Undeterred, the Beatles plunged on headlong into project after abortive project. There was a full-length cartoon film, *Yellow Submarine*, which died in England and cleaned up in the States. There was a stage adaptation of John Lennon's *In His Own Write*, which was successful, and there was also a John Lennon art exhibition, which wasn't. There was an excursion into boutique management, which was catastrophic. Finally, there was a mammoth double album, ninety minutes and thirty tracks long, which was mostly just boring. And John Lennon got divorced from his wife and took up with Yoko Ono, a Japanese lady; between them, they came up with an album full of squeaks and squawks, *Two Virgins*, with nude pictures of themselves all over its cover. And Paul McCartney called Lennon a saint. And George Harrison wrote further mock-Orientalisms on the soundtrack of a film called *Wonderwall*. And Ringo Starr, of course, went right on shooting snooker.

In America and England they have become two entirely separate things: in the States, where pop is followed with great solemnity by almost everyone intelligent under the age of thirty, there are still many people who take them seriously, who see them as divinities and hang upon their every utterance; in England, where pop remains mostly entertainment, they're seen as cranks, millionaire eccentrics in the grand manner—vaguely regrettable, maybe, but quite harmless.

Either way, they're the Beatles, and they continue to sell records in millions. They're still flying; they're up so high by now that nothing can bring them back down again. Simply, they've gone beyond.

The thing that fascinates me most in all this is that it's happened so fast, that it's taken only five years for ultimate hard-headedness to change into ultimate inanity, and I'm puzzled. There are, of course, lots of easy explanations—too much acid, too many ego-trips, too much money and success and wastable time—and maybe the easiest answers are the right ones after all, but I'm not so sure. I sense that there's something here that I don't yet understand, that's going to become clear only in retrospect.

In any case, they're still young; they have time to return inside their skulls, and then just possibly they'll do what they promised in the first place: they'll purge pop of pretension. Meanwhile, though, they've only killed off one style of bullshit to replace it with another.

From here on in, I have only one or two final evaluations to make and then I'm through. First, their music.

What do I say? They're good. They have talent, and Lennon/McCartney are infinitely the most inventive, wide-ranging, and melodically ingenious writers that pop has produced. They've added whole new dimensions to pop; they have introduced unthought-of sophistications, complexities, and subtleties. And *Sergeant Pepper's Lonely Hearts Club Band,* their best album, really was quite an impressive achievement.

For all this, I don't enjoy them much, and I'm not at all convinced that they've been good for pop. So, all right, the Beatles make good music, they really do—but since when was pop anything to do with good music?

Sergeant Pepper was genuinely a breakthrough; it was the first try ever at making a pop album into something more than just twelve songs bundled together at random. It was an overall concept, an attitude: we are the Lonely Hearts Club Band, everyone is, and these are our songs. It was ideas, allusions, pastiches, ironies. In other words, it was more than noise.

Some of the songs were dire *(Lucy in the Sky with Diamonds, She's Leaving Home, Within You Without You);* others were pretty but nothing *(When I'm 64, With a Little Help from My Friends);* a few really worked out *(Lovely Rita, A Day in the Life, I'm Fixing a Hole,* and *Sergeant Pepper* itself). In any case, the individual tracks didn't matter much; what counted was that it all hung together, that it made sense as a whole. Added up, it came to something quite ambitious; it made strange images of isolation, and it sustained. It was flawed but, finally, it worked.

So, if Sergeant Pepper passes, what am I grousing for? Well, it did work in itself; it was cool and clever and controlled. Only it wasn't much like pop. It wasn't fast, flash, sexual, loud, vulgar, monstrous, or violent. It made no myths.

And why should the Beatles limit themselves to pop? Why can't they just expand and progress as they want, not thinking about categories? No reason—they're responsible only to themselves, and they can work whichever way they like.

The only thing is that, without pop, without its image and its flash and its myths, they don't add up to much. They lose their magic boots, and then they're human like anyone else;

they become updated Cole Porters, smooth and sophisticated, boring as hell. Admitted, the posh Sundays say they're Art, and that's true, but after all what's so great about Art? What does it have on Superpop?

The way I like it, pop is all teenage property, and it mirrors everything that happens to teenagers in this time, in this American twentieth century. It is about clothes and cars and dancing; it's about parents and high school and being tied and breaking loose; it's about getting sex and getting rich and getting old; it's about America; it's about cities and noise. Get right down to it, it's all about Coca Cola.

And in the beginning, that's what the Beatles were about, too, and they had gimmick haircuts, gimmick uniforms, gimmick accents to prove it. They were, at last, the great British pop explosion, and even when their songs were trash, you could hear them and know it was mid-twentieth century, Liverpool U.S.A., and these boys were coke drinkers from way back.

They've changed. They don't belong to their own time or place any more; they've flown away into limbo. And there are maybe a million acid-heads, pseudo-intellectuals, muddled schoolchildren, and generalized freaks who have followed them there, but the mass teen public has been shafted.

What's more, because the Beatles are so greatly worshiped by the rest of pop, almost every group in the world pursues them and apes them and kneels at their feet, and that's why there's no more good fierce rock and roll music now, no more honest trash.

And at least, with the Beatles, there has always been a certain talent and wit at work, but with their successors, there's been nothing but pretension. Groups like Family and the Nice in England, the Grateful Dead and Spirit in America—they're crambos by nature and that's fine; they could be knocking out three-chord rock and everyone would be happy. But after the Beatles and Bob Dylan, they've felt themselves obliged to get into Art, and so they've wallowed in third-form poetries, fifth-hand philosophies, ninth-rate perceptions—and who've lost out? Teenagers have.

In America, admittedly, kids have tended to take anything they've been given and like it. They've come to talk in the same crapola terms as their groups. But in England, they've mostly shrugged and walked away; record sales have crashed, and everything's gone stale.

It's bad: originally, in the fifties, the whole point about rock was its honesty, the way it talked so straight after all those years of showbiz blag, and now it's become just as fake as Doris Day ever was.

So it isn't really their fault, you could hardly blame them, but, indirectly, the Beatles have brought pop to its knees. It'll get back up again—it must, because somehow it's needed—but I don't think it'll be the Beatles who'll revive it; I think it's already too late for that.

In some sense they have opted out, and they can hardly come back in again. They'll keep progressing, they'll make better music yet, and they won't ever fall. Only, in thirty years, I don't think they'll have meant as much as Elvis Presley.

In the end, Bert Berns may still have summed them up better than anyone.

As I mentioned in an earlier chapter, Berns was a most shrewd man, and he understood pop perfectly. And one afternoon, about three years ago, he sat in some decaying West Hampstead café and looked gloomy over a picture of the Beatles. Then he shook his head in infinite sage sadness. "Those boys have genius," he said. "They may be the ruin of us all."

15.　The Rolling Stones

IN LIVERPOOL one time, about four years ago, I was sitting in some pub, just next to the Odeon cinema, and I heard a noise like thunder.

I went outside and looked around, but I couldn't see a thing. Just this noise of thunder, slowly getting closer, and also, more faint, another noise like a wailing siren. So I waited but nothing happened. The street stayed empty.

Finally, after maybe five full minutes, a car came around the corner, a big flash limousine; it was followed by police cars, police on foot, and police on motorbikes, and they were followed by several hundred teenage girls. And these girls made a continuous high-pitched keening sound, and their shoes banged down against the stone. They ran like hell, their hair down in their eyes, and they stretched their arms out pleadingly as they went. They were desperate.

The limousine came up the street toward me and stopped directly outside the Odeon stage door. The police formed cordons. Then the car door opened and the Rolling Stones got out, all five of them with Andrew Loog Oldham, their manager, and they weren't real. They had hair down past their shoulders, and they wore clothes of every color imaginable, and they looked mean, they looked just impossibly evil.

In this gray street, they shone like sun gods. They didn't seem human: they were like creatures off another planet, impossible to reach or understand, but most exotic, most beautiful in their ugliness.

They crossed toward the stage door, and this was the chance the girls had been waiting for, so they began to surge and scream and clutch. But then they stopped, they just froze. The Stones stared straight ahead, didn't twitch once, and the girls only gaped. Almost as if the Stones weren't touchable, as if they were protected by some invisible metal ring. So they moved on and disappeared. And the girls went limp behind them and were quiet. After a few seconds, some of them began to cry.

In this way, whatever else, the Stones had style and presence and real control. They are my favorite group. They always have been.

To begin with, they used to play the Crawdaddy Club in Richmond, and they laid down something very violent in the line of rhythm 'n' blues. They were enthusiasts then; they cared a lot about their music. Really, that was the only thing that linked them, because they'd come from different backgrounds, very different situations, but they'd all grown up to dig the blues, and for a time they got along.

At this point, they were only archtetypal dropouts. I mean, they weren't art students but they should have been. They had all the symptoms: that aggression, that scruffiness and calculated cool, that post-beat bohemianism. And in these very early sixties, before the age of T-shirts and baseball boots, the heavy art school cults were Ray Charles and Chuck Berry and Bo Diddley, Muddy Waters, Charlie Mingus and Monk, Allen Ginsberg and Jack Kerouac, Robert Johnson. If you were pretentious about it, you might stretch to a paperback translation of Rimbaud or Dostoevsky, strictly for display. But the Stones weren't pretentious—they were mean and nasty, full-blooded, very tasty, and they beat out the toughest, crudest, most offensive noise any English band had ever made.

(Up to this, the British R & B scene had been desperately thin. Chris Barber, the trad trombonist, had started a few sessions in the late fifties, but by 1960 the obvious boss was a harmonica blower called Cyril Davies, who died just as the blues boom was finally lifting off the ground. Davies was an earnest man and a good musician, but he mostly rehashed the Americans; he made almost no attempt to translate things into English terms, and that limited him. Still, he laid foundations.)

At any rate, the Stones were at the Crawdaddy, peddling stuff about midway between the bedrock Chicago blues of Muddy Waters and the pop-blues of Chuck Berry, and they built themselves a following. Naughty but nice, they were liked by Aldermaston marchers and hitchhikers, beards and freaks and preneanderthal Mods everywhere. Simply, they were turning into the voice of hooliganism.

As groups go, they were definitely motley: Mick Jagger, who sang, came out of a solid middle-class background and had been to the London School of Economics; Keith Richard came from Tottenham and was quite tough; Brian Jones wasn't tough at all—he was from Cheltenham, very safe, but he was insecure, highly intelligent, wildly neurotic. Charlie Watts had worked in an ad agency and, being a drummer, never talked; Bill Wyman was older, was married—he didn't quite belong.

Unlike the Beatles, they didn't balance out but niggled, jarred, and hardly ever relaxed. At all times, there was tension to them—you always felt there was a background chance of a public holocaust. That was partly what made them exciting.

In 1963, Andrew Loog Oldham became their manager. Oldham, without doubt, was the most flash personality that British pop has ever had, the most anarchic and obsessive and imaginative hustler of all. Whenever he was good, he was quite magnificent.

His father having been killed in the war, he'd grown up with his mother, quite rich; and he was expelled from school for sneaking out after hours to catch Cliff Richard movies and for being generally objectionable. By the time he was sixteen, he was doing window displays for Mary Quant, the clothes designer, and then he spent a year bumming round the South of France before he came back to work in the cloakroom at the Ronnie Scott Club and be a publicist with Brian Epstein's NEMS. And that was the whole sum of his achievement at the time he first met the Stones. He was then nineteen years old.

What he had going for him was mostly a frantic yen to get up and out: he loathed slowness and drabness, age and caution and incompetence, mediocrity of all kinds, and he couldn't stand to work his way up steady like everyone else.

Instead, he barnstormed; he came on quite outrageous. He slabbed his face with make-up and wore amazing clothes and hid his eyes behind eternal shades. He was all camp, and when he was batting off nothing at all, he still shot fat lines and always played everything as ultimate big-time.

The great thing was, the way he pushed himself, he could either clean up or bomb completely. He couldn't possibly get caught by compromise.

Anyhow, the Stones were obviously just his meat. He caught them at Richmond and got hooked by their truculence, their built-in offensiveness. Also, he struck up immediate contact with Mick Jagger, who was greatly impressed by him and became almost his disciple, his dedicated follower in the ways of outrage.

So Oldham brought in Eric Easton, who was his partner and had capital. Easton, a stock businessman who handled such showbiz stuff as Bert Weedon and Julie Grant, wasn't unimpressed. "But the singer'll have to go," he said. "The B.B.C. won't like him."

As manager, what Oldham did was to take everything implicit in the Stones and blow it up one hundred times. Long-haired and ugly and anarchic as they were, Oldham made them more so; he turned them into everything that parents would most hate, most be frightened by. All the time, he goaded them to be wilder, nastier, fouler in every way, and they were—they swore, sneered, snarled and, deliberately, they came on cretinous.

It was good basic psychology: kids might see them the first time and not be sure about them, but then they'd hear their parents whining about those animals, those filthy long-haired morons, and suddenly they'd be converted; they'd identify like mad. This, of course, is bedrock pop formula: find yourself something that truly makes adults squirm, and you have a guaranteed smash on your hands. Johnnie Ray, Elvis, P. J. Proby, Jimi Hendrix—it never fails.

In one way, though, the Rolling Stones were a break-through; they acted just as mean off-stage as on. Elvis, say, might have been sexual and slimy in a spotlight, but at any other time he loved his mother, his country, and his God. The Stones weren't like that—they looked mean, talked mean, and they were mean. They were revolt in the crudest, most vicious style possible, and they were loved like that, they caught fire.

Their first single, *Come On,* got to the edge of the twenty, and then *I Wanna Be Your Man* was number ten, and *Not Fade Away* was number three, and finally, *It's All Over Now* was number one. Their initial album did a hundred thousand in a week; by this time they were running hot second to the Beatles, and they kept it like that for two years solid. Later on, in America, they even temporarily went ahead.

All this time, Oldham hustled them strong: he was hectic, inventive, and he pulled strokes daily. Less obviously, he was also thorough; he worked everything out to the smallest spontaneous detail. Well, the Stones were really his fantasy, his private dreamchild, and healthy narcissist that he was, he needed them to be entirely perfect.

The bit I liked best, both about Oldham and about the Stones themselves, was the stage act. In every way, both individually and collectively, it expressed them just right.

Charlie Watts played the all-time bombhead drummer, mouth open and jaw sagging, moronic beyond belief, and Bill Wyman stood way out to one side, virtually in the wings, completely isolated, his bass held up vertically in front of his face for protection; he chewed gum endlessly and his eyes were glazed and he looked just impossibly bored.

Keith Richard wore T-shirts. All the time, he kept winding and unwinding his legs, ugly like a crab; he was shut-in, shuffling, the classic school dropout. Simply, he spelled Borstal.

Brian Jones had beautiful silky yellow hair to his shoulders, exactly like a Breck ad. He wasn't queer, very much the opposite, but he camped it up like mad; he did the whole feminine thing, and for climax he'd rush the front of the stage and make to jump off, flouncing and flitting like a gym-suited schoolgirl.

And then Mick Jagger: he had lips like bumpers, red and fat and shiny, and they covered his face. He looked like an updated Elvis Presley, in fact, skinny legs and all, and he moved like him, so fast and flash he flickered. When he came on out, he went bang. He'd shake his hair all down in his eyes and dance like a whitewash James Brown; he flapped those tarpaulin lips and, grotesque, he was all sex.

He sang, but you couldn't hear him for screams; you only got some background blur, the beat, and all you knew was his lips. His lips and his moving legs, bound up in sausage-skin pants. And he was outrageous: he spun himself blind, he smashed himself, and he'd turn his back on the audience, jack-knife from the waist so that his ass stuck straight up in the air, and shake himself; he'd vibrate like a motor, and he'd reach the hand mike through his legs at you, he'd push it right in your face. Well, he was obscene, he was excessive. Of course, he was beautiful.

The weird thing was, Jagger on-stage wasn't like Jagger off-stage, but he was very much like Andrew Oldham. Andrew Loog Oldham. I mean, he was more a projection of Oldham than of himself. This happens often. For various obvious physical reasons, most managers aren't capable of getting out and being stars themselves, but they're often more narcissistic, insecure, and image-obsessed than the singers they handle, and then they use the singers as transmitters, as dream machines. Possibly that's the way it was with Jagger and Oldham.

Anyhow, what I was saying, the Stones had a wild stage act, and that time in Liverpool, the night I mentioned before, they put on maybe the best pop show I ever saw: final bonanza, hysterical and violent and sick but always stylized, always full of hype, and Jagger shaped up genuinely as a second Elvis, as heroic and impossible as that.

After the show, I hung around in the dressing rooms and wasted time. The Stones were being ritually vicious to everyone, fans and journalists and hangers-on regardless, and I got bored. So I went down into the auditorium; it was empty, quite deserted, but there was this weird smell. Piss: the small girls had screamed too hard and wet themselves. Not just one or two of them, but many, so that the floor was sodden and the stench was overwhelming. Well, it was disgusting. No, it wasn't all that disgusting, but it was strange—the empty cinema (chocolate boxes, cigarette packs, popsicle sticks) and this sad sour smell.

Throughout this chapter, I've kept on saying how great the Stones were, but all I've shown is evil, and the question finally needs to be asked: what's so good about bad?

No question, of course, the Stones were more loutish than they had to be, but after all, each pop generation must go further than the one before, must feel as if it's doing everything for the first time. Always, it must be arrogant and vain and boorish. Otherwise, it's not being healthy, and the whole essential teen revolt gets dammed up, that whole bit of breaking away and making it by oneself, and then it's stored up in frustration: it twists itself and, most likely, it comes out ugly later on.

The best thing about the Stones, the most important, was their huge sense of independence, uncompromised.

In the first chapter, I said that pop had originally been just that, a movement toward teen independence, and that Elvis was its first great leader. Well, compared to Elvis, the Stones were entirely different class: they were as far ahead of him as Elvis himself had been ahead of the young Sinatra.

No mashed banana sandwiches, middle-aged managers, G.I. blues, teddy bears, Gods, or obediences—the Stones were a teenage industry all by themselves, self-contained, and the adult world simply wasn't relevant. That's why they were so loathed inside the business, because they threatened the structure, because they threatened the way in which pop was controlled by old men, by men over thirty.

That's also why they mattered, that's why Andrew Oldham mattered in particular—because they meant that you didn't need to soften up to make it any more. You didn't need to be pretty, you didn't need to simper or drool or suck up—the old men might hate you in every way possible, and you could still make yourself a million dollars.

Really, the Stones were quite major liberators: they stirred up a whole new mood of teen arrogance, and the change was reflected in the rise of Mod, in Carnaby Street and Radio

Caroline, in Cathy McGowan and the Who, and later, in Twiggy. These weren't purely teenage happenings, of course, but almost everyone involved in them was under thirty, and none of them could possibly have happened in the fifties. For the first time, England had something like a private teen society going, and I think it was the Stones rather than the Beatles who led it.

Certainly the Beatles were much the bigger group, but until they turned to Love in 1967, they never greatly changed the way that anyone thought. They were self-assured, cocky, and they took no shit, but they were always full of compromise, and they appealed as much to adults as to kids. They weren't committed. The Stones were.

In this way, then, the Stones were the final group of the sixties, and their image was the final image; Jagger was the final face, and their records were the final records. More than anyone, more even than Bob Dylan, they became their time.

Apart from anything else, they made marvelous music.

In the early R & B phase, they were wildly exciting but also crude, derivative, very limited, and they shaped up only as a short-term craze. But then, just as things were wearing thin, Jagger and Keith Richards suddenly upped and exploded as writers. Out of nowhere, they started churning out monsters: *The Last Time, Satisfaction, Get Off of My Cloud, Mother's Little Helper, Under My Thumb, Paint It Black.*

They weren't much on melody, their words were mostly slogans, and a lot of their songs were simply crap. None of that mattered. All that counted was the new sound—an adapted Spectorsound but less symphonic, less inflated—and the murderous mood it made. All din and mad atmosphere. Really, it was nothing but beat, smashed and crunched and hammered home like some amazing stampede. The words were lost and the song was lost. You were only left with chaos, beautiful anarchy. You drowned in noise.

There were some fierce songs written, cruel, and the girls in them caught solid hell, were put down and hit and discarded like total trash. The dominant fantasy had the singer as randy working class, surly and always dissatisfied, cold, entirely ruthless, who picked up debs like dust, loved to make them break.

All right, so this was childishness, but who cared? It worked. It got home to the masochist in girls, the fantasist in boys. And in any case, the sound destroyed you, raped you regardless, and you had no defenses left.

Their best record was probably *Satisfaction*. Their most archetypal was *Get Off of My Cloud,* which did in the sixties what *Blue Suede Shoes* had done in the fifties, which sloganized a whole decade.

According to the story line, Jagger lives in an apartment on the ninety-ninth floor of his block and sits alone by the window, imagining the world has stopped. He plays records incredibly loud, makes holocausts of noise, and nobody can reach him, nobody can turn his volume down. People from below try to shut him up, but he takes no notice. He sits and plays records and watches and floats. He can't be touched. He's on his cloud.

From Autumn 1966, though, the Stones began to slide.

Basically, they'd become too familiar. They'd come to be accepted, and new people came along (the Who, Jimi Hendrix, the Mothers of Invention) who went beyond them in outrage and made them look tame. Suddenly, when the Stones came out to do their thing, they looked dated and a bit comic— Jagger's cavortings even had a certain charm to them. That's how fast pop is: the anarchists of one year are the boring old farts of the next.

Beyond that, they'd gone badly stale in themselves; they'd lost pace and direction. Like the Beatles, they'd gotten lazy and stopped touring. Unlike the Beatles, they didn't use the extra time to make better music—their records went flabby and gutless instead.

Finally, they made an album called *Their Satanic Majesties Request,* very experimental; they commissioned a 3-D cover and pushed the whole operation like mad; they peddled it as a major musical breakthrough. And it was only boring. It wasn't freakish or dire or nauseous—it was a drag. It had no rage or arrogance left, no image. In every way, it was toothless.

Also, they weren't too much of a group any more: Watts and Wyman were married and settled; Brian Jones was going through big neurotic troubles on his own; only Jagger and Richard were still close. Andrew Oldham wasn't much in evidence at all.

Fatally, they'd made no films, and without movies nobody can really sustain. The Stones had had chances—they'd bought a property, they'd had deals set up, but they'd never brought anything through. The right moment went, and still they fannied about. When they finally got straight, it was already too late.

In the summer of 1967, Jagger and Richard were given jail sentences on drug charges; later they got off on appeal. Shortly afterward, Brian Jones went through roughly the same thing.

That could have saved them: they'd been made martyrs again, and they were hounded by authority, by respectability, by the uglies in general. They were saints in the true cause of pot, teen symbol of that year, and they were most dignified, and they held their cool. In theory, they should have won everything back.

It didn't work—they rushed out a new record, *We Love You,* complete with sound effects of prison doors slamming, and it badly failed to hit number one. Well, it was a lousy record, but that wasn't the point. In such a situation, it should have scored regardless. Obviously, the time for dramatic savers had gone.

The same winter, Andrew Oldham stopped being their manager.

No question, the second half of his management had been infinitely less impressive than the first. Really, he'd run out of targets—after all, he'd come out of nowhere and found the Stones and made them happen; he'd earned himself a million dollars and started Immediate Records, his own independent label, the first indie in England. He'd cleaned up. He'd entirely made it, and he was now twenty-one years old. So what did he do next? How did he fill in the rest of his life?

Not surprisingly, he turned a bit lazy. He hung out in Hollywood a lot and squandered much money and didn't necessarily get the right things done. For one, it was his job to bring a film through, and he didn't make it. He was aimless, and whenever I saw him, he looked bored, vaguely unhappy.

The Stones weren't much pleased by this, and relations got very strained indeed. The clincher came when Oldham didn't fly back from Hollywood for the Jagger/Richard drug trial. Even Jagger, who'd always been closest to him, was finished by this, and not long afterward the split was made official.

Oldham doesn't starve—he still owns Immediate, and he has the Beach Boys' publishing in England. At the worst, he survives. But he is much changed, very much deflated.

At the time of his bust-up with the Stones, he went through some quite bad times, and he spent various rests in nursing homes, getting himself tranquillized. When he came back, he was almost unrecognizable. No make-up, no camp, no outrage— he'd turned into a businessman.

He wasn't objectionable. He was quiet and thoughtful, very polite, and he wasn't even rude to waiters. He wanted to get into films; he wanted to be solid inside the pop industry. On his office wall he had a small photo of himself and his partner, Tony Calder, solemnly shaking hands with some middle-aged American record chief.

In every way, he was a more adult, responsible, and admirable man, but myself, I'd preferred the ancient monster. He used to be messianic. And now he was a merchant. So Andrew Oldham lived, but Loog was very dead.

And the Stones? They handle their own affairs these days and, mostly, they lose out. In the last eighteen months, they've appeared in a Jean-Luc Godard film, *One By One,* and they've done a few television appearances, and they've got themselves involved in umpteen projects that have come to nothing, and that's just about all; they've done nothing.

Musically, they've veered away from the artiness of *Their Satanic Majesties Request* and gone back to the basics, the bedrock aggression that they've always been so good at. In this style, they've produced one fine album, *Beggar's Banquet,* and two fine singles, *Jumping Jack Flash* and *Street Fighting Man.* No question, they still have what it takes; they remain the best rock band in the world.

Tactically, though, they've wasted themselves—there was a time when they could have been as heavy and powerful as the Beatles, when Jagger could have become bigger than anyone since Elvis, when the Stones could have led their whole generation. But now it's not going to be like that; there have been too many miscues and cul-de-sacs, too much unused time, too much assorted fucking about.

They're hardly suffering. They still sell records and make headlines, and even now they probably run second behind the Beatles. The only thing is, they could have been more than that.

Predictably, Jagger has come off best. He's settled himself down nicely as an international gossip-column face, a trusty; he's seen at the opera and the theater, he makes trends, and he gets his face in the papers every time he catches a plane. He'll always be around. He'll make it in the movies and he'll guest on TV shows and he'll go to premieres. Gradually, he'll lose his hair. Never mind, he's safe.

On the whole, things have worked out fine.

So, all right, the Stones could have been smarter, they could probably have upped their status a bit but, finally, what would be the point? They could slowly twist themselves into family entertainers (a song, a dance, and twenty-two tricks with a banana), or they could hang on to become elder statesmen in pop, sage old maestros like the Beatles will be. What for? Either way, they'd bore everyone stiff.

The way things are, they most likely won't last, and I'm pleased: I think that's right. They weren't meant to, they weren't made to get old. They existed only to go bang one time and then disappear again. And if they have any sense of neatness, they'll get themselves killed in an air crash, three days before their thirtieth birthdays.

16.   R & B England

OUTSIDE of mainstream pop fans, there is a separate sub-breed of English teenager, roughly classifiable as The Art Student, which goes in for violent bouts of musical insanity, one-shot fads that come out of nowhere and explode into huge obsessions and then drop dead quite suddenly, never again to be mentioned.

Along this tradition, there was Skiffle in the mid-fifties and Trad around 1960 and R & B in 1964 and, in the summer of 1967, of course, there was Flower Power.

The symptoms haven't varied much: the subject regards itself as several cuts above teenagers in general, being more intellectual and altogether more soulful, and it gets very scornful about any pop outside of its own cult of the moment. Mostly, it isn't an Art student at all, it's only a weekend dropout, but it has the mannerisms, even the uniforms, and you have to be a bit fly to spot the difference.

Over the years it has usually gone big for beards and nuclear disarmament, hitchhiking, all-night raves, pop, and getting its picture in The News of the World.

Numerically, of course, it has only been a small minority, a stable hundred thousand or so, but it has always been a fanatic, it has punched much more than its fair weight, and I wouldn't be right not to give it space.

Anyhow, its most golden age was the early sixties. First, it got itself hooked on Trad, a definitely sick bowdlerization of New Orleans jazz, all banjoes and fancy waistcoats and boozy vocals, and there was much assorted high jinking on Aldermaston Marches. Everyone wore jeans and baggy sweaters and dirty toenails, and Mr. Acker Bilk was king.

In due course, Trad died its death, and after a seemly pause, R & B took its place. The Rolling Stones were the major sponsors, of course, and Saturday night Soho used to be jammed tight with mean boys and moody girls, all long-haired, singing infinite choruses of *I've Got My Mojo Working* and blowing mouth-organs out of tune.

What did R & B add up to? In English terms, it was most anything from rock to bedrock country blues, from Chuck Berry and Bo Diddley through Muddy Waters, John Lee Hooker, and Little Walter, all the way along to the gutbucket stumblings of Sonny Boy Williamson. Stirring times—old bluesmen kept getting dug out of their Delta obscurity and shipped across in bulk to bang out a few random chords, sing us their forgotten favorites, get drunk out of their heads, and finally lose their teeth in the middle of their acts.

Like you'd expect, most of our home-grown bluesmen were lousy. They'd come out of Surbiton, their hair down in their eyes and their Mick Jagger maracas up by their ears, and they'd sing their blues, dem lawdy-lawdy blues, all about those cotton-fields back home: the Dagenham Delta.

The most classic were the Pretty Things, who'd been deliberately designed to make the Rolling Stones look like that proverbial vicarage tea party. Man, they were ugly. I mean, really ugly—Phil May, the singer, had a fat frog face, entirely covered by hair, and he'd bang about the stage like some maimed gorilla. The others looked even badder. And their music was all chaos: the big bad blues. Actually it wasn't either big or the blues. Bad it was, however.

The Animals were something different again.

I spent my early teenage years in Newcastle, and the Animals were my local group—only they were still called the Alan Price Combo then—and they used to play Saturday all-nights at the Downbeat Club. Later on, they moved to somewhere more elegant, the Club A Go-Go, but I always liked the Downbeat best.

It was stuck on top of some kind of disused warehouse,

down toward the docks, and the railway bridge ran right outside it, making it shake. It was cramped, wet, ratty, and music made its walls buckle. And it was a fierce atmosphere, it burned, and I used to go dancing there with two short-sighted sisters. I never had quite such good nights again.

The Animals sounded good then. Musically, they were quite limited, but they came across angry, they hit so hard. Nothing else mattered much but drive. Also, Alan Price played very tough organ. Then there was Eric Burdon, who sang, and he was odd.

Burdon was small and round, looked like Just William; he didn't sing in tune much, but he had a wild passionate yell. Always, he was fanatical. He'd been to Art school and he worshiped Ray Charles. No other word applies—he worshiped him. And he fell about on stage like some exploding doughnut, tubby and ecstatic, howling the blues, and he was a good boozy boy then, he had real talents.

In due course, they went south to London and made it: Alan Price did a new arrangement for *The House of the Rising Sun,* and Burdon sang it quite beautifully, and inevitably, it turned into a worldwide smash. So they had a couple of lush years in there, and they made fortunes in America. But somehow they never got around to making another good record, and in the end they came to be just another group.

What went wrong? Nothing very much—they used up their talents and got lazy and turned bitchy; they hung out in too many discotheques, and they went flabby. Alan Price left to form his own group and got successful all over again. John Steele, the drummer, went back to Newcastle. Finally, the whole group broke up.

Eric Burdon himself is greatly changed.

He used to be an early morning madman, hard drinker, and hard talker, always bursting out of himself, and he collected war relics, guns and helmets and so forth, but now he preaches Love and smiles angelic smiles for everyone. He went through acid and that changed him, that softened him up. Then he toted beads and bells and San Francisco, the whole bit, and he turned prophetic. These days, his records are tracts and his interviews are gospels. He sermonizes endlessly. Kid, he's pious.

The strange thing is, he's always been both trendy and painfully sincere, a tough combination to handle. Whatever has been fashionable, Ray Charles or Newcastle Brown or acid or love, he's moved with it and believed in it. Really, he is the instant sixties' saint.

Also, there were the Yardbirds (*Most Blueswailing*).

There were five of them, and they took over from the Rolling Stones at the Crawdaddy Club. In the beginning, their big strength was Eric Clapton, who played the best blues guitar in England and just about disguised the fact that the rest of the group was stone cold. Never mind, they built up a strong following around the clubs, and then they went commercial, swallowed the blues, and had hits instead.

Eric Clapton cut out—he wanted to play the blues, nothing but, and the Yardbirds played mostly pulp those days. So Clapton set off to hitchhike around the world, and he did, and when he got back, his playing had become quite sensational. He joined John Mayall's Bluesbreakers, a purist blues band, and built up a big following underground. Finally, in 1966, he formed Cream and became famous.

Meanwhile, he was replaced by Jeff Beck, who was also good, and the Yardbirds racked up maybe half a dozen hits straight. At this point, they started being managed by Simon Napier-Bell.

Napier-Bell was a smooth man, in his middle twenties, and he'd worked in films. He lived in a most lush flat high above Gorringes and drove a Thunderbird, and nobody knew exactly where he'd got his money from. No question, he was flash.

Truthfully, I couldn't call him a great manager, great producer, great songwriter, great anything. He was a great line-shooter, that's all. He was an outrageous cosmic talker, a true mouth, and he'd sell you anything. Well, he was an English Nick Venet, and in his time, he pulled real strokes. Only he was too tricky; he always overelaborated and wound up nowhere.

So, by the time he stopped being their manager, the Yardbirds weren't having hits. Could they complain? They couldn't: they'd been entertained, they'd been sold the Eiffel Tower three times over, and they'd finished up wiser than when they started. Would anyone really ask for more?

Again, there was Manfred Mann.

Manfred Mann himself was a South African organist, an earnest jazzman with a beard and horn-rimmed glasses, and he ran a band that played around one-third the blues, one-third jazz, one-third straight pop. They were musicians, what's more. Nothing earth-shattering, but they knew their stuff, and over four years they've churned out one automatic hit after another. Offhand, I can't think of anything I've liked much, but then I can't think of anything I've disliked much either. They're professionals, that's all.

Their singer, Paul Jones, got himself turned into pop's most resident intellectual. He'd done a year at Oxford, you see, and he wore a nuclear disarmament badge and he read books. He was nicely spoke, he even used quite long words. By pop standards, he was truly deep.

The thinking man's pop star: very soon, he was writing articles for the posh Sundays and punditing on TV shows. Later, he went solo and talked some more and finally starred in *Privilege*, Peter Watkins' Art movie. By this time, he had the solemnity stakes all wrapped up.

He was ideal. He allowed left-wing intellectuals to feel hip without scaring them, without making them sweat at all. He was a varsity man, after all, and quite civilized. So they could go to him, ask him about Vietnam, and they were safe; they risked no unpleasantness of any kind. No clowning, no yobbism, no embarrassment: that nice Paul Jones, he only smiled and answered them well, a clean machine. In this way, he became the Sidney Poitier of pop. It was hardly his fault, but he did.

Finally, in this batch, there were the Kinks, who started out like they'd be the worst of all but who wound up being easily the best.

They came out in ridiculous red hunting coats, and they had long ratty hair like everyone else, and live, they only sounded bad. Their first records were predictable dogs. But then Ray Davies, the singer, started writing their singles for them, and he was good.

Davies has never been fashionable; he has always been greatly scorned by hipsters and hippies everywhere, but almost everything he's done has been a hit, and I'd rate him very high indeed.

Whatever else, he's been an original: he has his own areas, his own private progression, and nothing intrudes, nothing deflects him. At all times, he is entirely separate from the rest of pop; he does his walkabouts by himself. And, as pop in general has gotten more complex, so he's gotten simpler, always more childlike, until his songs have become as pared as nursery rhymes.

His lyrics are all understatements, small simplistic slogans, and he uses bass lines like trombones, trundling along like so many elephants, and fast falsetto hooks over the top. His own voice is flat and awkward, quavering along like some pop George Formby. The whole thing is lobsided, crablike, one step from chaos, but somehow it balances out, it makes sense.

He writes about nothing much: streets and houses and pubs, days at the seaside, little bits of love, drabness and things that don't change—stuff like that. Mostly, he writes about small lives, small pleasures, and he's an open romantic but there's always a slyness in it, some self-mockery ("As long as I gaze on Waterloo sunset, I am in paradise").

With his gappy teeth and his grin all twisted, he looks clownish, and he seems always doubtful, unsure of himself, so that you expect him to split his pants or trip over his feet at any time. He even wears white socks. And he's childlike (not childish); he has the most intense butterfly concentration; he'll get all wrapped up in something one moment and be equally obsessed by something new the next.

He gets horribly brought down by the smallest things; he can't stand hassle and has to hide. He's depressive, exhausting. But he's also funny, and I like him immensely.

So that was English R & B, a far cry from the American

article, but it was quite enjoyable; a good and filthy time was had by all. Four years ago, it was, but I walked into a northern club not long ago and the group was still doing the blues, long hair and maracas and all. I couldn't believe them, I could hardly believe myself. Only four years and, already, they were like a walking museum.

17.   *Bob Dylan*

FIRST of all, some basics: Bob Dylan was born Bob Zimmerman in Minnesota, 1941.

He came out of a Midwest Jewish background, quite straight, and through his teens, he ran away seven times from home and high school and college; according to a legend which may well be true, he was on the road at eighteen, a hobo in the romantic Beat tradition, a teenage Sal Paradise. He played guitar, he wrote poems, he traveled. When he changed his name, he called himself after Dylan Thomas.

He was a folk singer by trade, and when he came East in 1961, he sat by the bedside of the dying Woody Guthrie. Then he went down inside Greenwich Village and joined the circuit.

Folk, at this time, was going through a major revival: there was a whole new generation coming through, young and political and ardent, people like Joan Baez and Tom Rush and Phil Ochs, Judy Collins and Tom Paxton, and they'd already established strong colonies in Boston and the West Village. They were radical, romantic, full of beliefs. Among them, they made up quite a powerful movement and Dylan became part of it; he hung around the bars and coffee houses and very quickly got noticed.

He was strange. Technically, he was nothing at all: he played bad guitar and blew bad mouth organ. He hardly even sang in tune, and his voice was ugly; it came through his nose and whined. Still, it was oddly mesmeric; it wriggled inside your head. Even when you didn't like it, it bruised you.

As for his songs, they started out immensely worthy—they were anti-war and anti-establishment and anti-mammon, full of easy answers. Stylistically, they were a mingling of very many things: folk/blues and Beat and Dada, Woody Guthrie and Robert Johnson and Allen Ginsberg, Big Joe Williams and Rimbaud. "Open your ears," said Dylan, "and you're influenced."

Sophomoric propaganda apart, he was impressive. He had imagination and energy and sweep, a fast way with words, a vivid feel for imagery, and coming out of nowhere, aged twenty, he seemed like something special. And down in the Village, he grew into a cult; he began to dominate, and already there were people who called him a genius, a primitive prophet.

He was cute: he had curly hair and smooth flesh; he seemed shy and shuffled his feet and acted gentle. Just sometimes, he'd turn around and be vicious instead, but mostly he was immensely charming. Allen Ginsberg thought he was sweet; Joan Baez thought he had true inner beauty.

In this style, he took New York and made records and then he wrote *Blowing in the Wind,* which became a hit for Peter, Paul, and Mary, and he sold a lot of albums; by late 1963, having torn up that year's Newport Festival, he'd emerged as the new leader of American folk.

But then he went beyond being a folk singer—he became more important than Woody Guthrie or Pete Seeger or Joan Baez ever were—just because he sold outside the normal folk audience and got through to a mass teen public, to kids who'd probably never even listened to folk before, but who'd come to look down on Top Forty pop as pulp and wanted music that was honest, halfway intelligent.

Ten years earlier, they might have been modern jazz fans: they'd have worn shades and covered their bedroom walls with pictures of Bird, but by the sixties, jazz had gotten boring or incomprehensible or both. Dylan filled the gap.

He was young and pretty, very cool, and he wasn't manufactured: he was no part of any system. Instead, he came on like a Dharma Bum, most romantic, and his songs were filled with all the right kinds of dissent. Above all, he used words; his lyrics went way beyond the slogans of rock 'n' roll (Awopbopaloobop). For the first time, he fed kids with songs that actually meant something, that expressed revolt through something more complex than a big cock, and many of the kids liked this.

In all of these ways, Dylan was natural hero-food, and by 1964 he'd come to be the mouthpiece of teen discontent all over the world. As teen discontents go, what's more, the 1964 strain was fierce.

In the past, in the times of Sinatra and Johnnie Ray and Elvis, mass pop dissent had mostly been as crude and superficial as a brick thrown through a plate glass window: my dad's a square, I hate him, I hate you too, I'll smash your face in.

By '64, that kind of revolt had survived in groups like the Stones and the Who, but now it had been joined by something new, something much more radical: that was a basic contempt for the whole Americanese life style, for its greed and smugness and stupidities, its wars and its ghettoes, its heroes and villains.

Agreed, this was expressed in great starry-eyed generalizations, all naive, but it mattered just the same; it carried weight just because it wasn't only a small intelligentsia that felt this way any more but mainline kids as well, millions of them.

In this way, Dylan at the helm, *Blowing in the Wind* became the first anti-war song ever to make the charts. Truthfully, it was possibly the worst song that he's written, embarrassing in its mimsiness, but that wasn't the point: it changed the whole concept of what could or couldn't be attempted in a hit song. Suddenly, pop writers could go beyond three-chord love songs; they didn't have to act mindless any more. Mostly, they could say what they meant.

By any standards, this was a heavy breakthrough, and all kinds of people moved in behind it. The Beatles, the Stones, Sonny & Cher, Donovan, P.F. Sloan—everyone had hits with songs that would have been inconceivable before, everyone took to peddling politics and philosophies and social profundities by the pound. Inevitably, most of it was a joke, most of it was total foolishness, but just the same it moved pop forward into its second phase and shut down rock and roll, the golden age of pulp.

Right then, pop began to be something more than simple

auto-noise; it developed pretensions, turned into an art form, a religion even, and in all of this, Dylan was the mover.

At the time when the Beatles were still the Mersey Moptop Marvels, when the Rolling Stones were still a Crawdaddy blues band, Dylan was writing verse and getting hits with it. Good verse, bad verse—what did it matter? The point was that, without even trying, he'd put pop through bigger changes than anyone since Elvis.

As for himself, most of his early hits—*Masters of War, The Times They Are A-Changing*—were tracts, very simple-minded, but then as he got more and more successful, he grew out of his innocence fast, and his music turned tough.

In place of the Minnesota boy scout, a whole new face emerged, watchful and withdrawn, cold and arrogant and often mean, full of conscious hipness. In particular, he became secret —he stonewalled and played games and pulled faces, let nobody intrude, and when he decided to put someone down, he'd stare at them without expression until they crawled, he'd be merciless. Definitely, this machine could kill.

Still, mixed in with all the amateur enigmatics, he was also subject to spasms of great sudden gentleness, odd tenderness, and then without warning he'd be so charming it wasn't possible; he'd get himself forgiven for almost anything.

At any rate, if his changes made him paranoid, they also improved his writing out of all recognition. No more schoolboy sermons and no more good intentions—his songs now were sharper, fiercer, stronger in every way. His melody lines got less hackneyed, his imagery less obvious, his jokes less cute. Instead, he was harsh and self-mocking and hurt; he laughed with his teeth; he packed real punch.

So all right, he was maybe less than the cosmic genius that his supporters claimed; if, like me, you were turned off by the physical sound of him, by the changeless wail of his mouth organ and by his voice itself, it was still possible not to dig him as a performer. As a writer, though, he was getting formidable.

Mostly, his best songs were also his cruelest, the ones where he let paranoia run wild, where he did nothing but bitch, both at his ladies and at himself. There were, of course, still times when he played his love songs straight—*Just Like a Woman, She Belongs to Me*—but more often he was malicious. He sounded disgusted, and it suited him.

More exactly, he sounded tired. Where his earlier work had been so full of certainties and self-congratulations, his new songs were sunk in distaste, a sense of waste. And he was still only in his early twenties, but there were times when he sounded quite defeated.

Inevitably, as his influence on pop grew, he got influenced back: he rode in limousines, surrounded himself with hangers-on, ran around with the Beatles, had a fast intense friendship with John Lennon, did the entire superstar thing, in fact, and, finally, he hired a rock 'n' roll backing band.

By this time, having got so full of sass, he'd managed to alienate most of his friends in folk; getting himself hooked on pop was the clincher. When he brought his rock group out on stage with him, purists everywhere booed out loud.

It didn't matter: any ethnic following that he'd lost was swamped by the vast new pop markets he'd opened up, and in any case his rock group did him great good, and he came up with his best and most powerful records yet: *Subterranean Homesick Blues, Positively 4th Street, Like a Rolling Stone*.

By this time, deliberately or not, he'd turned himself very much into the Elvis of the sixties, remote and unreachable, and almost everyone you met had some strange story about him, some monstrous saga that at once explained all of his secrets—except that each new story entirely contradicted the one before.

All that anyone could say for sure was that he had image, lots of it, and late in 1966 he had a motorbike crash and broke his neck and took a whole year to get better again. Or maybe he didn't have a crash at all—there are differing versions on that. Whatever, he went into hiding and wrote a novel called *Tarantula* and saw nobody, not the press, not his record company, not his friends, not anyone.

When he emerged again, he got friendly with Johnny Cash, the C & W singer, and showed much of his influence in *John*

Wesley Hardin, his first comeback album. This had a couple of fine songs on it—*Dear Landlord, All Along the Watchtower*—and went further down the line he'd drawn earlier, was more secret and more hurt and more paranoid than ever: "There must be some way out of here." Even with its overtones of Nashville, hoedown, and Grand Ole Opry, it was grim.

And that, to the time of writing, is the saga just about complete. He's done a few further recording sessions, he appeared at a Woody Guthrie Memorial Concert, and every so often he suddenly shows, maybe in New York, maybe out West, and spends a night or two in public; then he hides again. In Big Pink, outside of New York, he sits and doesn't smile at visitors.

How do I rate him? Quite simply, I don't—he bores me stiff. Under pressure, I can see that he's an original, that he writes good melodies and makes some funny jokes, that he has a pretty face, that his influence on pop has been immense—but still I can't enjoy him; he turns me off. Just the noise he makes, his whine and his sneer, he loses me.

As a poet, he's had his moments of real vision—*Gates of Eden, Its All Over Now Baby Blue*—but more often I've found him flabby and sentimental, much overblown. As a propagandist, I've always thought him ridiculous.

Really, I suppose it's been more his supporters' fault than his own: if he'd been put forward merely as a good young songwriter, a clever lyricist, a heavy image, I'd have been all sympathy. Well, I still wouldn't have bought his records, perhaps, but I'd never have put him down.

What I can't take is the vision of Dylan as seer, as teenage messiah, as everything else he's been worshiped as. The way I see him, he's a minor talent with a major gift for self-hype, for amateur mythmaking, which is the same equation that Elvis had, or Mick Jagger, or Jim Morrison, or anyone else that's broken rock up. The only bringdown is, Dylan's been pushed as so much more than that.

At any rate, that's why I haven't attempted any detailed evaluation of his music or tried to explain him—simply because there's nothing helpful I could possibly say on him. In my own life, the Monotones have meant more in one line of *Book of Love* than Dylan did in the whole of *Blonde on Blonde*—what hope could there be for me?

Just the same, his effect on pop remains enormous. Almost everyone has been pushed by him—the Beatles and the Stones, Jimi Hendrix and Cream and the Doors, Donovan and the Byrds—and almost everything new that happens now goes back to his source. Simply, he has grown pop up; he has given it brains.

In the end, he hasn't so much changed rock as he's killed off one kind and substituted another. And if the kind he killed was also the kind I love—well, that was hardly his fault.

18. *Folk Rock*

IF THE Beatles meant a lot in England, they meant very much more in America.

They changed everything. They happened at a time when American pop was bossed by trash, by dance crazes and slop ballads, and they let all of that bad air out. They were foreign, they talked strange. They played harsh and clean, and they weren't phony. Just as they'd done in England, they brought back reality.

Beyond that, they happened at a time when the whole of American teenage life was bogged down, when there was an urgent need for new leaders, and along with Bob Dylan, that's just what they became.

Because they weren't fake or computerized themselves, they brought home exactly how conformist America had really become; they woke people up; they crystallized all kinds of vague discontents. They didn't sermonize, they didn't have to. Just by existing, they played a major part in turning dissent from an intellectual left-wing indulgence into something that involved maybe thirty per cent of all American teens.

Still, that's roughly what they'd done in England, too, so how come they meant much more in America? Mostly, it was a question of scale.

In England, after all, teenage rebellion has always been something quite amiable and formalized. It starts fashions, sells records, makes fun for the people—but it doesn't change much, it causes no revolutions. Over the years, it moves things very gently along, but then England simply isn't ugly enough to make white kids feel passionate.

But in America, in the sixties, teen dissent has become something more than fashionable. On the whole, it's about real diseases, real social insanities, and it's going to end up making changes. And, as its patron saints, the Beatles have become more than they'll ever be in Britain; they've gone beyond entertainment and turned into serious social influences: they matter.

At a less exalted level, when they first broke through, they stirred a hysterical cult for all things British, a fad that's only just dying down now.

This was simple: one look at the Beatles, long hair and all, and America decided that something strange must be going on, that London must be some kind of continuous space-age funfair, one endless parade of boutiques and discotheques and hip trattorias, Carnaby Streets, and King's Roads.

Immediately, England became the epitome of everything elegant, enlightened, deeply switched-on, and its exports became automatic triumphs.

English pop had it fat in there and almost everyone cleaned up: the Rolling Stones, the Animals, the Yardbirds, the Kinks, Manfred Mann, Donovan, Dusty Springfield. And not only pop but actors, designers, hair stylists, models—Julie Christie, Mary Quant, Vidal Sassoon, Michael Caine, and, climactically, Twiggy.

Two groups, in particular, made it much bigger in the States than they'd ever done at home—the Dave Clark Five and Herman's Hermits.

Dave Clark had been a film extra; he was handsome, he had smooth skin and white teeth and a dazzling smile, he was clean-cut as hell. He played a bit of drums, and he formed his own semi-professional group around Tottenham.

After a time, they made records, very crude and chaotic but quite danceable, and soon they had a number one hit, *Glad All Over*. They had no pretensions to musical class; they were only basic noise-machines, and predictably, after they'd lost their first impetus, they found the going erratic.

When they got to America, though, Dave Clark smiled just once, flashed those perfect teeth of his, and they were made.

For two years, they were hardly ever gone from the American charts; every time they wavered, Clark only flashed his smile one time, and they went right back on top again.

The odd thing was, he had no manager. He was advised by Harold Davidson, his agent, but nobody controlled him ever, nobody made his decisions for him. All on his own, he'd realized his potential and pursued it; he'd grabbed everything possible. And it was really quite an impressive thing, any young boy being so sure of himself that he could set up as a million dollar industry and not be conned, not stumble for a second. It was almost indecent.

Herman's Hermits were another strike for Mickie Most.

Herman himself was really called Peter Noone, and he was a very young, very innocent-looking boy from Manchester. He had buck teeth and dimples, he looked about twelve years old, and he'd sometimes stick his finger in his mouth as he sang.

America being as matriarchal as it is, such little boy antics could hardly miss and they didn't. Mickie Most, who knows where the money is and has always concentrated on America more than anywhere, handed him one hit song after another, and Herman came to be bigger than Dave Clark.

Throughout this British invasion, the American scene stood stock still. It grew its hair long, produced a few halfhearted imitations of the Beatles, and left it at that. For one year, the English ruled unchallenged.

Outside of Berry Gordy's Tamla/Motown empire, the only American who was thriving was Burt Bacharach.

Bacharach was a Hollywood writer/arranger, a smooth man, already in his thirties, and he was musical director for Marlene Dietrich. He'd been quietly making it for years, but now, in partnership with lyricist Hal David, he began to churn out hits in clusters.

His stuff didn't vary much. Always, it was tasteful, attractive, a bit gutless. Seemingly, he could turn out hit songs almost at will, complex melody lines and cute backings, full of cellos and French horns and so forth; taken one at a time, they were very pretty music, but when you heard them at length, they sounded limp.

His successes were endless—*Walk On By, Anyone Who Had a Heart, I Say a Little Prayer, Always Something There to Remind Me, Do You Know the Way to San Jose?*—and he won awards, wrote film themes, and got called a genius by lady singers in skintight sequined dresses and men singers in toupees, by the showbiz establishment in general.

Most of his best songs went to Dionne Warwick, a lantern-jawed Negress with a fast voice and perfect control. She interpreted him just right; she was smooth and tricky, quite flawless and quite empty. Very musical she was, and entirely emotionless. Between them, she and Bacharach brought muzak to its highest point ever.

Roughly in the same bag, a bit later, there was Herb Alpert and his Tijuana Brass, who sold more albums through the mid-sixties than anyone outside the Beatles.

Alpert himself was a very lean and beautiful-looking man, a true matinee idol, and he played trumpet pretty for the people. Mostly, his music was mock-Spanish, staccato and quite delicate, and each new record of his sounded just like the one before. In terms of content, he simply didn't exist. He was harmless, that's all, and he sold.

When the American comeback did finally happen, though, neither Bacharach nor Alpert had much to do with it. Instead, the breakthrough came with folk/rock, which was exactly what its name suggested, a grafting of serious folk lyrics onto a basic hardrock beat. It exploded commercially early in 1965.

In immediate terms, folk/rock was fired by Bob Dylan and the Beatles, but its roots reached back into the middle fifties.

At that time, the folk scene had been split into two very distinct camps. On one side there were the ethnics, and on the other there were the commercials, and between them there was a seemingly unbridgeable gulf. Simply, they made no contact.

The ethnics were people like Woody Guthrie and Pete Seeger, and the material they used was part traditional, part self-composed. They were mostly middle-aged, unglamorous, strictly non-showbiz. Almost always, they were left-wing and showed it in their music; for all these reasons, their age and their politics and their basic seriousness, they didn't have hits, but they commanded a steady following and sold albums and didn't starve.

As for the commercials, they were folkniks, they were fakers; their basic routine was to take ethnic material and castrate it, swamp it in marshmallow. Beaming all over their toothpaste faces, the Kingston Trio would dig up some old warhorse like *Tom Dooley*, full of stabbings and hangings, and turn it into a Shirley Temple nursery rhyme.

Approximately, folkniks were equivalent to Highschool and they didn't mean anything. Just occasionally, though, they'd look soulful and attempt something portentous, something like *Where Have All the Flowers Gone?*, bedraggled gestures at significance.

As you might expect, these solemnities weren't much better than the straightforward crap, but rather surprisingly, they sold a lot of records. Simply, they had snob appeal—kids who thought themselves above Fabian or Frankie Avalon could buy folk and feel all smooth inside.

This move to seriousness hit its peak with the emergence of Peter, Paul, and Mary, who bossed commercial folk right through the early sixties and had whole strings of hits with stuff that was sometimes very earnest indeed. And all right, so they were less than anarchic—their sound was gutless, their looks antiseptic, and they were capable of *Puff, the Magic Dragon*, one of the true monstrosities of pop history—but they were still a step forward from the Kingston Trio; at least they tried.

In particular, they provided a link between hardline folk and the public in general. They pushed unknown writers, used quite tough material, even peddled politics, but they were always so limp that not Ed Sullivan himself could have been offended.

In this way, they got away with stuff that would have got most people deep into trouble. For instance, they did Dylan's *Blowing in the Wind* when Dylan himself was still very much an underground cult and no anti-war song had ever made the charts before, but they so deballsed it as to make it almost meaningless, and it became a hit. Musically, of course, this might have been sacrilegious, but at least it gave Dylan an introduction, it got his name through to a mass pop public, and when he came out in person, people were ready for him.

At the same time that Peter, Paul and Mary were emerging in commercial folk, a whole new generation had been coming through at a more serious level. Dylan was the most crucial of these, of course, but there were others; Phil Ochs and Joan Baez and Tom Paxton, Tim Hardin and Dave Von Ronk. Most of them were post-Beats: they wrote poems and wore blue jeans and hung around the Village, dug Allen Ginsberg, thought that America was sick, and smoked pot. And they were passionately political; they had a raw intensity that had been missing in folk for decades, and that's how they broke through, that's how they reached a teenage audience that would normally have put folk down, thinking it tired and dated.

So Dylan happened, and behind him, Baez and Ochs and Tim Hardin, and among them they shut the folkniks down. At least, after ten slow years of education, the pop public was ready to take its medicine neat, and fakers became obsolete. Quietly, they slid away to Las Vegas and plugged in to the middle-aged circuit, where they clapped hands and cavorted and sang fifty choruses of *If I Had a Hammer* nightly.

Meanwhile, folk proper got very big indeed. It was the perfect antidote to highschool and the mindlessness that had bossed the American charts these last years; it was articulate and raw and romantic, and it made its audiences feel cool just to dig it.

The way it most affected teenage music, though, was that it made lyrics count. For the first time, words became as important as melody, and groups like the Beatles or Stones, who'd started out just as sounds, quit talking in slogans and began to write real lines. Simply, pop developed a head.

So far, the influence was all one way: pop groups heard Dylan and were put through changes by him. But then, when groups began to write songs that meant something and smashed them out over a gutrot rock beat, the process was somewhat reversed: folk singers, who'd always thought that rock was crapola by definition, found themselves hooked on the Beatles, and they hired backing groups, stoked up a beat behind them, and turned electric. So rock moved toward folk, folk moved toward rock, and where they met, what else, that got called folk/rock.

The first group to bring folk/rock through as a solid concept were the Byrds, who came from California and had themselves a worldwide number one hit with Dylan's *Mr. Tambourine Man*.

They had image: they were, in fact, the first really outrageous group in America, long-haired and arrogant and mean, and their stance was classic West Coast cool, meaning that they were deadpan and remote, that their putdowns were merciless, and that they thought it was sinful to be fun.

Jim McGuinn, their lead singer, wore pince-nez and smiled strange crooked smiles over the top of them, squinting like some moth-eaten Dickensian lawyer, very devious; the rest of the group slouched in the background, staring straight ahead, stoned and uncaring, and none of them gave off any warmth, any signs of life at all.

Musically, though, they started out strong—*Mr. Tambourine Man* was brilliant and their first album even better. They made odd insidious noises, quite soft but sneaky and sinister, and McGuinn phrased sideways like a musical crab. They weren't exciting, they weren't meant to be, but their sound crept in on you and nagged you; they made you itch.

Above all, they made no concessions, they went as far beyond Peter, Paul, and Mary as PP&M themselves had gone beyond the Kingston Trio, and they shaped up like something really big; they looked as if they might make the same league as the Beatles and Stones.

It didn't happen, that's all—a series of ego wars broke out inside the group, everyone hated everyone else, and all that good energy got wasted on dirt-flinging. Then there was a bad tour of England, a few substandard singles, a rash of personnel changes, umpteen policy changes. One year solid of that and they'd done themselves in; they didn't get hits any more. Still they weren't satisfied; they went on hassling and quitting and starting over, gesturing and bullshitting until everyone was sick to death of them.

At the time of writing, the Byrds are a trio and play mostly country. In six months, it's a safe bet they'll be something entirely else. As for their music, it isn't bad; it's strictly competent, but the spark is gone, and truthfully, the Byrds are all through.

Back East, very much the same thing happened to the Lovin' Spoonful, who were even better, who were quite the best group in folk/rock, but who wasted themselves just as badly as the Byrds.

They were built around John Sebastian, who sang and blew mouth organ and wrote songs, and he was people. He wore small round glasses and looked like a sleepy John Lennon; he smiled very gentle and wrote the laziest songs you ever heard. Musically, he had his roots in the country blues and Nashville C & W and the Memphis jug bands, in Fats Waller and Rambling Jack Elliott and any kind of good-time music he came across. And his lyrics were splendid; his melody lines curled up and purred like so many drowsy cats.

Younger Girl, Do You Believe in Magic, Did You Ever Have to Make Up Your Mind?, Daydream, Bad-Headed Lena, Summer in the City—they were beautiful, all of them, and he wrote one line in particular that I loved: "It's like trying to tell a stranger about rock and roll."

Always and always, the Spoonful were fun: Zal Yanovsky, who played guitar, lunaticked around like something from the Marx Brothers, a cross between Groucho and Harpo, and Sebastian's glasses teetered on the end of his nose, and everything was mellow, everyone got stoned.

If they'd only gone on like they started, they'd have been monsters, but Sebastian and Yanovsky, who'd put the group together, fell out and pulled it all to pieces. There were a couple of bad singles, where laziness degenerated into total inertia. Then Yanovsky quit, Sebastian did nothing in particular, and the Spoonful got finally ruined.

Records are still issued from time to time, and Sebastian still does some lovely things—*Money, She's Still a Mystery*—

but he doesn't get big hits with them, and the Spoonful, just like the Byrds, are sunk.

Whatever their failures, though, both the Byrds and the Spoonful were at least originals. They used a lot of influences, whether Dylan or Hank Williams, the Beatles or Gus Cannon, but they wound up with a flavor of their own, they weren't ever bowdlerizers. The same thing couldn't be said of Sonny and Cher.

Sonny was Sonny Bono, and he'd worked with Phil Spector; he was an established writer/producer, and Cher was his wife. And the way he made it, he took the messages of Bob Dylan and cut out anything serious in them, any stuff about wars and ghettoes and sick Americas, any foolings with pain and waste and death. Then he picked up what remained, called it Protest, and turned it into very big hit records. Him and Cher, they grew their hair long and dressed like teenybop tramps; they looked outrageous, and this was meant to pass for dissent, the soul cry of an oppressed generation.

Commercially, it was perfect format—kids who felt rebellious but found Dylan too heavy, who wanted to smash a few windows without having to wade through all that poetry and paradox and philosophic discussion, thought Sonny and Cher were truly peachy-keen and made them the hottest new act of 1965.

Throughout the summer, Sonny and Cher swamped the charts two or three at a time, and *I Got You Babe* was a monster, all about how everyone put them down for their long hair and their clothes and their general freakishness, but at least they had each other, their love was true, and nothing could pull them apart. In other words, the oldest and corniest routine in showbiz. Under all the hair and hype, Sonny and Cher emerged as pop-age answers to Jeanette Macdonald and Nelson Eddy.

Predictably, they had a fat six months and then they began to die. Sonny Bono had one shrewd head, however, and he came up with savers. As soon as the going got tough, he put Protest behind him and dived back fast into straight pop. Next, he put himself in the background and concentrated on Cher, who could sing and who looked good—half-Indian with great sloe eyes and wild hair hanging halfway down her back. And finally, he came through with natural hit songs, maudlin flowerpots that couldn't miss—*Bang Bang, You'd Better Sit Down Kids,* and campest of all, *Mama (When My Dollies Have Babies).*

In the end, inevitably, the datedness of their image did them in and the hits dried up, but by that time they had a mansion in Bel Air; they could afford not to give a damn.

If Sonny turned protest into vaudeville, however, Lou Adler's Dunhill label built it into a full-scale industry.

Adler, as I mentioned earlier, is one smooth operator, and he rode folk/rock hard. In the past, what with Johnny Rivers and Jan & Dean, he'd been less than famous as an idealist, but now, with dissent suddenly selling in millions, he revealed himself as a true believer and became a one-man protest factory.

In particular, he set a songwriter called P. F. Sloan to churning out searing indictments of society at a rate of roughly one a week, and together they were responsible for *Eve of Destruction,* a round-trip diatribe against everything. This was sung by Barry McGuire, an ex-New Christy Minstrel, and became a worldwide smash.

Adler's most successful folk/rock act, though, were the Mamas and the Papas, all of whom had hung around the West Village and sung in various folk groups and played bohemians.

One by one, they were John Phillips, who wrote their songs, and his wife Michelle Gilliam, who was very beautiful, and Denny Doherty, who balanced things out, and Cass Elliott, who weighed around 250 pounds. By the time they got to Dunhill, they'd worked out a sound all their own, light and spacious, full of intricate harmonies, with the Papas singing the basic melody lines down below and the Mamas soaring way high over the top. When they were bad, they sounded like a hip Ray Conniff. When they were good, though, which was often, they'd make the most musicianly noises in the whole of pop, and they'd be exhilarating.

John Phillips wrote good and witty songs for them, commercial songs for them, but their strongest selling point was Mamma Cass, who was maybe a gimmick, agreed, but who was also splendid; huge and tough and very funny she was, and she developed into a true heroine. She posed nude for Cheetah magazine. She had a child and turned its paternity into a national comic-strip mystery. She was a big old girl, she had fun, and she signaled something nice about pop—just the fact that someone that fat could now make it.

The only trouble was, the Mamas and the Papas got bored. They'd had some very big hits—*California Dreaming* and *Monday Monday* and *Dedicated to the One I Love*—but then they ran out of energy, stopped working, and stayed home in Hollywood; they hung out and made a few records and bickered; they got stoned and did nothing in particular. In the end, they broke up. Mama Cass went solo and did a disastrous gig in a Las Vegas cabaret. The others only swung loose.

The Byrds, the Lovin' Spoonful, the Mamas and the Papas—the three best and most successful of the folk/rock groups, and all of them, they blew it. The basic reason was, they weren't equipped for pop; they weren't mean or hungry enough. They enjoyed their music and they enjoyed their money, but they weren't obsessive. They liked gigging in some small club on Bleeker, all high and surrounded by their friends, but when it came to ninety-day barnstormers and Greyhounds and teenybop one-nighters in Columbus, Ohio, they lost interest fast. Having got famous and fat, they ran short on need, and they formed themselves into cliques, bitched among themselves, and did nothing ever afterward.

The only other folk/rock figures that mattered much were Simon and Garfunkel.

Paul Simon was a small, serious man who came out of a straight folk background and wrote songs about loneliness: *The Sound of Silence, Richard Cory, Homeward Bound, Mrs. Robinson.*

Melodically, his songs were most attractive, all tenderness and regret and gentle irony, very wistful, and he sold albums by the truckload, working his way up steady until, by 1968, he'd become one of the heaviest sellers anywhere in pop.

What's more, there were critics who thought that he was a major talent, a roadrunner second only to Dylan. Myself, I couldn't see it, but then his talents mostly fell across my blind spots, his softness and tenderness, his wistful ironies.

Under pressure, I liked *Fakin' It* and *Mrs. Robinson,* but that was just about my limit. I flagged on *At the Zoo* and bombed out entirely on *Scarborough Fair.* Still, that was most likely my fault, not Simon's.

So what, after all that, about folk/rock?

On the whole, considering how much talent went into it, its results were less than sensational, and its final importance probably wasn't so much in its own achievement as in its effects on pop in general.

One of these effects, obviously, was that it brought through lyrics. Another was that it canonized drugs.

Of course, in popular legend, all jazzmen had been dope fiends for years, and part of that reputation had carried over into pop, but in reality, most of the fifties' rockers had much preferred alcohol, and even in the early sixties, when groups had begun to use pills and maybe a little grass on the side, nobody had gotten very much excited.

Folk took it more seriously: the Beats had always been solemn smokers, and they'd handed down their message to Dylan and the East Village; from there it had spread to the Byrds, and from there into the rest of rock. The Byrds' *Mr. Tambourine Man* became the first ever drug hit, and grass grew into one of the major pop obsessions, a symbol of everything that separates hip from square. It stopped being just something that you smoked and was made mystical, was turned into a full-scale religion.

As for folk/rock itself, the style passed, as it was bound to—it was too soft, too subtle, to hold the attention of a mass teen audience for long—and pop resolved back into hard rock again. But the motivation that produced folk/rock survived, the urge toward a pop that would be uncomputerized and unsweetened, that would be personal and halfway honest, and this took hold and built and, finally, burst through with the Love Crowd.

19.   *London 1964-65*

THROUGH ten years, England had done nothing in pop, only trash, and now it had come across with the Beatles, the Rolling Stones, and the Who, three heavies out of nowhere.

Also there were the Animals, the Kinks, the Yardbirds, Manfred Mann—every time you turned around, there was someone new sneaking up on you. From nothing, London had made itself almost the pop center of the world.

Why? What was going on?

Always, there's no simple answer to any question like that. These moods just break out regardless, and you can't explain them. But partly it was a product of the fat fifties, those greasy Macmillan years, when everyone was smug and thought they'd never see trouble in their lives again.

During this time, there'd seemed to be space for everything, there'd been no such word as Freeze, and you'd been free to dedicate yourself to nothing but decadence. That's why kids went into pop. That's why they became photographers or hair stylists or interior decorators or models or, like me, gave their lives to pinball.

Of course the lot of them made only a tiny minority, and most of them were huddled tight into London. Still, it never takes much, just a quorum, and there were enough to make a surface sheen, to give an atmosphere of something happening.

Then it was partly a matter of timing—Mick Jagger, Paul McCartney, Ray Davies, Pete Townshend, and so forth, they'd all been in the first teen generation to grow up through rock; they'd had pop pumped into them deep; they'd got it properly assimilated.

So when Jailhouse Rock came out, say, Cliff Richard was sixteen, but Pete Townshend was only eleven. It was an important gap—Cliff was already too old to adjust himself, and he always sounded like someone speaking in a foreign language; he could only ape Americans. With Townshend, though, that sense of strain didn't exist. He had pop off by heart; he thought in it instinctively. He didn't have to copy, he could just relax and say whatever he liked.

Anyhow, it didn't matter how it had happened, the pop boom was fact, and especially in London, it made teen life pretty good. All of a sudden, you could dress like a rainbow, grow your hair down your back, make noise, act almost any way you felt like, and you didn't automatically get your face pushed in. Sometimes, you didn't even get called dirty names in the street.

For the first time, there was some real sense of teenage action, teen speed, teen style, and a lot of it came from the pirate radio stations operating off ships moored just outside English territorial waters. They really mattered.

The first station to open was Radio Caroline, and it was run by a young Irishman called Ronan O'Rahilly.

O'Rahilly had been around; he'd been involved in the early Animals, but this was his first big breakout, and he was quite messianic about it, he did truly believe.

He had a handsome, foxy face and passionate eyes, and he didn't stop talking. And he saw Caroline as a crusade, an embryo revolution, a great uprising of the young against the massed tyrannies of authority.

His grandfather had fallen on the barricades of the Easter rising, and so his station opened on Easter Sunday, 1964. According to O'Rahilly, it was everything he wanted to get across —youth, health, energy, joy in life. In Latin, he said, Caroline meant happiness.

After all that, he ran a bum radio station; it was just too slow and it played bad records. Much better was Radio London, which had none of Caroline's idealism but which was most professional—almost as good as an American station, and American stations are great. All it did was devise good jingles, use good commercials, and play good music all the time.

Why was it important? Only because it was private—you could jam that transistor way up tight against your ear, and you'd hear nothing but righteous music all day long. Nobody intruded. Nothing unpop, no crap broke in on you.

Also, Radio London was marvelous for the industry itself, just because it used to play any record that was good, no matter how unknown the group or how small the record label or how strange the sound. For the first time, you could try something experimental and still get a hit with it.

For a mixture of legal and emotional reasons, the government hated pirate radio always and finally, summer 1967, made the whole thing illegal. Well, it listed reasons, but it did a dirty thing to pop, half killed it off. After three years everything was right back where it had started—you switched your radio on and you couldn't hear pop when you wanted it; you were stuck with Tom Jones and Englebert Humperdinck instead. You were fed by the corporation, government-sponsored pop, the very thought, and the B.B.C. didn't understand pop anyhow, never had, never would.

Typically, though, even after he'd been outlawed, O'Rahilly soldiered on.

Working out of Amsterdam, he kept howling defiance at the nations, and he broadcast prophetic visions of the Caroline ship floating up the Thames one day, watched by cheering crowds and honored by the world.

All right, so he was comic—but he believed it, he put his wallet right behind it. Against all the probabilities, he held out alone for almost a year. In the end, inevitably, he had to quit, but he'd had a genuine heroic quality. A bit Don Quixote but heroic just the same.

One other breakthrough was *Ready, Steady, Go!*, which was the only genuinely teen TV show this country ever had.

At first glance, it looked like any other pop program ever made—a resident compère, a string of groups, a few hundred teenyboppers milling round the studio and looking lost—the whole package as routine and dead as school prayers. What made RSG different was, one, the quality of its music and two, Cathy McGowan.

The good music happened because RSG threw out that

stock TV format of hiring anyone who'd made the charts, balladeer or comedian or ventriloquist regardless, and having them mime through their latest hit. Instead, it worked to a hard-core pop public and booked nobody that wasn't a bit hip, that didn't stand some chance of catching fire.

Naturally, there was still some dross left, but there were also occasional full-scale happenings. Every so often you'd get someone like the Stones, James Brown, Ike and Tina Turner, the Who, doing four or five songs straight off, and then there'd be some kind of general freak-out.

On such nights, the teenyboppers would stop milling and come alive, they'd fall about, and there'd be an atmosphere built up, speed and sweat, real action, and it would all jump out of its box at you.

Cathy McGowan was central in this. Before she was made compère, she'd been one of the original Mods; she was a long gangling streak with a lot of teeth and long black hair and a fringe down in her eyes.

She was amateur. She kept stumbling on her lines, stammering and blushing, grinning pointlessly. This is a Super record, she'd say, with a Swinging beat by a Smashing artist. Holy trinity: Super, Swinging, and Smashing. And when someone truly famous came on her show, John Lennon or Mick Jagger, she'd get tongue-tied and agonized; she'd flutter just like any fan.

That was the point—she was like some fan. She wasn't some fat middle-aged DJ with a toupee and a plastic smile; she was almost a teenybopper herself, and she was genuinely thrilled because she met pop stars. So young girls could watch her and they'd think, that Cathy McGowan, she's like me, I'm like her, we both want Elvis Presley's autograph. And look at her, she's on TV. That means I could be on TV myself.

In this way, she became one of the great heroines, an embryo Twiggy, and she got rich. Naturally, she wasn't quite as ingenuous as she looked—she did play her gawkiness up— but she wasn't phony either. When she said Super, she meant exactly that.

After the pop boom faded and RSG was taken off, she

didn't starve. She put her name to a lot of fashion products, shoes and so forth, and she sat behind a big desk in a big office. So she was a tycoon, but she didn't change too much. She still giggled and squeaked; she still shook her fringe out of her eyes. In the end, she became twenty-five.

Around this time, 1964, pop was breaking up fast into two very separate scenes, one fashionable and the other square, one In and the other Out.

In the fifties, no one had bothered with such stuff. Just so long as you had hits and got rich, that was all that counted. You were pop or you weren't. Period.

Then, after the Beatles, the concept of quality crept in, and that changed things entirely. Very fast, the business resolved itself into two distinct schools: one just trying to sell records regardless, and the other trying to sell records and make good music both.

Inevitably, nothing stopped there—the quality team soon found out that some among them were more quality than others, altogether more hip, and there was much frantic reshuffling at the end of which there emerged a definite elite, an In crowd.

Most nights, this new aristocracy used to hang out at the Adlib Club, getting stoned on whiskey and coke, and they'd wait intently for the Beatles to show. They'd slump around in the half-dark and not move until it got light outside. After a few hours, they'd go into a kind of stupefied dream and they'd sit there blind, not talking much, not looking and not hearing, just steadily boozing and nodding their heads. Through everything, music played incredibly loud.

In the very end, everyone would decide who was going to bed with whom, and they'd go home. Next night, they'd do the same thing again.

After a few months, the Adlib was all used up, and they moved to somewhere new, the Scotch of St. James. Later on, they turned briefly to Sybillas, the Bag O' Nails, the Speakeasy, and the Revolution. All of these places have looked different; all of them look the same.

It got to be quite addictive—groups would even cut down on gigging, flunk out on work, all because they wanted to hang around the discotheques, get smashed, and stay up past their bedtimes.

When you walked into the Scotch, you'd see the entire group world assembled there. So who was out in the dark, playing for the people? Nobody at all.

Just the same, there was a lot of talent around, whole battalions of new names: Donovan, Tom Jones, Dusty Springfield, Lulu, Georgie Fame, the Walker Brothers, the Small Faces, the Hollies, Marianne Faithful, Dave Berry, Petula Clark. And no doubt, if I had a proper sense of responsibility, I'd go into one long catalogue and bore everyone to tears. I won't though; I'll stick to the people that interested me.

For a start, the Walker Brothers.

They were Californians, and their real names were Scott Engel, John Maus, and Gary Leeds. All of them had hung around and been known in Hollywood. Finally, they'd noticed that things were happening in Britain, many people were making it, so they groomed themselves, grew their hair very long, and invaded.

They could hardly miss: Engel and Maus both were beautiful, Engel could even sing. More, Engel was a natural-born heart-throb.

He was a light golden color, and he had all the equipment: the tragic mouth and misted eyes and fluttery lashes, the thin hands and soft hair, and he never managed more than a small sad smile. When he sang, his hands went up in front of his grieving face and, delicately, his body curled up like a lettuce leaf.

He looked like he needed mothering, in fact, and what more has any pop singer ever needed? In one throw, 1965, the Walker Brothers were made. They kept racking up hits, one doomed ballad after another, and they became more hysterically screamed over than anyone outside the Stones.

The only snag was, Engel was almost as unhappy as he

looked. He was a bit like a new Johnnie Ray—he surrounded himself with heavies, spoke to hardly anyone, and lived in a room with all the curtains drawn, huddled tight into himself, playing romantic music very loudly, Wagner or Jacques Brel or Tony Bennett.

He didn't want to be just a pop singer; he had visions of quality. In the meantime, he toured with the Walkers, but he didn't dig it; he was contemptuous of being screamed at, and he had very fraught relations with John Maus. In the end he broke the group up and went solo.

Since then he has removed himself from straight pop; he's devoted himself entirely to flowerpots. He has a fine voice, delicate and always musical, and he's a natural for international cabaret, a throwback to the times of Sinatra, Mel Tormé, and Andy Williams.

Like you might expect, he peddles some very solemn stuff, standards and Brel translations and songs of his own, atmospheric enough but top-heavy and maudlin. Everything is painted black. Never mind—he's a moody bastard, he still looks beautiful, and he has lots of image.

More to my own taste, though, were the Small Faces.

Originally the Faces came out of the East End, and they were ultimate Mods, small and neat and schnide, very spotty. In the first place, they made it by bowdlerizing the Who, and they were small ravers, loud and brash and really a bit dire. Once they'd settled down, though, they turned out not to be dire after all.

Their singer and lead guitarist, Steve Marriott, had once most suitably played the Artful Dodger in *Oliver!* Now he looked like a teddy bear and showed a fine shamelessness, screaming himself purple and hurling himself at the mike as if he meant to swallow it whole. He sang well, too, wild and strangled. Bopping up and back, his knees clamped tight and his eyes screwed up, he'd be berserk and he'd be good. He'd have everything it took.

In many ways, the Faces have been the group that sums up

all groups: they have that classic group gift for self-delusion. They've thought themselves artists when they've only been loons, they've talked endlessly about getting themselves together and making masterpieces, but somehow they've wound up in discotheques instead. They've jumped aboard every arty fad possible, but they've never quite got the point, and in the end they've always made solid old-fashioned noises after all.

Finally, none of the crap has mattered: they've meant fun and they've lasted. Little and fierce and pantomime, they've come to be one of my most favorite acts.

Among the girl singers, by far the best was Sandie Shaw. Originally, she came from Dagenham, and she was skinny and shortsighted, but she was sexy. She sang in her bare feet, and she had a curious myopic vulnerability going for her; she made people turn very soft.

Technically, she could hardly sing at all but she had some built-in ache to her voice, a tunelessness that worked exactly right, a beautiful creak. Also, she had a songwriter, Chris Andrews, and he gave her hits every time. Between them, they turned out one of the best streaks any English act ever had: *Girl Don't Come, I'll Stop at Nothing, Message Understood, I've Heard About Him.*

One time, I saw her do cabaret and realized just how good she really was. Most of the time she sat on a stool and sang too soft, bare feet dangling, bunions and all, and she was nothing but bones and angles.

Objectively, she was lousy. When she had a high note to hit, she missed it, and when she had a low note to hit, she gave up altogether. Still, she trapped me regardless; I thought she was sexy. No question, she had it going, and every mistake she made, the more I was hooked and the more I agonized for her. In the end I got so bruised that any time I saw a tough bit coming up, I couldn't stand it and had to hide my face.

At one time, she introduced a ballad and sang a few notes, and suddenly she began to shed tears. Just a few, three drips and one sniff, and then she wiped her eyes, sang her song.

Maybe it was fake, of course, and then maybe it wasn't. Whichever, it did me in.

In due course, though, having first cut two mother records by himself—*Yesterday Man* and *To Whom It Concerns*—Chris Andrews stopped writing good songs. Probably, he'd simply used himself up. At any rate, he broke his streak, and Sandie Shaw has never made a good record since.

Still, she kept trotting out on bum TV variety shows and singing pulp. She seemed bored and you'd be disillusioned; you'd forget to feel sloppy any more. Only every so often, you'd catch a fast flash of her bunions, just one glimpse, and you'd be caught all over again.

Through everything, she was steered and mothered by Eve Taylor, who also managed Adam Faith. Miss Taylor, a warm-hearted lady, perpetuated Sandie's name and loved her, spoiled her, suffered for her. In return, Sandie was grateful.

I only spoke to her twice. First time out, I asked her questions; she, having just had her first hit, didn't answer much. "Dunno," she kept saying.

The second time, some eighteen months later, I asked her more questions; she still didn't answer much, but she had changed, she belonged to new words. "Ça va," she kept saying. "Comme ci, comme ça."

Marianne Faithful epitomized everything that had changed in pop.

Her mother was a baroness, true class, and Marianne had been to convent school. When she got out, Andrew Loog Oldham saw her at a party and employed her on the spot.

You could see his point—she was the perfect face. She had long yellow hair falling all around her, and she looked incredibly virginal, incredibly sexual, and she had the strangest sad smile you ever saw. When she sang, she sighed and she drooped her eyelids in poses of infinite lustful purity.

She didn't naturally belong in pop; she was high above it. In the fifties, she'd have passed it by without thinking, but this was after the Beatles, pop was the most fun thing, and not only scrubbers from Wigan played the game. So she made records and, looking like she did, she got hits.

As it turned out, she was interested in sex; she talked about it most freely, and she quickly became something like a resident TV pundit on it. Kid, she was frank and unashamed. Even after she stopped having hits, she was gladly accepted as an expert, and she was used by journalists everywhere as the authoritative voice of trendy, deeply switched-on, sinful female youth.

She got married to a man called John Dunbar, who ran an art gallery, and she had a child. They broke up; later she went out with Mick Jagger, and they became the most celebrated couple, holidaying in Positano and dining in Alvaro's and arriving late at Covent Garden. Approximately, they became the Lord and Lady Docker of their decade.

On her own, she played Chekhov at the Royal Court and made sexy films, dressed up in ballet drag and black leather suits. Beyond that, she was a personage, she was symbolic of the scene. Most of the time she didn't do much, but she was famous just the same.

Why? For the same reason as Paul Jones was famous—she was reassuring. She might be shocking, but she did it in a nice accent; she wasn't vulgar with it. She could be coped with. Even in disgrace, she was still a lady.

She kept talking sex. For instance, she gave interviews saying that blue films should be legal and that sensitive actors would turn the sex act into something truly inspiring. What films, what actors? Umm, she said, me and Mick on a high bare rock.

Among the men singers of this time, the ones that meant most were Donovan and Tom Jones.

Donovan began as a carbon Bob Dylan. He was born in Glasgow and he was another dropout; he'd spent a long time bumming around the nation with his friend Gypsy Dave. He wrote songs and poems, and finally he arrived in London.

When Dylanesque came into vogue, he was launched on

RSG, wearing a cap and singing in an oddly familiar retard's whine. Inevitably, everyone and me leaped at him, accused him of cynically cashing in. What's more, everyone and me were wrong.

For a start, he had none of Dylan's harshness. He was one gentle person, naive and kindly and well-meaning, desperately sincere, and he wrote limp little nursery rhymes, all poetical and minstrelsy.

The same things that made him attractive in himself, his innocence and real sweetness, made his music unbearable. Always, he sounded angelic and folksy and fey, almost like an updating of one of those sentimental heroes in Dostoevsky, Alyosha or Prince Myshkin, the Holy Fools. In no time, he'd become pop's best answer to Patience Strong.

After he'd first made it, he went through a bad phase when he wasn't being promoted right and wasn't even making records. Also, he got busted on a drug charge and badly blew his cool by leaping nude aboard a policeman's back. But then he came into the factory of Mickie Most, who is a walking hit machine, and Most brought him all the way back again.

Most is a record producer, and apart from Donovan, he's cut hits for the Animals, Herman's Hermits, Lulu, the Yardbirds and Jeff Beck. He is the most successful producer in the world.

In the whole of pop, he's the only man I can think of who has unnatural powers, who really knows what will hit and what won't. He hardly misses.

In his time, he's picked up some desperate lame ducks, real scrap-heap rejects, and always he's rescued them, pulled them back from nowhere. Over the years, inevitably, he's had failures, but they've been peripheral, they've never come when they've mattered. Under pressure, he wins out every time.

The strange thing is, he used to be a singer, and in those days he had no knack whatever. Once I saw him open the show on an Everly Brothers/Little Richard/Bo Diddley/Rolling Stones tour, and he was bad, he really was. He did that whole hilarious rock routine, leaping about and falling on his knees and groveling, but he hadn't the figure for it; he hadn't the voice either, and he got laughed at. If ever I saw one loser, he was it.

The next thing I heard, he'd just made *The House of the Rising Sun* with the Animals, was collecting Rolls Royces like stamps, and had bought a yacht.

Anyhow, he isn't earnest; he thinks that making records is just like making soapsuds. He never talks about Art, but he's a minor miracle worker; at times he's even cut some good records. And he rescued Donovan and built him back into a hero and put a rock beat behind him; between them they made the best English folk/rock singles: *Sunshine Superman, Mellow Yellow,* and *Hurdy Gurdy Man.*

These days, Donovan lives in a cottage and wears robes, looks beatific, and preaches a return to the sun and the earth, the basic simplicities. Everyone likes him. A lot of people think he has talent and a few people even think he's a genius, a true prophet of gentleness. In America, he's huge, he's a real influence. Myself, though, I can't take him seriously at all. I think he's a writer of commercial melodies and I'm glad he survives, but as a poet, I don't think he begins.

In contrast, Tom Jones was pure beefcake.

He was the son of a Welsh miner, and he was six feet tall, with huge shoulders and a busted nose. By any standards he was a virile hunk, a throwback; small Mods detested him, but their Moms adored him.

What's more, he could sing. Technically, in fact, he was infinitely the best singer we've had, and he'd storm through anything you put in front of him, pop or country or standard. Also, he was already into his middle twenties by the time he made it, and he was truly professional; he had range and control and command. Face it, he was good.

As soon as he'd got a couple of hits behind him, he went into film songs, country songs, big ballads, and he was hardly pop any more. Instead, he became conventional showbiz, the Rolls and the champagne and the cigar, the whole bit, and he was incredibly successful all over the world. He was inevitable:

by 1967 he'd become the biggest-earning singer in England, one of the biggest-earning singers anywhere.

He is unfashionable. He's so butch, so square, and all right, he does make some very tedious records. But I like him; he's an amiable man and he knows what he's doing. First and last, he can sing, and that, in England, makes him something.

And that's where I'm going to end this list. No doubt I'm going to get multiple brickbats for not giving space to the other big names of this time, but I really can't think of anything even marginally interesting to say on them. Dusty Springfield was a competent singer who wore too much make-up; Georgie Fame started out as high level R & B, a cool voice backed by a compact and driving band, but then he grew pretensions as a jazz singer and wound up sounding like a poor man's Jon Hendricks; the Hollies were a flawless hit machine—they never missed, and they were very boring; Dave Berry was fun—he moved like a spider, all arms and legs, very spooky in black, and he said he was going to be reincarnated as a snake; Lulu and Petula Clark were both quite dreadful. All of them had hits and built up big followings and made much money, but none of them had any great influence on pop in general.

Above and around all this there was Mod, and Mod got colder, tighter, more obsessive all the time.

Mods had enemies who were called Rockers, and Rockers were updated Teds—they were in that same tradition, black leather and motorbikes and grease—and Mods dominated most of the southern cities, but Rockers held the countryside.

Mods thought that Rockers were yobs; Rockers thought that Mods were ponces. They hated each other deeply. Both of them were fanatic sects, and their fights became holy wars, each truly believing that right was might, that the gods were on their side.

Through 1964, every bank holiday, Mods and Rockers would pick one of the southern seaside resorts, Hastings or Margate or Brighton, and they'd descend on it in their thousands, stage a three-day running battle. They'd roam along the front in packs, smashing and pillaging at random, and all the people who lived there would hide indoors and peep out from behind their curtains. The police would make a few arrests, and they'd change nothing.

Ecstatic weekends—seventy-two hours without sleep, and all you did was run around, catcall, swallow pills, and put the boot in. For the first time in your life, the only time, you were under no limitations and nobody controlled you and you caught sight of nirvana.

When it was all over, Rockers didn't change: they were solid, and they went on exactly the same way they'd always done, riding their bikes and getting lushed and brawling. But Mods were edgier, more neurotic, and everything that happened now was anticlimax. Going their rounds, just making themselves beautiful, and staring—they were bored and they couldn't sustain. They lost their dedication. Very soon, they began to fall apart.

Always, when you look back, you make things better than they really were. That's a cliché by now. But with that in mind, I'd still say that Mod was fun to live through.

At any rate, I have a memory of two fat years, 1964 and 1965, when you did nothing but run loose and waste time, buy new clothes and overeat and gab, when you thought you'd never have to work in your life again. It was futile, of course—pop has always been futile—but it seemed elegant, it was easy living, and English pop was better then than it's ever been, than it's ever likely to be again.

No doubt there'll be great records made, heftier achievements racked up. It's just that there won't be any time when you can open your Melody Maker, scan the clubs, walk down the street, and hear so much noise for seven and sixpence.

By this time, America was back in control; California was the new pop center. England just took the signals as they were given and followed the best it could.

Simply, London had run out of steam. It had used itself up. It had produced a lot of heavy talent in one flurry, and now it had nothing left in the bag. So when an established act turned boring, nobody new came up instead. Everything slowed down, everything petrified.

Neither the Beatles nor the Stones played concerts any more, groups spent more time in discotheques than they did on the road, and you were left with a nucleus of maybe ten acts coming around time after time, the same faces and the same tired songs. Running through everything, there was a persistent sense that something had ended.

The atmosphere had changed. The economic crisis and the freeze, these things didn't actually change people's standard of living much, but they shifted the mood. When you went abroad and came back again, you noticed something like defeat in the air, a growing drabness and depression. Really, it was only a return to sanity, to responsibility. And sanity, of course, is purest poison to everything pop.

As I said in my opening chapter, entertainment always turns soft when times turn tough. Accordingly there was a massive swing back to old-fashioned balladeering. Even at the height of the pop boom, there'd been occasional freak ballad hits, but now the charts were completely swamped in the stuff. Ken Dodd, Harry Secombe, Frankie Vaughn—all the old comedians, they cleaned up. Tom Jones was never out of the hit parade.

After Jones, the biggest success of the lot was Englebert Humperdinck. He was really a dance band singer called Gerry Dorsey, and he'd been around for a full decade, scrabbling and halfway starving. Finally, in 1966, he became managed by Gordon Mills, who also handled Tom Jones, and Mills changed his name for him.

Englebert Humperdinck—it was good backdated gag publicity, and immediately he was joke fodder for every bad comedian in the country ("Has Englebert got the hump?"). Then he came on TV and he was a matinee idol from way back, hollowed cheeks and big mournful eyes, Regency suits and moody side-burns. He looked exactly like some hero in Georgette Heyer, the man who has known sadness, and he mooched around in poses of graceful melancholy, one hand stirring small gestures of resignation. Mostly, he reminded me of a King Charles spaniel.

With all that riding for him, how could he miss? Early in 1967 he made a record called *Release Me,* an archetypal big ballad from any time in the last forty years, and it went to number one. A bit later he made something else called *The Last Waltz,* and that did even better; it sold a million without even being a hit in America, and that hardly ever happens. Delicate and droopy, he stared back at you every time you turned your TV on. And by the beginning of 1968, he was the hottest thing in England.

All this time, he lived in a low income apartment in Hammersmith. He was into his thirties and he was married; he even had children. He was a throwback, an afterthought on the Sinatra line, and he didn't get screamed at much; he was more swooned for. He posed with his fans, women of all ages. On stage he'd look mournful, be gorgeous, stretch out one hand and let it fall. Out in the dark, everyone sighed.

While the monster ballad was taking over, pop itself was splitting into two distinct approaches, just as it had in the States.

On one side, there were the straight noise-machines, angled at a mass teen public and at sub-teens, ages six to twelve. These were just old auto-pop from any time in the last ten years: simple songs, one-line lyrics, gimmicks, big smiles, and a dash of good clean filth for flavoring. It's a format that's changed only fractionally with time, and some new groups did very well with it—the Troggs, the Tremeloes, the Love Affair and the dreaded Dave Dee, Dozy, Beaky, Mick, and Tich—but there's nothing I could possibly say on any of them except that they had hits.

On the other side, there were specialists: soul bands, blues bands, folk singers, freaks, and just people who wanted to make good music. In the middle of this, there was a small avant-garde of musical experimenters. Most of them took their bearings from the Beatles and were hip to everything that came out of America; they tagged along with California. Among them they formed something approaching an underground, flabby and untogether but going in one direction, trying to make pop expand and progress.

Around the end of 1966, they climbed aboard Psychedelphia. This was the first fashion that England had stolen from the States in years, the first time that London had had to look outside itself for novelty, and the result was only a bowdlerization of the American original. Nothing fresh was added—British mind-expansion meant not much more than a few flashing lights, a bit of back-projection, a handful of discords, and some smoke bombs thrown in for luck. In any case, nobody was sure what psychedelic actually meant.

By far the most serious attempt at local psychedelphia were the Pink Floyd. Most of the time they played instrumentals, twenty-minute scream-ups, formless and tuneless and colorless but always incredibly loud. And they were into electronics, free form and all sorts—very solemn, they were, most artistic, and boring almost beyond belief.

As it happened, buried under all the crap, there was a good singer/songwriter called Syd Barrett, and he came up with one fine single, *Arnold Layne*. After a time, though, he quit, and from then on the proceedings were all dire.

Much more to the point was the Jimi Hendrix Experience.

Hendrix was an American Negro, born Seattle 1946, and he'd spent most of his late teens touring the States near the bottom of mammoth package shows, picking them up at one town and quitting them at another. Then he had a spell in Greenwich Village playing blues guitar and singing a bit, and finally, 1966, he was brought to England by Chas Chandler, who'd played bass with the Animals and who now became his manager.

As blues guitarists go, he was hardly mainstream. He had none of that repose, that inevitability you get from people like B. B. King or John Lee Hooker. Instead, he squealed and squittered all over the place. He played guitar behind his back and above his head and between his legs, he played it with his teeth, he rubbed it against his amps. A lot of the time, he used it as crude sex, his clean machine.

He was all image, Hendrix, he had long tight-napped hair that stuck up all around his head like some grotesque fuzzy halo, and he was most cool, he had one slow schnide smile, and he talked very drawled. Superspade—he knew exactly what he was doing.

He was an outrageous ham showman, of course; he camped it up like mad. Still, he was good. He had presence. Under the gimmickry, he had it all going. And he did play fine guitar, after all, he carried real exhilaration. He was mesmeric. He was ferocious and sexy. He was an ugly man and he had endless charm.

Also, he wrote strong songs. He stormed so hard on them that he half obscured his own quality, but they worked; they were an odd cross between the old tough blues and post-Dylan imagery, and he sang them in a non-voice, wry and one-note, strangely effective. So he was a conman, a black cliché, but it finally didn't matter much; he freaked out regardless, and he was real excitement.

Among the home-grown groups the best was Cream.

Cream was Eric Clapton, who'd played guitar with the Yardbirds and the fine blues band of John Mayall; Ginger Baker, who'd drummed with the Graham Bond Organization, the toughest, most evil jazz/blues noise we ever had; and Jack Bruce, who sang, played bass, and had worked with almost everyone.

Within the business, each was generally regarded as the best man going on his particular instrument. Themselves, they agreed with this, and that's why they used Cream.

Basically they were an updated blues band, but they borrowed from anything that caught their minds, rock 'n' roll or jazz or Dylan. Always, they stormed. Always, they crunched and burned and sweated.

Ginger Baker had long red hair hanging lankly all down his face and a matted red beard and the most agonized face you'd ever see, his cheeks all cavernous and his teeth rotted and his eyes quite cancelled. He was the final drummer, head lolling and mouth open and schizo eyes staring out into nothing, but he was no phony; he laid down one brutal churning beat, all looped and doubled back on itself, the deepest pulse imaginable. Sunken and suffering, he was epic.

Around him, Jack Bruce pumped out nothing but goose-grease bass, and way over the top, Clapton played the best guitar in Europe. Probably he was musically stronger than Hendrix, but he had none of that flash. Instead, he hunched in tight and watched nothing but his guitar. He concentrated so hard, he worked so much, that you'd get hooked by his own obsession; you'd start to ride on him. Held by him, you'd listen very hard, you'd be stretched. When you walked out at the end, you'd be exhausted.

On stage they'd be magnificent, and both in Britain and the States they were huge. But on record, they never quite came off. They weren't strong writers, and canned, they lost most of their impact; they didn't get you fully involved.

In two years, they cut one great single, *I Feel Fine,* and that's the only time they worked out their full potential. Finally, Clapton got bored and they disbanded.

Hendrix and Cream—they've both had mass followings, they've both sold albums by the ton, but they've never had number one hits. At the best, they've made the ten. That's the way that pop has drifted, that's how much ballads hold control, and even the best, the most successful progressives are only allowed the leavings.

The Move came from Birmingham and they took over from the Stones and the Who as rabble-rousers-in-chief.

They were managed by Tony Secunda, a King's Road hustler from the early sixties, and Secunda was one fast stroke-puller. Any bandwagon that passed, he'd been up on top of it so fast you couldn't blink. And he was clever with it; what's more, he had bursts of true inventiveness. At the least, he was entertainment.

In 1966 he launched the Move from the Marquee, and they were impressive. They stood in a straight line, four-part harmony, and they were natural rockers; they wore Capone gangster suits, and they looked mean as hell. Eternal Brummers, dour and monosyllabic. And Carl Wayne, their lead singer, did a nice line in mike-throwing and Ace Kefford, a guitarist, was the singing skull itself, his flesh eaten away, his jaws clamping endlessly on gum, his face set rigid in infinite boredom. So they were the nastiest looking bunch you could hope to meet, and they sang well, they made a big bad noise.

When Psychedelphia came in, Secunda made his first jump —he set them to smashing TV sets on stage, assaulting them with an axe, and destroying images of Hitler, Ian Smith, and such. This, if you hadn't guessed, was a comment on the society in which we live, and meshed with a few flashing lights, it spelled mind-expansion. It was all poor man's Who, of course, and, on their own admission, the Move weren't too sold on it. But it got them publicity; it freaked them into their first hits.

In summer 1967, Psychedelphia was replaced by Flower Power, and Secunda jumped again—the Move forgot their gangster suits, their axes, and their snarls, and they took to frolicking in cornfields, all robed and garlanded. Ace Kefford, Singing Skull, cast as a daisy chain—it wasn't a likely concept, but once more it worked.

They made a record called *Flowers in the Rain,* and to publicize it Secunda circularized what amounted to a dirty postcard of Harold Wilson. Inevitably, Wilson sued and they had to give all their royalties to charity. Still, it had been their biggest bonanza yet, and it finally got them established. With Secunda, you win when you lose. Or maybe you lose when you win.

By the winter, Flower Power had duly faded and there were signs of rock 'n' roll revival. So, you knew it, the Move suddenly had their snarls back, and they cut *Fire Brigade,* complete with Duane Eddy twang guitar. As it happened, this was their best record yet, and they were right back where they began, hard-core rockers again. That's what they'd always been good at, anyhow.

At a less exalted level, there were the Bee Gees, Traffic, and Procol Harum, all of them competent enough, but none of them so wild that I have to go into any great detail on them.

The Bee Gees were Australian, built around the three Gibb brothers, who wrote a lot of catchy, melodic, and maudlin ballads, heavily influenced by mid-period Beatles. More to the point, Barry Gibb was pretty.

Traffic were formed by Stevie Winwood, who was probably the closest thing to a soul singer that England had ever had and who had already racked up two number-ones with the Spencer Davis Group. On paper, Traffic were all musicians, and they should have been formidable, but somehow they never made it. They only functioned in spasms, and their first hit, *Paper Sun,* remained easily the best of them.

As for Procol Harum, they made one classic record, *A Whiter Shade of Pale,* and then kept reviving it under different names and disguises until everyone got sick to death of it.

A Whiter Shade of Pale, incidentally, was produced by Denny Cordell, the most successful new English producer since Mickie Most. Apart from Procol Harum, he handled the Move, the Moody Blues, and Georgie Fame and had hits with all of them. Ironically, though, his two best cuts—*Hush* by Jackie Edwards and *Marjorine* by Joe Cocker—failed· to make it.

On the whole, the progressive English groups had their fattest period in the Flower Power boom, summer 1967. As fads go, Flower Power was less than impressive. Just as it had done with psychedelphia, London was content mostly to ape California. Everyone wore kaftans and beads and bells. Everyone spoke in hushed tones of San Francisco and Monterey, of acid and Love and the Maharishi. Nobody threw fists any more. The whole city was cloaked in incense and the smoke of joss sticks. Every last groupie had turned prophet.

The center of the local hippie movement was U.F.O., a basement club in Tottenham Court Road, and its Saturday all-nighters turned into major weekly happenings. It was a nice atmosphere down there, very lazy, and the music was fine. Most everyone lay about, and if there was ostentation in it, if there was a lot of flash love-making and out-freaking, there were also some mellow times had.

After some months, though, U.F.O.'s lease ran out, and nothing so fresh ever happened again. There were other hippie clubs, of course, but they became stale, ritualistic. There was no fever in it any more. Instead, everyone stood and gawked and listlessly shook their beads. They were bored again.

Throughout the Flower Power fairy tale, the role of bad witch was played by the drug squad.

By their very nature, all teen movements need something

to be paranoid about; this time out, the fuzz asked for all the hate they got, because from the beginning of 1967, they got into the habit of raiding clubs and stopping kids in the street, searching them for drugs and pushing them around at random, bullying them and making them strip and lumbering them down to the station. Small stuff by American standards, of course, but fascist just the same.

I was stopped a couple of times myself; I didn't get hit, but there was a lot of shoving and grunting, a lot of unprovoked aggression flying about. Always, there was this basic resentment that I was young and wore tight pants, bright shirts. Before I opened my mouth, I was hated.

In the summer, there was the Jagger/Richards trial, and that hardly helped things. By this time, both sides were hysterical—smokers saw pot as some magic cure-all, the police saw it as a deadly plague. I mean, either way, marijuana is something so trivial, but it had become almost a national obsession, a professional bore.

Anyway, it was a warm summer and people believed in Love. But then autumn came and it turned cold, and suddenly people didn't believe in love after all.

In any case, Flower Power had always been very much a London thing—kids everywhere else had gone on hitting each other regardless, schnide and moody as ever. The summer's music, rarified and mimsy, all full of transcendental meditation, had meant less than nothing in the dance halls, and teenagers had been left with nothing they could understand or relate to. Trapped between Englebert Humperdinck's flowerpots on one side and George Harrison's curry powder on the other, they'd completely lost out.

Accordingly, in the winter, there was a swing back to basic pop, instant noise, and there was even a small revival in rock 'n' roll. Bill Haley, Jerry Lee Lewis, Buddy Holly, and Eddie Cochran—they all had their old hits reissued and did quite well with them. Nothing sensational, but they sold.

More to the point, present-day groups climbed down off their clouds a bit and went back to work. *Lady Madonna* by the Beatles, *I Can See for Miles* by the Who, *Fire Brigade*

by the Move, *Jumping Jack Flash* by the Rolling Stones—
it was renewed aggression, an intelligent mixing of basics and
progression.

These were only a few singles, though, and everything
else looked pretty grim.

For a start, the pirate stations had been outlawed, and
they'd been replaced by the B.B.C.'s Radio One, which was
only dire. Under the new regime, you got thin slices of pop
wedged in between great gobs of children's requests, recipes,
Joe Loss, mighty Wurlitzers, and Jimmy Young chatting with
housewives. No flair, no speed, no flash. No hard plugging,
either, and that meant that any weird sounds, any experiments,
were doomed before they even started. Everyone was forced
to play safe, nothing moved forward. By spring 1968, the
entire industry had ground to a standstill.

The only DJ peddling anything at all was the Emperor
Rosko, an American working out of Paris. His real name was
Mike Pasternak (he was the son of Joe Pasternak, the Hollywood producer), and he was a greyhound spieler, one slippery
mouth. He knew pop from the beginning; he played amazing
noise. Always and always, he was fast.

On French Radio Luxembourg he had a daily hour-long
show and an epic three-hour freak-out every Saturday night,
a veritable mind-snapper. On Radio One, he got exactly one
hour a week. Precisely, that was what had happened in Eng-
glish pop.

Since mid-1967, only one new group has emerged with really
heavy potential and that has been The Crazy World of Arthur
Brown.

Arthur Brown used to be a philosophy student at Reading
University, and he was one long gangling skinny streak, complete with haystack black hair and great staring eyes and an
elephant's nose. And when he came on stage, he was wearing
Sun God robes, a Bug-Eyed Thing mask, and his head was
on fire.

He wore a blazing crown, and it threw flames up high
toward the ceiling. When the fire burned low, he'd go into a
wild sideways-leaping dance, his head flickering, his robes flap-

ping like a shroud; and he screamed, he snarled, he howled. Then he tore off his mask and his face was painted with wode; he looked like something neanderthal, half man and half beast. His eyes burned up in the dark, and his head kept thrashing.

When he sang, he told you stories about black magic, about death and destruction, about fire and the way it cleanses, the way it heals. Mister witch-doctor, he made spells, and all the time he'd be dancing, whirling, his head kept spinning. So he was scary and he was comic, but he had these sad eyes and this big nose; he looked tragic, and the major fantasy he conjured was King Kong, big doomed monster.

Beyond all this, he could really sing. He had a freak range: he could go from a Boris Christoff rumble through a fat Tom Jones belt all the way up to a copyright Arthur Brown screech, a hysterical scream that he'd keep up through whole choruses, the killer.

During the same period, there have also emerged Julie Driscoll and Joe Cocker and the Incredible String Band.

Julie Driscoll is a skinny girl from east London, and she toured the circuits for years without getting anywhere in particular until, autumn 1967, she suddenly got herself a Jimi Hendrix hairstyle and called herself Jools and was launched as a new ultimate in London dollydom, deadpan and strange, very freaked.

She was a vegetarian and lived off carrot juice. She dressed up in improbable antiques bought in junk shops, all feathers and mangy furs. And she made up her eyes to look huge, and she moved her shoulders like a cobra nodding; she hardly ever smiled, she froze.

With all of this going for her, she came in for fast publicity, and in 1968 she had her first hit, Bob Dylan's *This Wheel's on Fire*, and she was voted Britain's top girl singer. What's more, many people thought she was a good singer and many people thought she was sexy. Myself, I thought she was even the best and sexiest thing in Europe, but that's no kind of competition, and truthfully, I thought she was mannered and monotonous, basically fake, and I detected no trace of feeling in her singing at all.

Joe Cocker was a fat and ugly ex-plumber from Sheffield, and I liked him very much. On stage, he was greasy and he sang white soul, very sweaty, and he waved his arms like some demented windmill; he was hilarious and he sang quite splendidly. His first record, *Marjorine,* was a small classic and bombed. His second, Lennon/McCartney's *With a Little Help from My Friends,* was less good and made number one.

Finally, purely in my role as chronicler, I should note the existence of the Incredible String Band, a folk duo whom several English critics described as the best songwriters since the Beatles. This mention made, I will make no further comment.

At any rate, forgetting the Incredibles, the good thing that Cocker and Jools and Arthur Brown all shared was that they worked hard, that they raved and rampaged some, and this alone made them exceptional. In this time, most English performers have gotten entirely lazy.

Typically, they'll be booked into some dance hall in the North; they'll drive up in their van and dash on stage and knock off one fast half-hour set, looking bored and playing crap, and then while you're turning around, they'll have gone again, disappeared into the night, desperate to get back to London before the discotheques shut. They've done nothing, they've only wasted time. What we've had here, as they say, is a failure to communicate.

So I'd say this was the worst phase that English pop has been through since before the Beatles, and it's not easy to see how things are going to get better again. Basically, as I said at the beginning, this isn't a pop age; it's much too insecure and careful. Get down to it—there simply aren't any heavy new talents coming up, and there's nothing anyone can do about it.

At a less bedrock level, though, there are changes that could be made. Two changes in particular. First, the government has to bring in commercial radio and let pop work as it wants. And second, the musicians themselves have to stop playing games, have to stop winking at each other's cleverness, and they have to get right back down in the alley, go back on the road, and start reaching their audience all over again.

20.   The Monkees

WHILE folk rock was unfolding on the intellectual front, mainline American pop ran on exactly the same as always. It was almost a separate industry, mindless and changeless, eternally wrapped in a vacuum of non-singers and non-songs. Highschool lived on.

Ten years after Elvis, the charts were still filled by fantasies of heartbreak and bliss, moonlight and hearts and roses. New singers came up and sounded like the old ones. Businessmen hyped, disc jockeys spieled, pluggers plugged. Everyone had his private gimmick. Everything was always new, always old.

The only thing that had changed was that the business had become more streamlined as it went along. In the middle sixties there was none of the knockabout farce that had brightened the fifties. Instead, pop had become safe and solid, very dull. All the time, it kept getting more computerized, and everyone just methodically mopped up: earn, baby, earn.

In this move toward machine-pop, the Monkees were in a whole class by themselves.

What happened was that a group of Californian businessmen set up a TV series about a pop group, 1966. They didn't want to use any established group, they wanted no possible hassles, and they decided to create a phenomenon out of nowhere. Accordingly, they advertised for young men.

Several hundred youths applied. They were interviewed one by one. Gradually they were all discarded until only four remained—Davy Jones, Mike Nesmith, Peter Tork, and Mickey Dolenz—and these four were chosen for their faces, for their ability to project, for the balance of their personalities. They were then called the Monkees.

Right away, they bore a strong resemblance to the Beatles: one of them was baby-faced and motherable (Davy Jones/ Paul McCartney), one was big and domineering (Mickey Dolenz/John Lennon), a third was lost-looking (Peter Tork/ Ringo), and the last was withdrawn, serious, the straight man (Mike Nesmith/George Harrison).

Both Davy Jones and Mickey Dolenz had been child actors and, later, had made records, not successfully. Mike Nesmith came from Texas and was married. Peter Tork had sung folk in Greenwich Village. None of them were exceptionally intelligent, talented, or even beautiful. On the other hand, none of them was moronic. All you could say was, they were very young.

Anyhow, they appeared in their TV series, and again they were very much like the Beatles. In general, their film format was on the same lines as *Hard Day's Night*—speeded-up chase sequences, much jump-cutting, a recurrent harking-back to the Marx Brothers and silent comedy.

The major difference was only that the Monkees were aimed at a more infant public, pre-teens, six to ten. There was a lot of dressing up and falling down, a lot of bangs and face-pulling and custard pies. Everything was kept dead simple, jokes and music and characters alike. If anything needed thinking about, it was left out.

At the beginning, the Monkees weren't musicians and they didn't play on their records. It didn't matter—their sponsors hired the best writers, arrangers, and producers available, and the Monkees themselves were hardly relevant. No matter what, they couldn't fail: they had a weekly TV show beamed all across America, and they had great armies of publicists, hyping and hustling them at all times. They had money behind them, talent and ambition and influence all forcing them upward. They only had to stand there and smile.

So they took off, they duly turned into an international industry, and they paid their investors back in full; they wound up making a big profit for them.

In the end, they learned their instruments and they played a few concerts. They even wrote songs. As it happened, they turned out to be not untalented after all.

But the point was, their talent was incidental. Even if they'd been tone deaf, they'd still have made it; they'd have worked out exactly the same. Simply, there was no way they could lose.

So the obvious question is, just how computerized can pop become? The simple answer is, very.

Always, it depends on exposure. If you have the basic equipment, meaning that you look good and you can talk and you don't pick your nose in public, and you are then hyped into something like your own TV show, you can hardly miss. If, on top of that, you're given a sustained press build-up and you don't make dumb records, you're foolproof.

Mind you, all this only holds good in the teenybop belt. In a more sophisticated market, too much blatant hype can be fatal.

For instance, there's the case of Moby Grape, a good American Coast group, approximately avant-garde, who were given a $200,000 build-up by Columbia, their record company. This involved all the standard stunts, posters and badges and brochures, blanket advertising in Cashbox and Billboard, plus no less than six singles issued simultaneously. And what happened? Exactly nothing: the progressive pop audience was far too hip to get bought by such crude ballyhoo, and they rejected the whole package.

There is, in any case, a persistent snobbery running right through the underground, a feeling that anything that makes the charts must automatically be a sell-out, and by coming on so strong, Columbia was jumping straight down the mineshaft.

The moral of this sad fable is only that, like any other sales technique, pop hype has to be applied with common sense. It's not at all true that the underground can't be steamrollered—Blue Cheer, Steppenwolf, and, as far as I'm concerned, the Doors are all good examples of bullshit at work—but it does take a certain subtlety. Where the way to break the bubblegum market is simply to shout, to be louder and flasher and more vulgar than the competition, the avant-garde has to be breached by stealth, by intellectual flattery, by the suggestion that only the very finest minds can understand the product offered. On that basis, though, the intelligentsia is possibly even more gullible than the kids.

Incidentally, while I'm on the subject, Moby Grape did finally make it—they went away and a year later came through with records strong enough to cancel all of Columbia's fog. Altogether, they've been quite an ironic saga.

In all hype, TV is crucial. Newspaper publicity and advertising are only so much flavoring. But when you get on that box, you're at the nitty-gritty.

In any case, it's much simpler in America than in England, where pop TV and/or radio hardly exist and what there is happens to be government-sponsored, just about incorruptible.

In the States, however, pop is run on a sensible commercial basis, and payola has been properly formalized; any businessman that comes along with enough money to win himself air space, plus the instinct to hire the right record makers, is going to clean up. All he has to do is to find a face.

That's hardly sinful; that's only what happens in any industry. At any rate, that's the direction that all commercial pop must increasingly take. Inevitably, it's going to get more standardized, more scientific, and more dreary all the time. It's going to stop being so open to passionate kids with hit songs in their satchels, to Phil Spectors and Andrew Oldhams, and it's going to be bossed by a few big organizations.

These organizations will hardly be the major record companies that exist already, E.M.I. and Decca and so forth. Instead, they'll be whole new setups, combining management and agency and records into one huge complex. There may be half a dozen of them, and among them they'll have everything neatly tied up.

In this way, pop will become an industry like any other. Experiments will be left to a small avant-garde, way out on the left, very solemn and romantic. The bubblegum business in general will regard this avant-garde with benevolence, will steal its best ideas and talents, but will otherwise ignore it.

21.   *Love*

IN AMERICA, acid really mattered.

In Britain, it never got much beyond being a one-shot curiosity, and only a few thousand people ever used it. It was a status symbol, certainly, but it moved in very limited circles, and it wasn't believed in as magic. So Paul McCartney might trip out and then announce that he'd been brought closer to God by his experiences, but when you talked to someone less eminent, some dumb post-Mod sitting on his scooter, he'd never used it. Pills and pot—he knew them well. Acid was another league, though, and everyone ran scared.

In the States it was all different; LSD was taken almost for granted. If you went there and moved through any kind of hip circles at all, acid turned up almost everywhere. You'd meet sweet little sixteen, some small dropout, and she was already bored by the whole pitch. She scorned one-time users as amateurs.

Beyond that, it was a cause. In the home of Dr. Timothy Leary, it became an organized religion, and even at less solemn levels, it was talked about as the cure of all trouble, the road to true nirvana. Users talked low and spoke of it in tones of mystic awe. They stared through the space above your head, and you'd guess they were watching infinity.

Why did it go down so big? Partly because of its own power, of course, the things it did to you, the way it changed you, and partly because it made the most perfect frontier ever between hip and square. After all, if you dropped out any other way, if you drank too much or dabbled in homosexuality, say, you had to share your situation with every kind of undesirable: bank managers and accountants and postmen. Maybe even your own father. But LSD was private—the plastic people left it severely alone. You were safe, and when you tripped, you knew that no losers would journey with you; no one would make you lose image.

Inevitably, you felt superior. After acid, you walked around bulging with your new perceptions, and you thought you'd been some place nobody else had ever seen. You knew all kinds of secret answers and you were smug, you couldn't help it.

In this way, acid formed its own aristocracy, and pop was part of it: pop was its mouthpiece. Not all of pop, of course. Just the underground.

The underground was anything experimental, anything outside the run of the industry, and it took in not only pop but newspapers, painting, poetry—anti-establishment expression of any kind. It was all very much in the tradition of fifties' Beat, but being laced with superpop, it reached an infinitely bigger public than Beat had ever done.

Its father figure was Allen Ginsberg, the poet. Ten years back, in poems like *Howl* and *America,* he'd already been peddling what amounted to hippie philosophies, and his messages still applied. Big-bearded and benevolent and exhibitionist, he was a bit of a joke but a good one. And he'd influenced Dylan; he influenced almost everyone.

Just as Beat had done in the late fifties, the underground came on strongest in California, where people are rich enough and time is relaxed enough and the weather is warm enough for such things to flourish. Through the early sixties, hip centers formed and grew across the state, notably in Venice, near Los Angeles, and in San Francisco's Haight Ashbury.

Always, they looked the same—streets full of sandals, cockroach apartments decorated with posters, overflowing trashcans, the smells of socks and stale hashish, cracks in the walls, beards. Generation to generation, nothing changes in bohemia. The heroes shift, that's all. Charlie Parker and Jack Kerouac, they give way to Kahlil Gibran and Dylan and Muhammed Ali, but underneath, the concept of romantic squalor remains the same.

At first pop didn't come into this much—the staple diet was

modern jazz and, later, folk. But after Dylan hired his rock 'n' roll band, pop suddenly became O.K. and the underground was swamped with groups, small armies of beards and matted hair and intense feet, who made big dirty noises and screamed obscenities at Mister America as he passed.

Specifically underground clubs started up, the best of them being the Fillmore Auditorium in San Francisco. They weren't like other dance halls; the audiences didn't just drift and shuffle and be bored; they really heard the music. Very often, there'd be a genuine involvement between the crowd and the band, a sudden meshing, and then strange nights would ensue. Even now, any group that played the Fillmore at its peak, 1966, will say it was the best gig they ever did.

The common denominator was acid, the fraternity pin, and it formed a huge subterranean brotherhood, freaks and dropouts everywhere united in their struggle against the ogre America, against its violence and greed and conformity, and so the term acid/rock came into use, a fairly meaningless phrase that got applied to any underground group, no matter what its style, but that at least summed up a feeling.

The other favorite word was psychedelic, which, in the dictionary, means mind-expansion. In practice, though, out in California, it only meant faking up a trip.

Instead of just standing up on stage and strumming, the psychedelic groups took to surrounding themselves with flashing lights, back-projected films, prerecorded tapes, freak dancers, and anything else they could think of; the idea was that, faced by all this, you'd be hit by a total experience, a simultaneous flowering of all your senses and, just like acid, you'd fly.

You didn't, of course. Instead, you watched the legs of them sexy go-go dancers and wound up with a headache. Never mind, it wasn't such a bad idea—at least it took away from the fixed boredom of staring at a group staring back at you.

On the whole, acid/rock groups tended not to come up with many monster singles, but they sold a lot of albums and they earned good gig money. Who were they? Jefferson Airplane, Love, the Doors, Captain Beefheart and his Magic

Band, Moby Grape, the Grateful Dead. And Country Joe and the Fish, who were good. And Janis Joplin with Big Brother and the Holding Company. And Frank Zappa with the Mothers Of Invention. And not only in California but back east as well, the Fugs and Andy Warhol's Velvet Underground, a massive volume of music.

Commercially, the biggest have been the Doors, out of Los Angeles, who revolved around Jim Morrison, the wildest white American act since Elvis itself.

He is tall and smooth and lean, quite innocent-looking, and he doesn't smile. Staring at his photograph, you'd think he was gentle, a bit melancholy. A nice man. Then he comes out on stage, and he's not a nice man after all; he's a phantom. He has black leather pants so tight that his machine shows through, and he's tortured: he looks as if his mind had gone away to lunch. He writhes, reels, staggers. He gropes for the mike like some blind man, and his face dissolves into rage and fear. Exactly, he looks like a man on a bad trip, driven insane by nightmares, by things he can't understand. First he pleads and then he's obscene and then he collapses and then he pleads again. He stammers, stumbles, can find no words. In turn, he is sadist and masochist. He blurs, his face turns into jelly. He's an ectoplasm. In the end, he's a psychopath: "Father? Yes, son? I want to kill you. Mother, I want to . . . Aaaaaaauuuugghh."

You guessed it, he's an exhibitionist. Off-stage he is surrounded by myths and legends, the heroic acts of Jim Morrison, all about how he's a sexual superman and how he brutalizes the groupies that hang around and how he used to swallow sugar cubes like so many candies and never even blink his eye. So his stage act is no uncontrollable fit—it's all theatrical, rehearsed, perfectly calculated, and it has become a ritual: the bit when he suddenly collapses, jack-knifes as if he's been kicked in the balls; the bit when he, umm, accidentally falls off the stage. Nothing's wrong with that, of course; it's all showbiz anyhow, and he burns you just the same.

And after all this, wouldn't you know it, it turns out that his father is in charge of a gaggle of Polaris submarines.

Musically, though, Morrison is no great singer and the Doors are no great band. They've made a couple of strong hardrock singles (*Light My Fire* and *Hello, I Love You*), and they've grown into probably the biggest and most influential live act current in America—they've spurred a whole resurgence of theatricality and sex and grotesquery among the groups there, they've revived the whole idea of pop as performance—but once you get inside their albums, their staying power is revealed as minimal, and a lot of Morrison's lyrics come across as pure pretentious bullshit. In fairness, they use some potent riffs, and instrumentally they're strictly competent, but still they get monotonous.

Really, they're another case of a potentially great rock band, full of sex and excitement but not too bright, getting dragged down by the post-Beatles need to get into Art.

Much more to the point has been Janis Joplin, who started out with Big Brother and the Holding Company but later went solo and who has become the most exhilarating white girl singer in the world.

She's something, she is really, a big tough woman out of Port Arthur, Texas, and she'd eat you alive for breakfast. On stage she stomps and pounds and grinds, she bosses, and she has a truly brutal voice, a killer. She's no lady. She picks up her songs and annihilates them, leaves them crippled ever after. Her face all twisted and scornful, she's fierce and she's sweet, a good old girl like they don't make any more, and you could love her easy, it wouldn't take you much at all. Just to hear her roar, watch her shake her stuff, that's enough.

Of all the underground groups, though, by far the most anarchic was Frank Zappa and his Mothers Of Invention.

Zappa himself was an adman, and he came through in 1966, a skinny man with a long nose, crows-nest hair, a droopy moustache, and a small dagger beard. By any standards, he was quite outstandingly ugly, but the Mothers, his group, left him looking like Robert Goulet. Bearded and gross and filthy, entirely obscene, they were the classic New Yorker cartoon of beatniks brought to life.

They were freaks. They were meant to be. They were playing the same old game again, *épater le bourgois,* but this time around it wasn't called Dada or Existentialism or Beat; it was Freak-Out.

"On a personal level," wrote Zappa, "freaking out is a process whereby an individual casts off outmoded and restricting standards of thinking, dress, and social etiquette in order to express CREATIVELY his relationship to his immediate environment and the social structure as a whole."

To this end, he assembled his Mother freaks and loosed them. On their first album, cutting a track called *The Return of the Son of Monster Magnet,* he went into the studio with a small army of auxiliaries, and the whole lot of them banged, strummed, pounded, and thrashed any musical instrument they could lay hands on, the total effect being a bit like a small army banging, strumming, pounding, and thrashing any musical instrument they could lay hands on. It worked, what's more. It made you wish you'd been in there yourself, banging and thrashing with the rest of them, and so it carried a sense of real release, exorcism.

Still, there was more solemn stuff involved: Zappa wrote songs and sang them, souped-up Dada visions of American follies, insanities, and nightmares. Some of it was earnest and some of it was a put-on; most of it was both.

His lyrics were tiresome, silly, melodramatic, or they were sharp, funny, true. His music was hardly existent, being a montage of mangled clichés from highschool, showbiz, and vaudeville, plus his own non-tunes. And taken through a whole album, he was pretentious, oppressive, imaginative, hilarious, foolish, spasmodically impressive. He was no fun person but he wasn't quite dismissable; he'd suddenly make you laugh or he'd bruise you. He was a drag, but that was almost the point.

Of the other West Coast groups, my own favorites were Jefferson Airplane, and Country Joe and the Fish.

Jefferson Airplane had a pretty girl called Grace Slick, with a foghorn voice, and she wrote some potent, vengeful-sounding songs, *White Rabbit* and *Two Heads. White Rabbit,* in fact, a dope-oriented version of *Alice in Wonderland,* was a small classic, and it remains by far the best thing they've done. But when Grace Slick steps back and the rest of the group take over, they're musical but they're cluttered and self-conscious, badly short of punch. They sell a lot of records. They aren't enjoyed by me.

As for the Fish, Country Joe McDonald is a roughneck with a bashed-in face, and at times he's comical. Stuff like *I'm Fixing to Die Rag* and his James Brown riff—they're the only true belly laughs in the whole of contemporary rock and, as such, are to be treasured. The only trouble is, Country Joe isn't all laughs; he has his poetical side as well, and that's not so hot, that's downright dire. With all of these groups, it's the same endless hang-up: when they stomp, they're fine, and when they turn profound, they're a pain in the ass.

Beyond all these there have been other good groups: Al Kooper's Blood, Sweat, and Tears, for instance, and Bob Dylan's one time backing group, the Band. Still and all, the American bands as a whole have been disappointing—there's too much inflation, too much crap, and too little real style. Get down on it, there's been far too little excitement, and then it's all been taken with absurd intensity; it has almost stopped being fun. The new breed of American fans, post-Beatles and post-Dylan, weaned on folk and social consciousness—they sit and get stoned with the lights off, they write treatises and split pedantics, just like jazz fans, and mostly they hardly remember Fats Domino's name; they think him trivial, and any suggestion that rock is a joke is greeted in shocked silence.

Anyhow times were good in there and the underground kept expanding, the music kept getting better, the movement kept growing. Somewhere along the line, the word hippie got used and it stuck.

The place that hippies flourished best was Haight Ashbury, 1966, and they formed a real community then; they forgot about possessions and shared almost everything they had. They believed they were beginning a whole new society, and the word they used was Love.

The rules were, you had to love everyone and everything; you had to turn your back on the bitch goddess, on materialism and war and all that stuff; and you had to get way back to the roots again, you had to rediscover the basic simplicities.

This was nothing new in itself, of course. It was the oldest chestnut imaginable. What was a bit different, though, was that something actually got done. This time, it wasn't just some poet preaching away in the woods; it was people, several thousand of them.

What's more, it caught, it sparked similar communities all across the country. "Hashbury" got famous, was much glorified. Journalists moved in and started to publicize it. So high school kids heard about it then, the way its streets were paved with pot, and they came down from suburbia for their vacations, and tourists came with cameras to watch the weirdies, and the admen and the record companies moved in for the kill. Within a few months, the whole thing had become a circus. The original hippies had all escaped, and what remained was an acid-burger nightmare. The streets were filled with beggars and pushers and pubertal panhandlers. Everything was filthy, decaying, rat-infested. Instant freaks sat on the sidewalks, munching hash sandwich, and the tourists took happysnaps.

Scott McKenzie, a folk singer straight out of a toothpaste ad, sang a song called *San Francisco* ("wear some flowers in your hair"), and it was a worldwide smash. In England, the Flowerpot Men did *Let's Go to San Francisco*. Everyone loved everyone else, everyone got rich. George Harrison visited Hashbury itself. Eric Jesus Burdon blessed us all.

And what remained of the original concept, the first flush of innocence? Hardly anything.

All over the world, kids walked around in rainbow robes and wore beads, bells, flowers in their hair, but it was all down to play-acting now; it was only a new toy, something on the level of Mods and Rockers.

It wasn't just confined to kids either; the game had spread through to young white liberals everywhere, even to academies and journalists and hip admen. So all right, they didn't go as far as robes, but they smoked pot and bought Sgt. Pepper, used words like groovy, filled their houses with joss sticks. They were flirting with wildness, that's all. Flower Power became a

one-night stand with bohemia. So much for the new society—
it was summer and everyone got stoned.

The high point of the whole junket was the Monterey Festival, June 1967, which ran right through a weekend and show-
cased the entire range of propressive pop: Eric Burdon and
Janis Joplin and Jimi Hendrix, the Who, the Mamas and the
Papas, Simon and Garfunkel, and even people like Otis Redding
and Ravi Shankar.

Maybe seventy thousand people went to it, the entire hippie
population of California, and they descended on Monterey like
some obscene plague. The city was scared out of its wits, of
course, but it didn't have to be; the love crowd was perfect.
It slept in the open and sang songs and got itself high. It broke
no windows, caused no riots. Everyone loved everyone. The
groups played for free; the music was endless and sometimes
marvelous. Everyone was flying, half on pot and half on sheer
idealism. Even the people who'd come to put it down, pressmen
and such, were caught and began to believe. By the end of
three days, the police themselves wore flowers.

Inevitably, as soon as it was over and everyone had gone
home again, hippie began to decline. Monterey had been wonderful, yes, but then the people went back to their jobs and
their lives, their sadder realities, and everything seemed anti-
climactic. Other attempts to catch the same excitement never
quite worked. Always, the first time is the only time. And when
autumn came and the sun went in, the whole thing fell apart.
In retrospect, Monterey had been the beginning and the end
at once.

After Monterey, the next step was transcendental meditation, a craze that blossomed exactly one day after the Beatles
took it up and dropped dead exactly one day after they abandoned it again.

While it lasted, though, it was big: meditation conters
sprang up all over America, and any rock musician that didn't
practice it got branded as bubblegum. The climax came when
the Beach Boys did a concert tour with the Maharishi Mahesh
Yogi, an act of faith that was both the high point and the
destruction of meditation as a cult, because most of the gigs

were half empty and even the people who'd turned up walked out in droves as soon as the Maharishi appeared.

Soon after this, the Beatles recanted, much to the general relief, and everyone went back to being quietly stoned again.

In any case, the whole meditation bit had been very much a legacy from LSD—pop had stuffed itself so full of acid that it addled its mind; it went light-headed and got itself mixed up in whimsicalities that it would normally have dismissed with a few fast farts. And then, after a year or so, the acid began to wear off, some semblance of sanity returned, and everyone went back into the discotheques.

So the last question remains, what next? Astrology? Roman Catholicism? Spiritualism? Even alcohol, perhaps? And the answer is, all of them and none of them—fashions change maybe three times a year, and they're hardly relevant; they're all jokes anyway. Only the underlying restlessness is stable and real.

It was this restlessness, this basic hunger for solutions, that gave rise to acid rock, love rock, and meditation, and that's going to give rise to the next move. And whatever that next move may be, it'll almost certainly be expressed through rock, because pop is the new American religion; it's the major rallying cry, and nothing is too hefty or too dumb to be foisted on it.

Just possibly, in fact, rock is going to be a real political factor in these next years. After all, maybe one in three American young do passionately believe in love and peace, a brave new world, and for almost all of them, pop is their natural medium.

It won't last, of course: within a decade, the intensity will have diffused, and this generation will have sunk into the same uneasy apathy as any other. In the meantime, though, rock may count.

22.

The Who

QUITE likely, the Who are the last great fling of Superpop.

I mean, most of the people one calls pop really aren't pop at all any more. The Beatles, the Stones, the Beach Boys—they've variously opted out, and they hardly make teen music now; they've moved on to something altogether more solemn. The Who remain.

They have it both ways. They're intelligent, musical, they do keep moving forward; but they're also flash, and they come on with all the noise and nonsense of some backdated rock 'n' roll group. They make good music and they're still pop. That's almost a contradiction in terms, but somehow they make it.

In the first place, they came out of Shepherd's Bush and they were Mods.

Mod came in from the beginning of the sixties and reached its peak in 1964. Very much, it was a reaction against the yobbishness of the Teds in the fifties.

Mods were small strange creatures, very neat and delicate, and they rode scooters, chewed gum, swallowed pills by the hundredweight. Most of all, they were hooked on clothes. Any money they got, it always went on making themselves look beautiful.

It was the Mods who first made Carnaby Street happen, 1962–3, and they used to change their clothes maybe four times each day. It was fierce, dedicated stuff. If you got caught in last night's sweater, you were finished, you were dead. By 1964, hyped too hard, Carnaby Street was all through—the clothes became badly made, hideously styled, and the whole thing deteriorated into one more American tourist trap.

Anyhow, Mod was a strictly male world, and you'd see them mooching around in big tribes, their girls trailing forgotten behind them, and they'd dance all by themselves, sunk deep in narcissistic dreams. They didn't smile. And if there was ever a mirror in the club, there'd be a frantic rush to get in front of it, and everyone would pose, pout, flounce about, and get high on themselves.

All right, so Mod was a new low in decadence, but then it was hard work, intense, truly obsessive, and that's the kind of atmosphere that breeds good pop.

At any rate, Shepherd's Bush was one of the most major Mod citadels, and the Who became the great Mod group.

The first thing, they were loud.

On stage they worked between great fortresses of amps, and they made that kind of noise that makes your eyes blur, that hits you and hits you, that halfway destroys you.

Always, they were murderous: Pete Townshend used to smash his guitar full into the amps, shattering it like kindling, and the amps would scream out feedback, squeal, and explode. And Roger Daltrey, who sang, used to swing his mike like a lariat and crash it against the drums, and Keith Moon used to play drums with twenty arms, mouth agape and eyes bugged, flailing and thrashing like some dervish, and John Entwistle used to play bass like Bill Wyman, bored as he could be, and he bound them down or else they'd have flown away. Or Townshend used to swing his arm in a great slow circle like a windmill, and he'd handle his guitar like a machine gun: he'd move very slowly along the faces of the audience, mowing them down one by one, and the people at the end of the line would cringe and cower, try to hide themselves. They didn't want to die. And by the end, the stage would look like a battlefield, all strewn with drum kit and busted guitar and bits of shattered amp, covered by smoke. Everybody sweated. The Who used to be wild in those days.

The second thing, they had image.

Moody bastards, the lot of them—they used to act like so many spoiled children; they threw tantrums and spat at each other and had fights on stage. They were violent. Well, they were only silly. They'd be obnoxious to almost everyone, and they'd cause endless hassle. But they spent a lot of money on clothes. Pete Townshend used to spend maybe $200 each week, just to make himself look right. They weren't pretty, but they had style.

From the beginning, Pete Townshend was the one that counted most.

His father had played in a dance band and, himself, he'd always hang around the far fringes of the industry. He wrote songs. He had a nose like a trowel and he didn't enjoy it. The way he explained it, his nose had got laughed at when he was a child, and later he thought he'd maybe take some revenge: he'd have his nose plastered all across every paper going; he'd push it right back in our faces. So he did. And when he got up on stage and machine-gunned his audience, it was camp but it was also meant; it carried real rage.

No matter what, he would have led a pop group and made them happen and been famous. He had that kind of drive; he couldn't miss.

As it was, he found Daltrey, Entwistle, and Moon, and they all called themselves the Hi-Numbers. This was 1963, when everyone was banging out R & B, but the Hi-Numbers used a mixture of Townshend's own songs and Tamla Motown things, all very advanced stuff in its time, and they were immediately good.

At this point, Kit Lambert and Chris Stamp came around.

Lambert was the son of Constant Lambert, the composer, and had been to Lancing and Trinity, Cambridge; Stamp was the son of an East End tugboatman and the brother of Terence, a film actor.

Both of them had gone into films, become quite successful as assistant directors. In due course, they met and became friends and went into partnership together.

Lambert was extrovert and insomniac and highly intelligent, too generous, and Stamp was hard and common-sense, approximately ruthless: they made a working combination, they rounded each other out. Anyway, they heard the Hi-Numbers in the back room of some pub and dug them and became their managers.

As solemn management, it's always been farcical. Lambert is neurotic, Townshend is neurotic, Keith Moon is neurotic. Almost everyone involved is a maniac, almost everyone is extremely bright, and for years hardly a week would go by without some kind of major trauma. Either the Who were going to break up, or the Who were going to leave Lambert/Stamp, or Lambert/Stamp were going to leave the Who, or everyone was just going to freak out regardless. Of course, nothing ever happened. It got to be something like a pop Coronation Street (Lambert as Elsie Tanner? Townshend as Annie Walker?), and the whole pantomime has always been the most inventive, comic and entirely admirable setup in English pop. Why? Because they've had fun. Because they're all clever people and they've never let things go dead.

The thing was, Townshend was intellectual, and Lambert wasn't exactly intellectual but he had the jargon. Between them, they looked at the things the Who did and analyzed them and thought up sassy names for them. If the Who smashed up their instruments and used feedback and acted like apes, was that violence? Certainly not: it was auto-destruction.

In the same way, if they wore jackets made out of Union Jacks and freaky T-shirts, that wasn't outrageousness, that was Pop Art. No less, Pop Art.

Well, it was all crap, of course, but they wrapped it up pretty, they talked most solemn, and it brought in vast publicity; it was a real stroke. Pop Art? Right away the Who were avant-garde, heavy; they drew big at the Marquee every Tuesday night, they were major Mod heroes, and they kept throwing smoke bombs, smashing stuff, and having fights. All image —they were wreckers, and they replaced the Stones as number one anarchists.

More to the point, Pete Townshend had begun to write some monster songs.

He used one recurrent framework: he cast himself as one teenage boy, and this boy was the archetypal Shepherd's Bush

Mod, a bit dumb, a bit aggressive, a bit baffled. His songs were about his scenes and his small hang-ups, his uncertainties, and Townshend got nothing wrong; he was imaginative and shrewd and funny; he caught everything exactly right:

> I'm a substitute for another guy,
> I look pretty tall but my heels are high.
> The simple things you see are all complicated,
> Look pretty young but I'm just backdated,
> Yeah . . .*

Often, the songs would carry quite heavy implications, but they never got flabby; their surface always gleamed. No sermonizing, no crap—Townshend kept everything tight and firm, very real, and he chronicled teen lives better than anyone since Eddie Cochran.

My Generation was typical: the Mod was trying to justify himself, wanted to lash back at everyone who'd ever put him down, but he'd taken too many pills and couldn't concentrate right. He only stammered. He was mad, frustrated, but he wasn't articulate; he couldn't say why. The harder he tried, the worse he stammered, the more he got confused. In the end, he got nowhere:

> People try to put us down
> Just because we get around,
> Things they do look awful cold,
> Hope I die before I get old.†

Townshend wasn't like this Mod hero at all, of course, but Roger Daltrey was. I mean, Daltrey wasn't stupid, but he was no theorizer; he was interested mostly in girls and cars, he wasn't too articulate, and Townshend used him like a mouthpiece. In fact, he used all of the Who like that: he *was* the Who.

He gave them hit songs, earned them money, made them famous; in return, they were used by him and were formed to

---

* Words of *Substitute* by permission of Fabulous Music Ltd., London.
† Words of *My Generation* by permission of Fabulous Music Ltd., London.

his image. Always, they've been like one walking Pete Town-shend fantasy.

He's been arrogant, generous, jumped-up, cruel, loyal, honest, complicated, always ultra-intelligent. He's kept his trowel nose, but he's come to accept it. He's played, and the Who has had hits.

They didn't have number-ones, but they kept hitting the top ten, and in due course they became safe. They even stopped punching each other. Like any other group, they got institutionalized and lost excitement. Mod had died, and by 1967 the Who had got to be one of the truly established groups, almost like the Beatles or the Stones, almost as rocklike and ignorable as that. Simply, they'd become solid citizens.

They happened in America as well. So all right, it took them three years scuffling, but they did finally make it, and then they spent a lot of time out of England, touring and getting rich.

In America, their image has been rather different. They haven't been seen so much as experimenters; they've gone down more as a classic hard rock band, almost as throwbacks. Working in a scene where almost everyone has gone mad for artiness, the Who come across as baddies in the great tradition of Eddie Cochran; they are the most basic group on the circuit.

Whenever you did catch up with them, they were disappointing—they were still going through the same old stunts, and they didn't seem loud any more; they sounded stale. In the end, they tended to be boring.

It didn't matter: Townshend himself got no worse.

Myself, I think he's the best writer British pop has produced, the most perceptive and the most original. Alone of all our major writers, he's kept close to what pop is really about; he's jumped on no post-Dylan bandwagons; he's always worked to and cared about a strictly teen public. Alone, he's written nothing phony. And, some time, I'd back him to produce something very impressive indeed.

So far, I'd say he's never quite lived up to his real potential. In his time, he's had maybe half a dozen mindbusts (*My Generation, Substitute, Mary Anne with the Shaky Hand, I'm A*

Boy, Tattoo, I Can See for Miles), but always he has been too pressured, too overworked to sustain right through an album.

For instance, the Who had an album to make, *The Who Sell Out*, and Townshend thought he'd turn the whole thing into one mammoth commercial, a wholesale ad fantasia, stuffed full of jingles and flashes and product hymns, all done as fast and loud and vulgar as it could possibly be.

Obviously, it could have been great; it could have been a music Claes Oldenburg; it could have summed up almost everything that surrounds us. It could even have been the first pop masterpiece. But then Townshend was touring America and gigging in England; he didn't get enough time to plan it out and it misfired. Half of it was brilliant and half of it was trash. It was a waste.

Recently the Who have done another album, and it justifies a lot of things I hoped for. Pete Townshend has finally written a full-scale pop opera, a project he's been threatening for years, and it's brilliant. In particular two of the songs in it— *Pinball Wizard* and *She's A Gypsy, She's An Acid Queen*— are as good as anything he's done, meaning that they're as good as anything anyone has done.

23.　　　　　　　　　　　*Superpop*

PROBABLY it's not been a bad time to write this book: rock is at its most important junction yet, it's in the gap between two major phases, and this has been quite a clean moment to make some interval notes on it.

What I've written about has been the rise and fall of Superpop, the noise machine, and the image, hype, and beautiful flash of rock 'n' roll music. Elvis riding on his golden Cadillac, James Brown throwing off his robes in a fit, Pete Townshend slaughtering his audience with his machine-gun guitar, Mick Jagger hanging off his mike like Tarzan Weismuller in the jungle, P. J. Proby—all the heroic acts of pulp.

Superpop? It hasn't been much, it's been simple always, silly and vulgar and fake, and it has been a noise, that's all. In the end, specific records and singers have hardly mattered. Instead, it's been pop itself, just the existence of it, the drone and bleat of it running through everything.

I was ten when it started; I'm twenty-two now, and it has bossed my life. It has surrounded me always, cut me off, and it has given me my heroes, it has made my myths. Almost, it has done my living for me. Six hours of trash every day, and it's meant more to me than anything else.

Superpop—it's been like a continuing Western; it's had that same classic simplicity, the same power to turn cliché into myth. It's had no mind of its own. All it's ever done has been to catch currents, moods, teen obsessions, and freeze them in images. It has made giant caricatures of lust, violence, romance, and revolt, and they've been the most powerful, most accurate fictions of this time. Jagger and James Brown and King Elvis—

249

they've been the ultimate heroes (only Muhammed Ali has equaled them, and he's pop himself; he works the same way).

And then, beyond the heroes, beyond anything, there's been the noise, the endless and perfect and changeless beat. Noise has been everything.

Anyhow, it's finished now, the first mindless explosion, and the second stage has begun. Pop has gotten complicated. That was inevitable: everything ends, nothing remains simple. Pop has split itself into factions and turned sophisticate. Part of it has a mind now, makes fine music. The other part is purely industrial, a bored and boring business like any other. Either way, there are no more heroes and no more Superpop. It has all been reduced to human beings.

What's left? In England, the industry is split roughly eighty per cent ugly and twenty per cent idealist.

The ugly eighty are mainline pop, computerized, and they hit a largely teenybop or pre-teen market, ages six to sixteen, plus a big pocket of middle-aged parents. They have a function, and they sell records. They make money.

The blue-eyed twenty are hardly even pop any more. With very few exceptions, notably the Beatles and the Stones, they don't sell records, and after all, what's pop about unpopularity? In ten years, they'll probably be called by another name entirely, electric music or something, and they'll relate to pop the way that art movies relate to Hollywood.

How good could they be? Logically, there's no limit—amplified music is an obvious art form for this century, and there's no reason whatever why it shouldn't produce major works.

Very soon, you'll have pop composers writing formal works for pop choirs, pop orchestras; you'll have pop concerts held in halls and the audience all seated in rows, not screaming or stamping but applauding politely with their hands; you'll have sounds and visuals combined, records that are played on something like a stereo system and TV set knocked into one, the music creating pictures and patterns. You'll have cleverness of every kind imaginable, and out of all this you'll get a lot of pretension and bullshit, but you'll also get masterworks.

It doesn't really matter to me. Not that I have anything

much against masterworks in principle, but I'm hooked on image, on heroics. It's like films—the best in art movies have no doubt been most sensitive, brilliant, and meaningful works of art, and where have I been? In the back row of the Roxy, of course, gawking at Hollywood. The art movie carries the quality, but Hollywood carries the myth.

The same thing with pop. If you're cutting great art and hardly anyone hears you, you're irrelevant. You're good and you're meaningless.

Pop is mass media, it is teen music always, it has to hit. Ideally, it has to do what Bogart and Brando and Monroe have done in films, John Ford and John Huston and Hitchcock: it has to be intelligent and simple both; it has to carry its implications lightly; and it has to be fast, funny, sexy, obsessive, a bit epic. Always, it has to be box-office.

Right now, there are signs that some of the English pop intelligentsia are coming down from the trees again, are getting back to hard business (in America, as yet, the problem hardly exists—there's a vast range of styles and almost all of them sell, almost all of them carry excitement). The Beatles and the Stones have both backtracked and cut recent basic rock. Pete Townshend, of course, has never been away, and he remains my white hope.

That's only a few individuals, though; it's not enough. There has to be a general resurgence of extravagance. There has to be insanity again.

The words of Little Richard still apply. They summed up what rock was about in 1956. They sum it up now and always: AWOPBOPALOOBOP ALOPBAMBOOM.